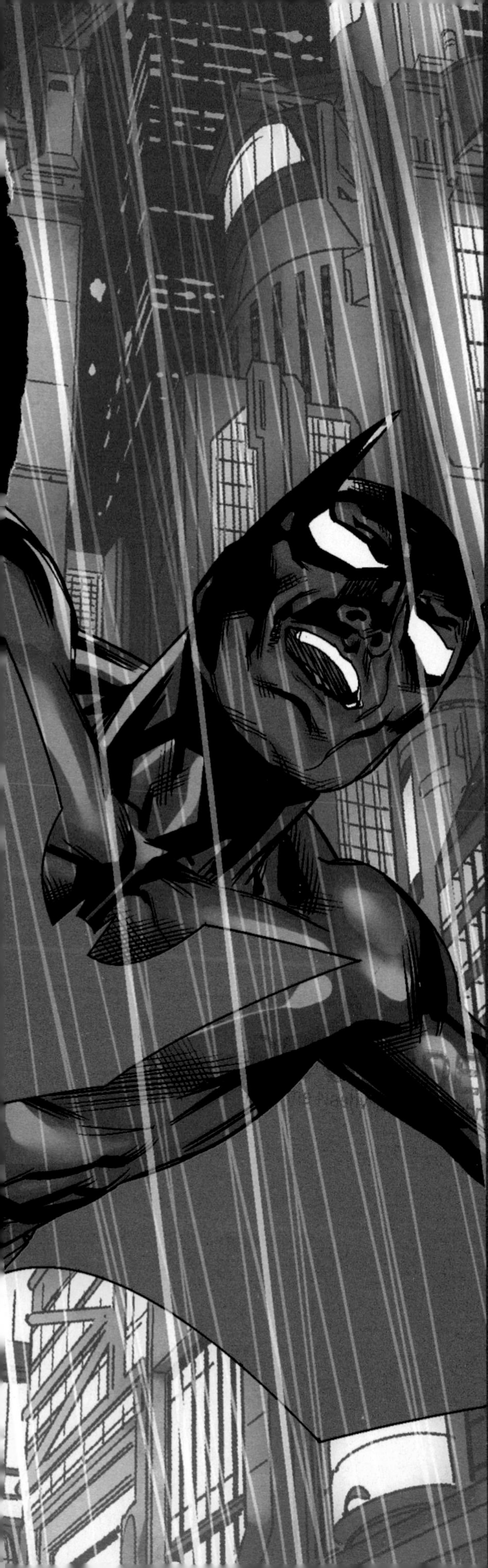

VOLUME 2

YESTERDAY

BATMAN BEYOND

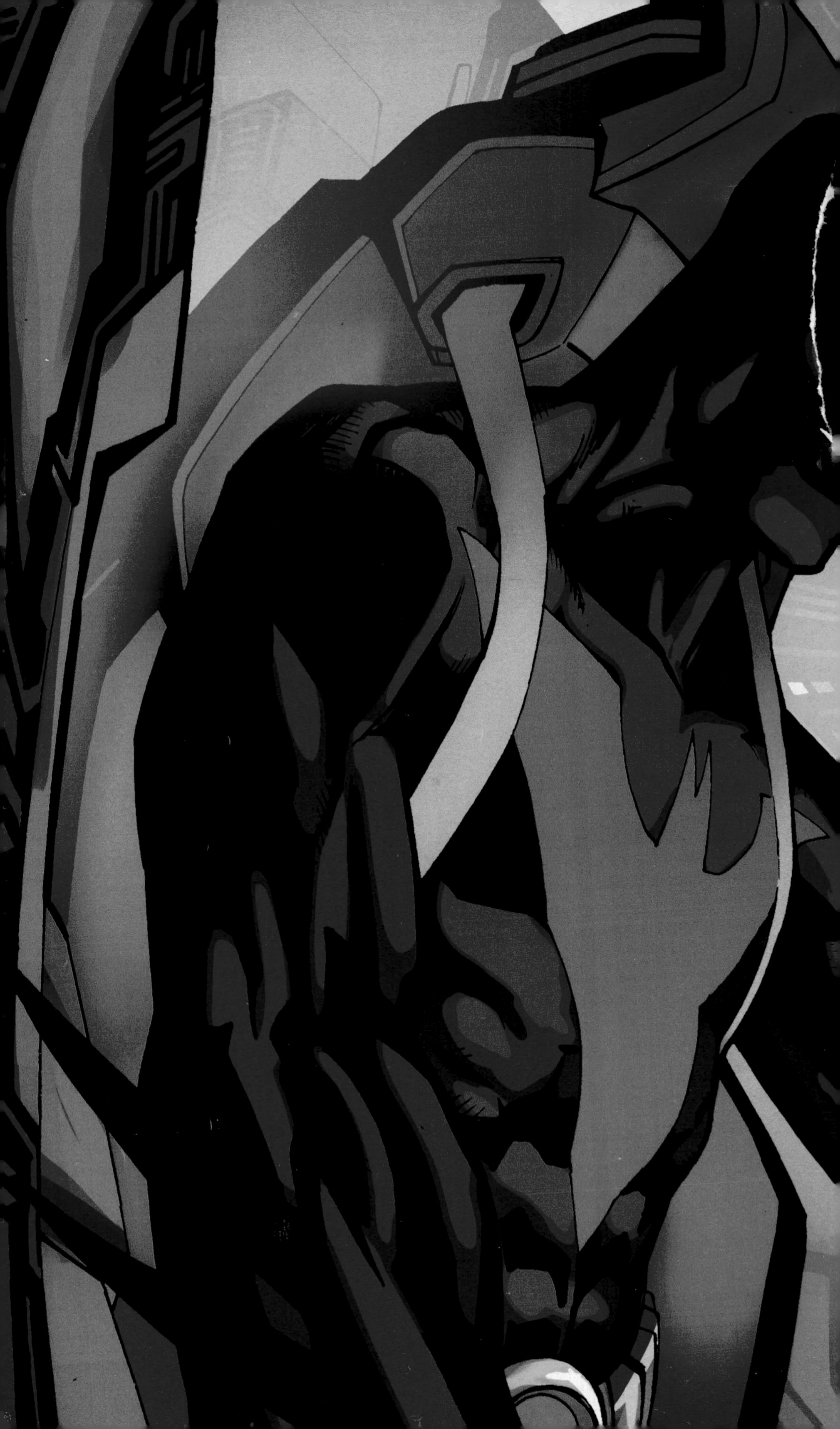

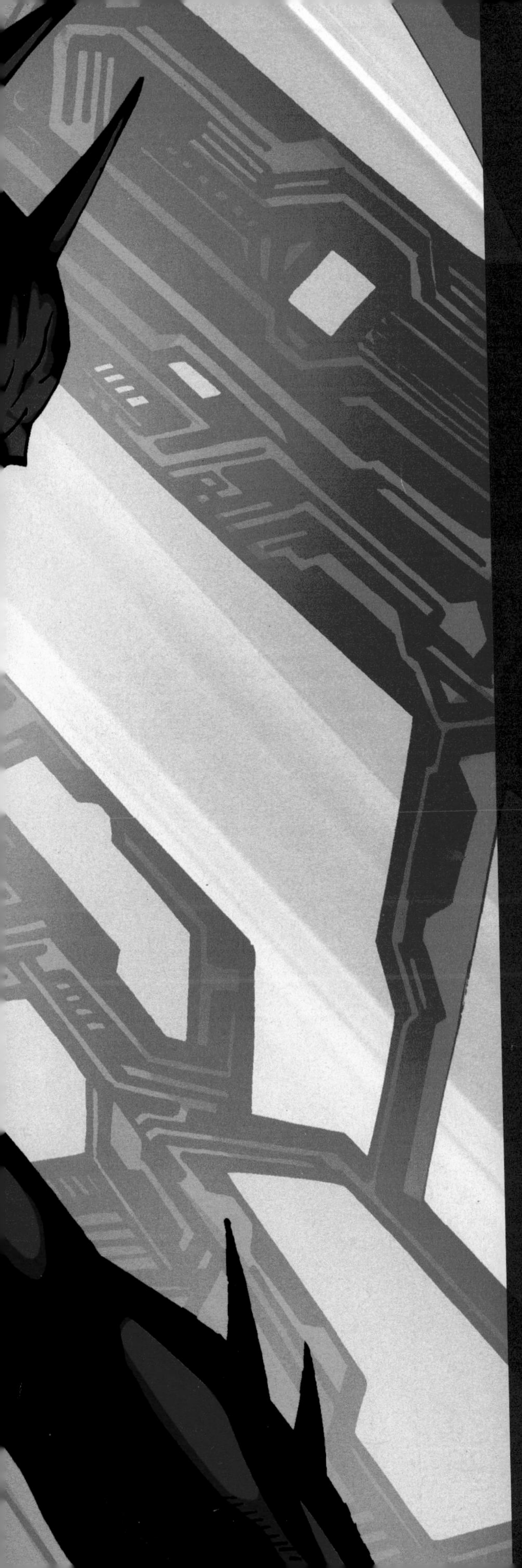

BATMAN BEYOND

VOLUME 2
CITY OF YESTERDAY

WRITTEN BY
DAN JURGENS

ART BY
BERNARD CHANG
STEPHEN THOMPSON

COLOR BY
MARCELO MAIOLO

LETTERS BY
DAVE SHARPE

SERIES & COLLECTION COVER ARTISTS
PHILIP TAN WITH
ELMER SANTOS

BATMAN CREATED BY
BOB KANE WITH
BILL FINGER

SUPERMAN CREATED BY
JERRY SIEGEL &
JOE SHUSTER
BY SPECIAL ARRANGEMENT
WITH THE JERRY SIEGEL FAMILY

DAVID PIÑA Editor - Original Series
JEB WOODARD Group Editor - Collected Editions
STEVE COOK Design Director - Books
DAMIAN RYLAND Publication Design

BOB HARRAS Senior VP - Editor-in-Chief, DC Comics

DIANE NELSON President
DAN DIDIO and JIM LEE Co-Publishers
GEOFF JOHNS Chief Creative Officer
AMIT DESAI Senior VP - Marketing & Global Franchise Management
NAIRI GARDINER Senior VP - Finance
SAM ADES VP - Digital Marketing
BOBBIE CHASE VP - Talent Development
MARK CHIARELLO Senior VP - Art, Design & Collected Editions
JOHN CUNNINGHAM VP - Content Strategy
ANNE DEPIES VP - Strategy Planning & Reporting
DON FALLETTI VP - Manufacturing Operations
LAWRENCE GANEM VP - Editorial Administration & Talent Relations
ALISON GILL Senior VP - Manufacturing & Operations
HANK KANALZ Senior VP - Editorial Strategy & Administration
JAY KOGAN VP - Legal Affairs
DEREK MADDALENA Senior VP - Sales & Business Development
JACK MAHAN VP - Business Affairs
DAN MIRON VP - Sales Planning & Trade Development
NICK NAPOLITANO VP - Manufacturing Administration
CAROL ROEDER VP - Marketing
EDDIE SCANNELL VP - Mass Account & Digital Sales
COURTNEY SIMMONS Senior VP - Publicity & Communications
JIM (SKI) SOKOLOWSKI VP - Comic Book Specialty & Newsstand Sales
SANDY YI Senior VP - Global Franchise Management

BATMAN BEYOND VOLUME 2: CITY OF YESTERDAY

DC Comics, 2900 West Alameda Ave., Burbank, CA 91505
Printed by RR Donnelley, Salem, VA, USA. 8/26/16. First Printing.
ISBN: 978-1-4012-6470-3

Library of Congress Cataloging-in-Publication Data is Available.

PEFC Certified
Printed on paper from sustainably managed forests and controlled sources
PEFC/29-31-75
www.pefc.org

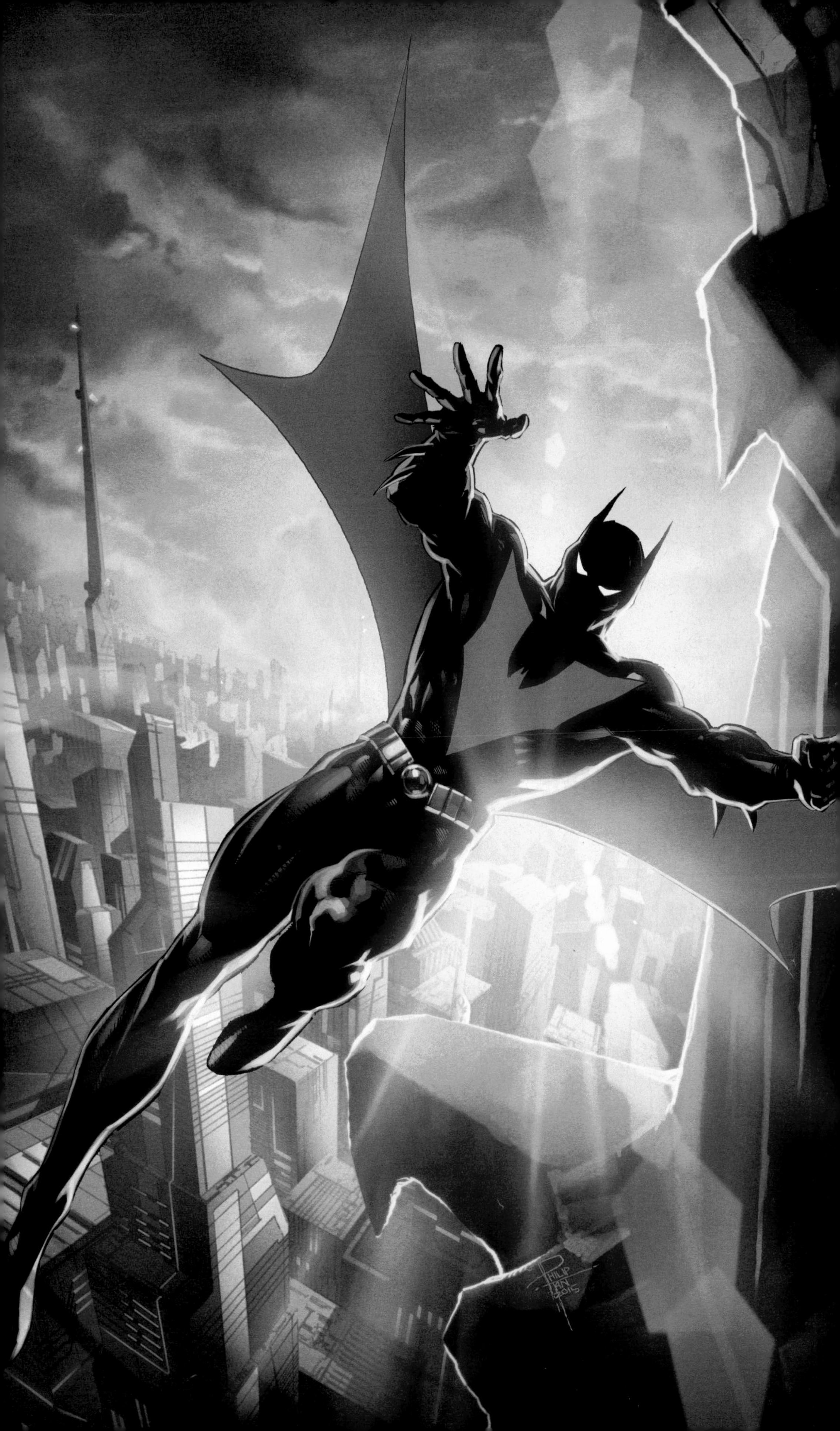
PHILIP TAN 2015

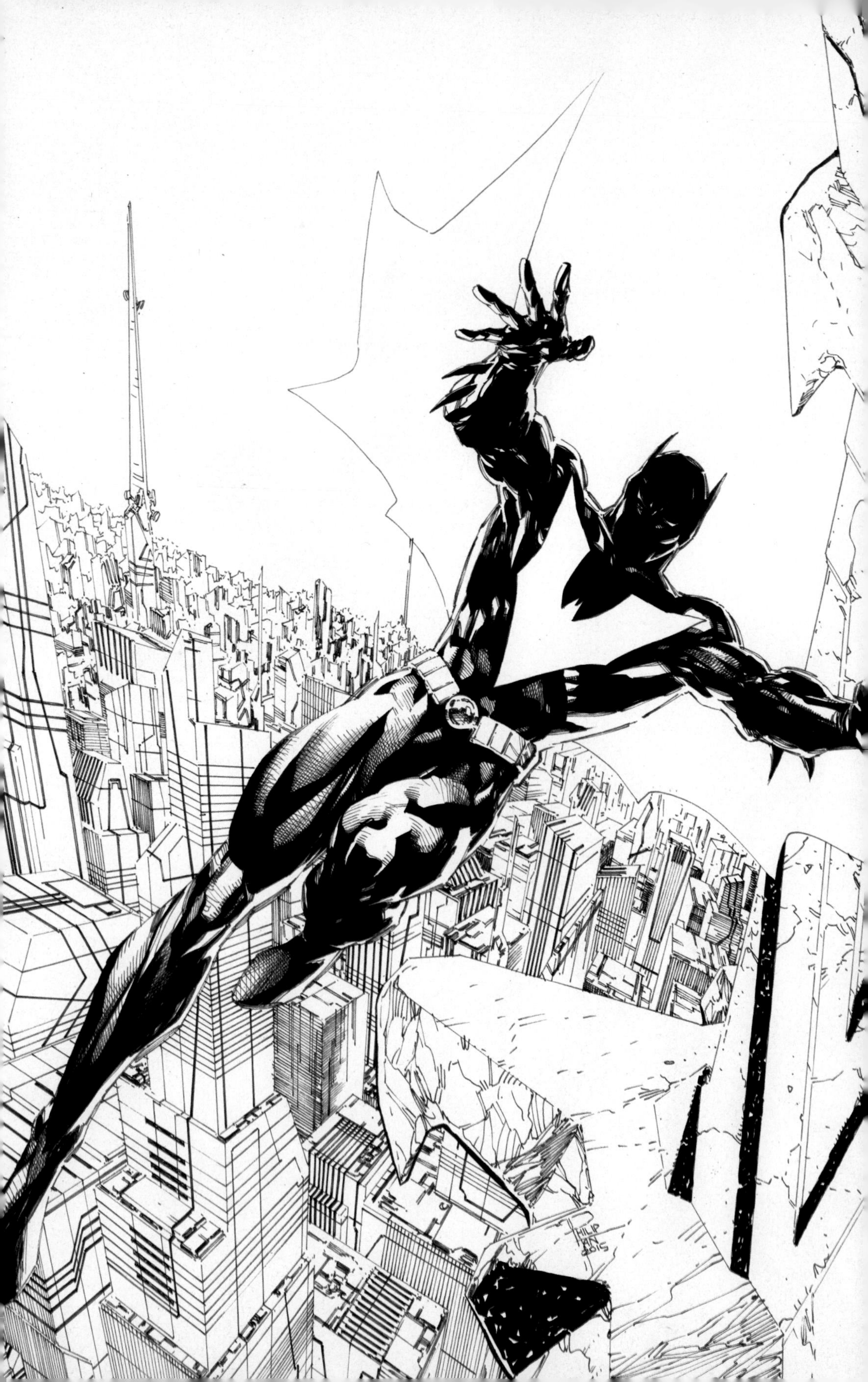

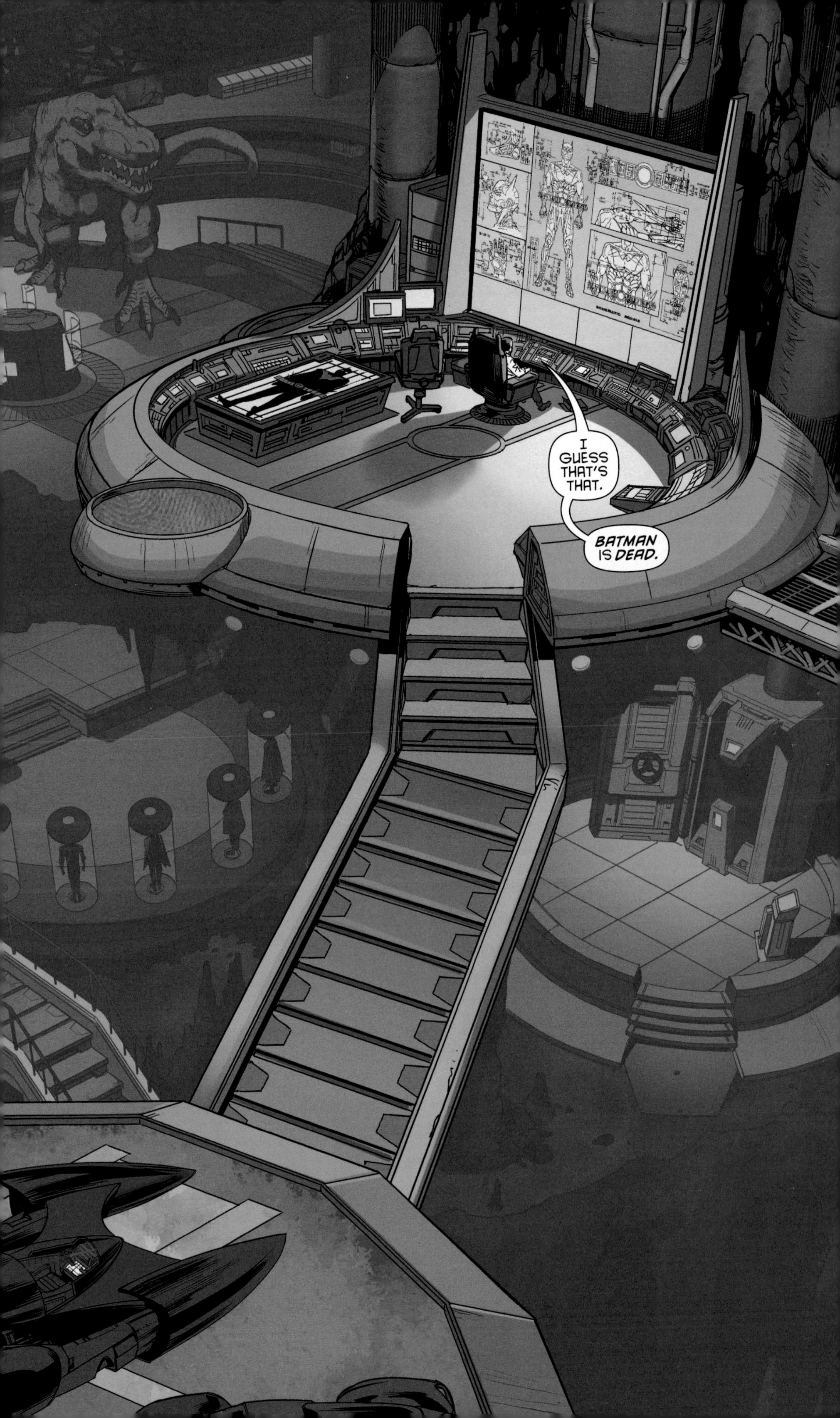
I GUESS THAT'S THAT.
BATMAN IS DEAD.

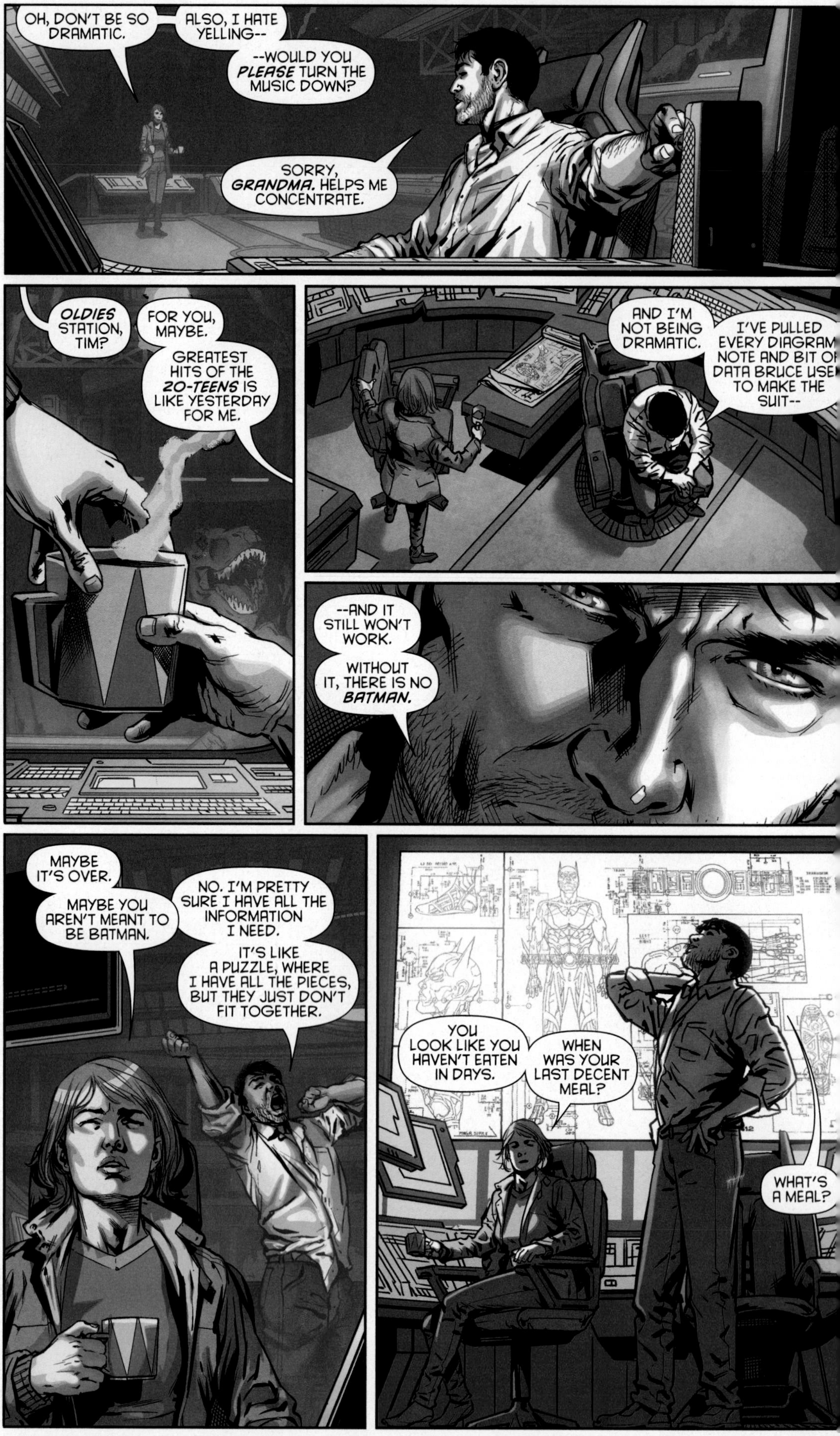

OH, DON'T BE SO DRAMATIC.
ALSO, I HATE YELLING--
--WOULD YOU PLEASE TURN THE MUSIC DOWN?
SORRY, GRANDMA. HELPS ME CONCENTRATE.
OLDIES STATION, TIM?
FOR YOU, MAYBE.
GREATEST HITS OF THE 20-TEENS IS LIKE YESTERDAY FOR ME.
AND I'M NOT BEING DRAMATIC.
I'VE PULLED EVERY DIAGRAM NOTE AND BIT OF DATA BRUCE USED TO MAKE THE SUIT--
--AND IT STILL WON'T WORK.
WITHOUT IT, THERE IS NO BATMAN.
MAYBE IT'S OVER.
MAYBE YOU AREN'T MEANT TO BE BATMAN.
NO. I'M PRETTY SURE I HAVE ALL THE INFORMATION I NEED.
IT'S LIKE A PUZZLE, WHERE I HAVE ALL THE PIECES, BUT THEY JUST DON'T FIT TOGETHER.
YOU LOOK LIKE YOU HAVEN'T EATEN IN DAYS.
WHEN WAS YOUR LAST DECENT MEAL?
WHAT'S A MEAL?

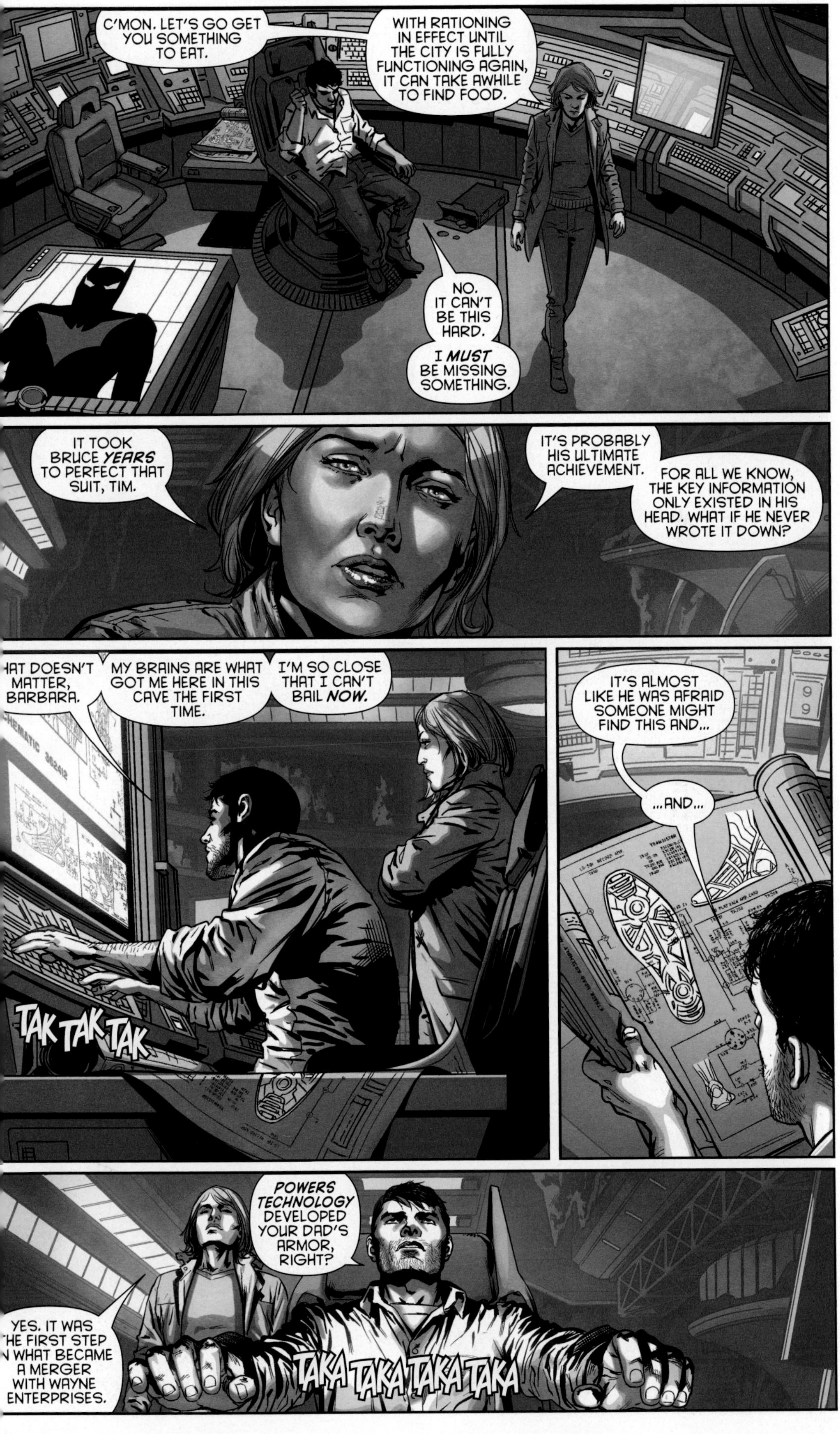
C'MON. LET'S GO GET YOU SOMETHING TO EAT.
WITH RATIONING IN EFFECT UNTIL THE CITY IS FULLY FUNCTIONING AGAIN, IT CAN TAKE AWHILE TO FIND FOOD.
NO. IT CAN'T BE THIS HARD.
I MUST BE MISSING SOMETHING.
IT TOOK BRUCE YEARS TO PERFECT THAT SUIT, TIM.
IT'S PROBABLY HIS ULTIMATE ACHIEVEMENT.
FOR ALL WE KNOW, THE KEY INFORMATION ONLY EXISTED IN HIS HEAD. WHAT IF HE NEVER WROTE IT DOWN?
HAT DOESN'T MATTER, BARBARA.
MY BRAINS ARE WHAT GOT ME HERE IN THIS CAVE THE FIRST TIME.
I'M SO CLOSE THAT I CAN'T BAIL NOW.
TAK TAK TAK
IT'S ALMOST LIKE HE WAS AFRAID SOMEONE MIGHT FIND THIS AND...
...AND...
POWERS TECHNOLOGY DEVELOPED YOUR DAD'S ARMOR, RIGHT?
YES. IT WAS HE FIRST STEP N WHAT BECAME A MERGER WITH WAYNE ENTERPRISES.
TAKA TAKA TAKA TAKA

BUT BRUCE DIDN'T *TRUST* DEREK POWERS.

IF HE FEARED THAT POWERS WOULD FIND HIS WORK...

...HE'D SABOTAGE HIS OWN DATA.

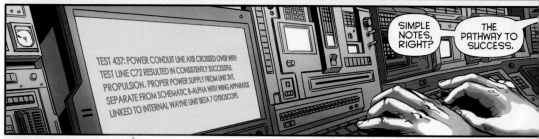

TEST 437: POWER CONDUIT LINE AXB CROSSED OVER WITH TEST LINE C72 RESULTED IN CONSISTENTLY SUCCESSFUL PROPULSION. PROPER POWER SUPPLY FROM UNIT 3VT, SEPARATE FROM SCHEMATIC B-ALPHA WITH WING APPARATUS LINKED TO INTERNAL WAYNE UNIT BETA 7 GYROSCOPE

SIMPLE NOTES, RIGHT?

THE PATHWAY TO SUCCESS.

TEST 437: **POWER** CONDUIT **LINE** AXB CROSSED **OVER** WITH TEST LINE **C72** RESULTED IN CONSISTENTLY SUCCESSFUL **PROPULSION. PROPER** POWER **SUPPLY** FROM UNIT **3VT,** SEPARATE FROM SCHEMATIC **B-ALPHA** WITH WING APPARATUS LINKED **TO** INTERNAL WAYNE UNIT BETA 7 GYROSCOPE

BUT APPLY ONE OF BRUCE'S CODES... SKIPPING ONE, TWO, THEN THREE WORDS PER SENTENCE...

EVERYTHING *CHANGES.*

THAT EASY?

ONLY IF YOU KNOW HOW THE MAN THINKS.

AND YOU CAN COUNT THOSE PEOPLE ON ONE HAND.

HOW DID I NOT SEE THAT?

WE'RE BOTH BEAT. IF I HADN'T NAILED IT, YOU WOULD HAVE.

NOW?

DIG DEEP AND PUSH--

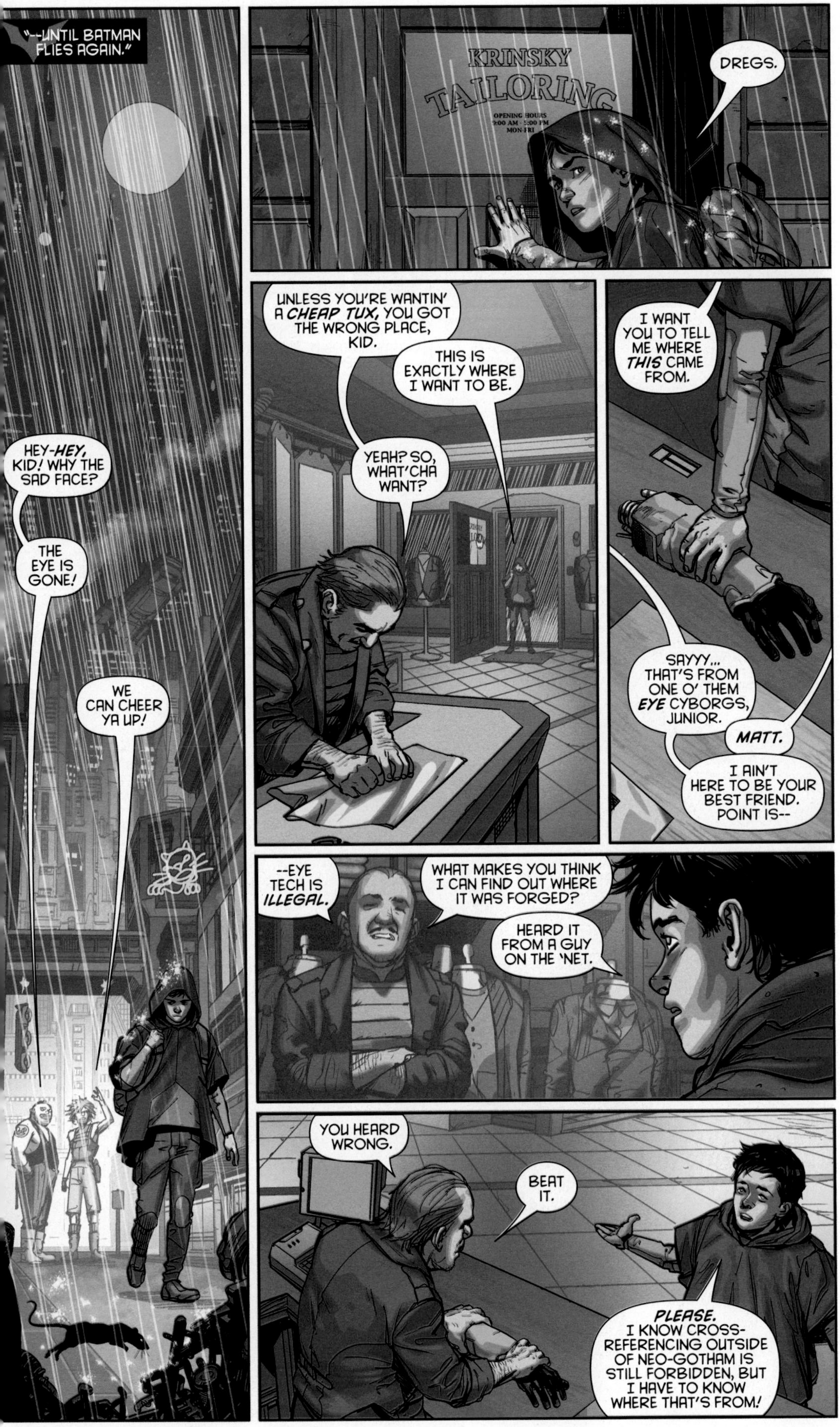
"--UNTIL BATMAN FLIES AGAIN."
HEY-HEY, KID! WHY THE SAD FACE?
THE EYE IS GONE!
WE CAN CHEER YA UP!
KRINSKY TAILORING
OPENING HOURS 9:00 AM - 5:00 PM MON-FRI
DREGS.
UNLESS YOU'RE WANTIN' A CHEAP TUX, YOU GOT THE WRONG PLACE, KID.
THIS IS EXACTLY WHERE I WANT TO BE.
YEAH? SO, WHAT'CHA WANT?
I WANT YOU TO TELL ME WHERE THIS CAME FROM.
SAYYY... THAT'S FROM ONE O' THEM EYE CYBORGS, JUNIOR.
MATT.
I AIN'T HERE TO BE YOUR BEST FRIEND. POINT IS--
--EYE TECH IS ILLEGAL.
WHAT MAKES YOU THINK I CAN FIND OUT WHERE IT WAS FORGED?
HEARD IT FROM A GUY ON THE 'NET.
YOU HEARD WRONG.
BEAT IT.
PLEASE. I KNOW CROSS-REFERENCING OUTSIDE OF NEO-GOTHAM IS STILL FORBIDDEN, BUT I HAVE TO KNOW WHERE THAT'S FROM!

SUPPOSE I DID HAVE A SCANALYZER.

WHAT'S IT *WORTH* TO YOU?

I DON'T HAVE ANY CREDITS.

BUT YOU CAN *KEEP IT.*

I JUST NEED TO KNOW WHERE IT'S FROM.

ONLY THE *GLOBAL PEACE AGENCY* IS ALLOWED TO HAVE 'BORG GEAR...

THAT'S WHAT MAKES IT VALUABLE.

FOR SOMEONE WITH THE RIGHT CONNECTIONS.

HEH. FEEL LIKE I SHOULD BE INSULTED BY THAT.

LET'S SEE WHAT WE GOT HERE...

ION IMPLANTATION TRACES TO ONE FOUNDRY.

METROPOLIS, NEAR AS I CAN TELL.

I *KNEW* IT!

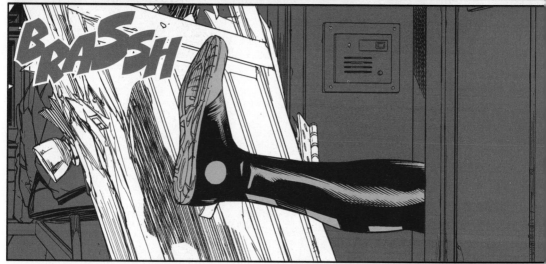

BRASSH

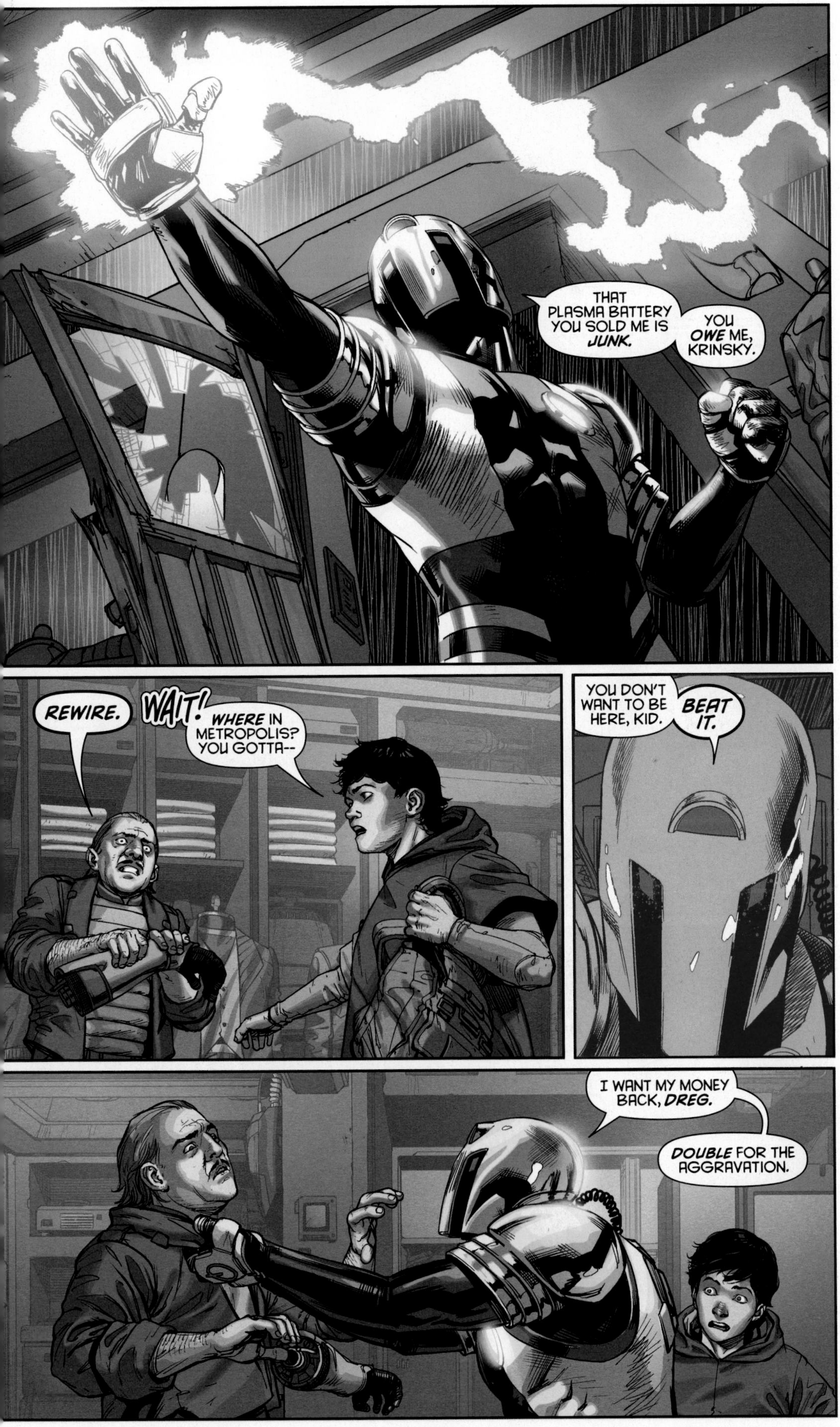
THAT PLASMA BATTERY YOU SOLD ME IS JUNK.
YOU OWE ME, KRINSKY.
REWIRE.
WAIT!
WHERE IN METROPOLIS? YOU GOTTA--
YOU DON'T WANT TO BE HERE, KID.
BEAT IT.
I WANT MY MONEY BACK, DREG.
DOUBLE FOR THE AGGRAVATION.

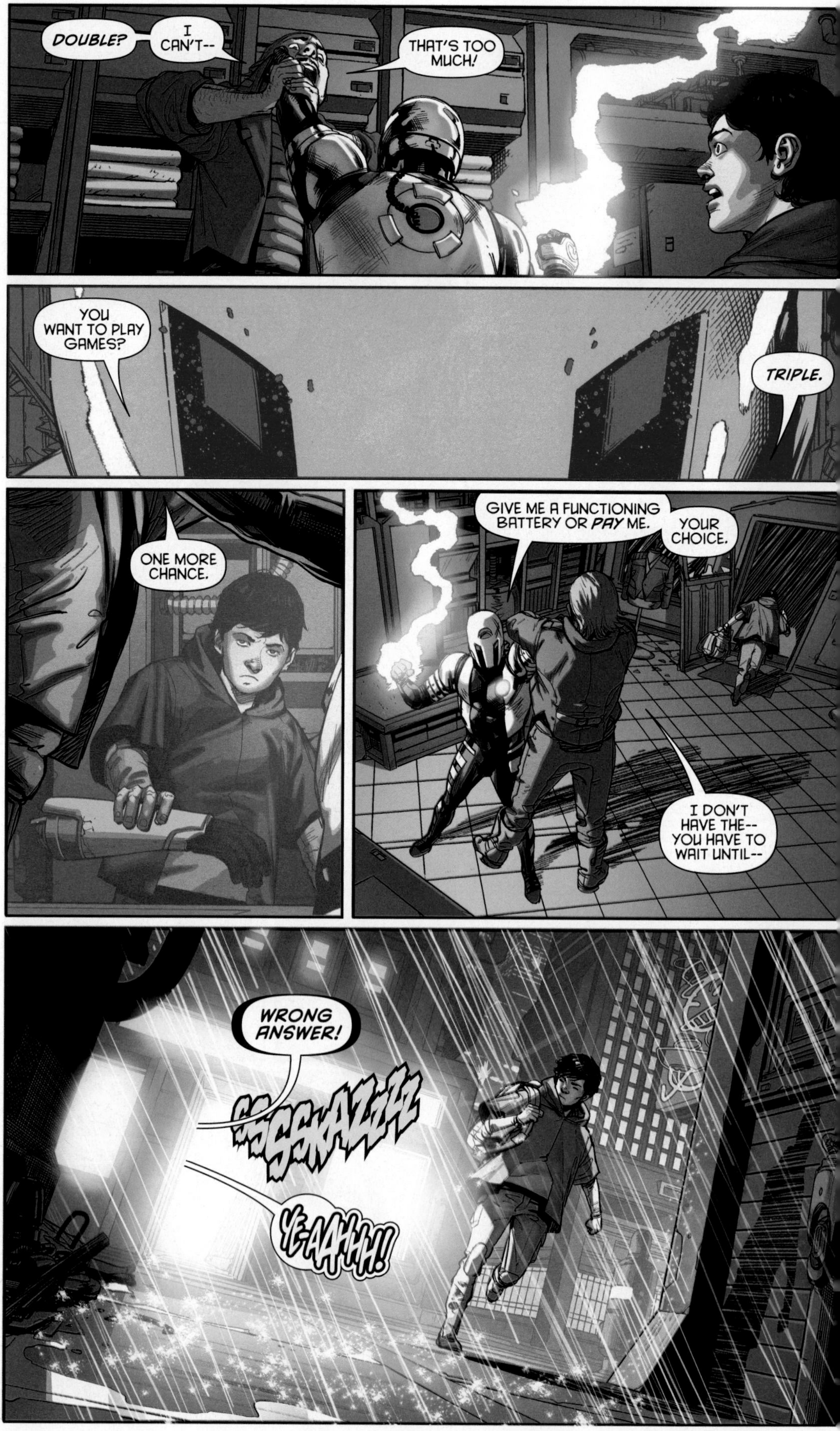
DOUBLE?
I CAN'T--
THAT'S TOO MUCH!
YOU WANT TO PLAY GAMES?
TRIPLE.
ONE MORE CHANCE.
GIVE ME A FUNCTIONING BATTERY OR PAY ME.
YOUR CHOICE.
I DON'T HAVE THE-- YOU HAVE TO WAIT UNTIL--
WRONG ANSWER!
SSSSKAZZZZ
YE-AAHHH!

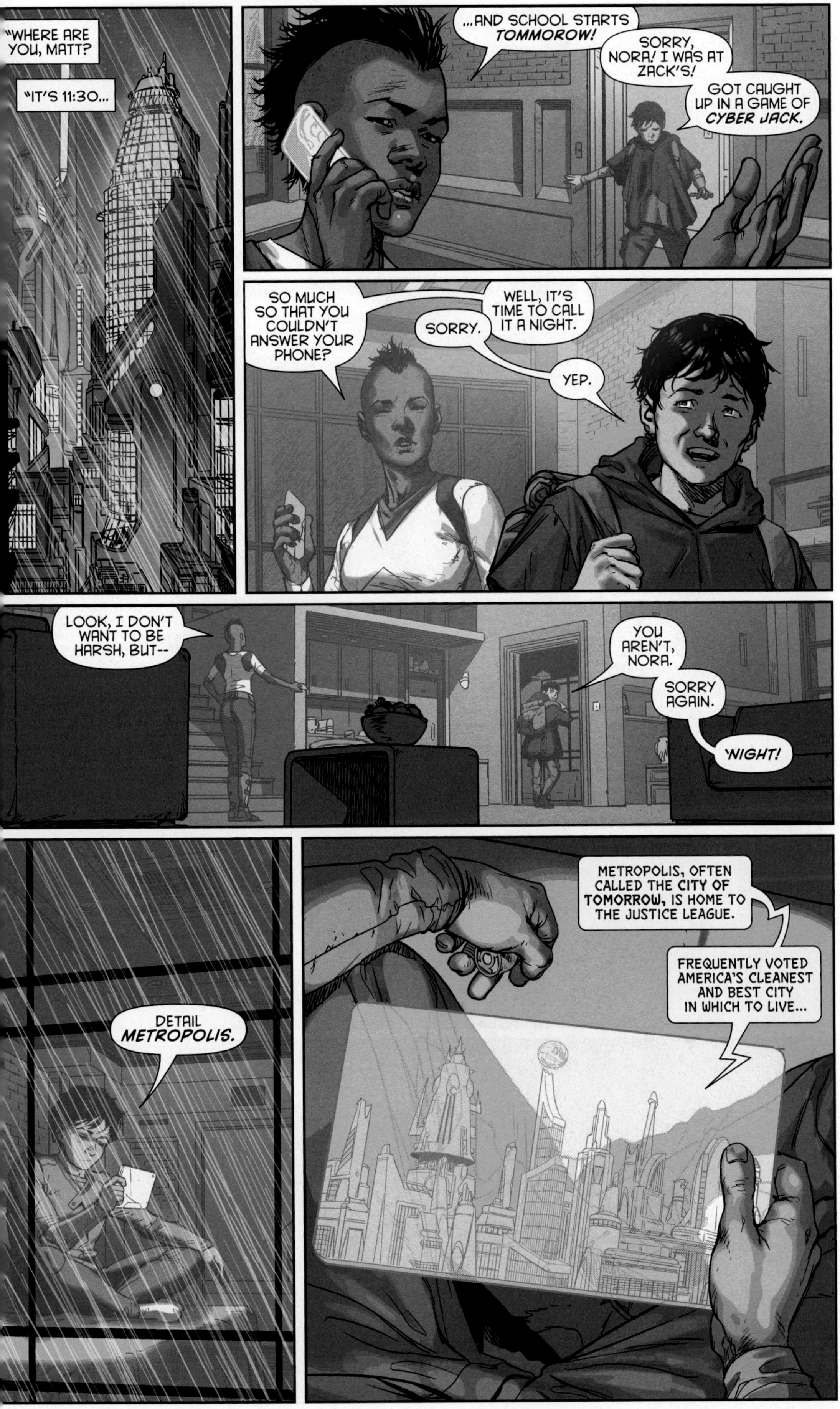
"WHERE ARE YOU, MATT?
"IT'S 11:30...
...AND SCHOOL STARTS TOMMOROW!
SORRY, NORA! I WAS AT ZACK'S!
GOT CAUGHT UP IN A GAME OF CYBER JACK.
SO MUCH SO THAT YOU COULDN'T ANSWER YOUR PHONE?
SORRY.
WELL, IT'S TIME TO CALL IT A NIGHT.
YEP.
LOOK, I DON'T WANT TO BE HARSH, BUT--
YOU AREN'T, NORA.
SORRY AGAIN.
'NIGHT!
DETAIL METROPOLIS.
METROPOLIS, OFTEN CALLED THE CITY OF TOMORROW, IS HOME TO THE JUSTICE LEAGUE.
FREQUENTLY VOTED AMERICA'S CLEANEST AND BEST CITY IN WHICH TO LIVE...

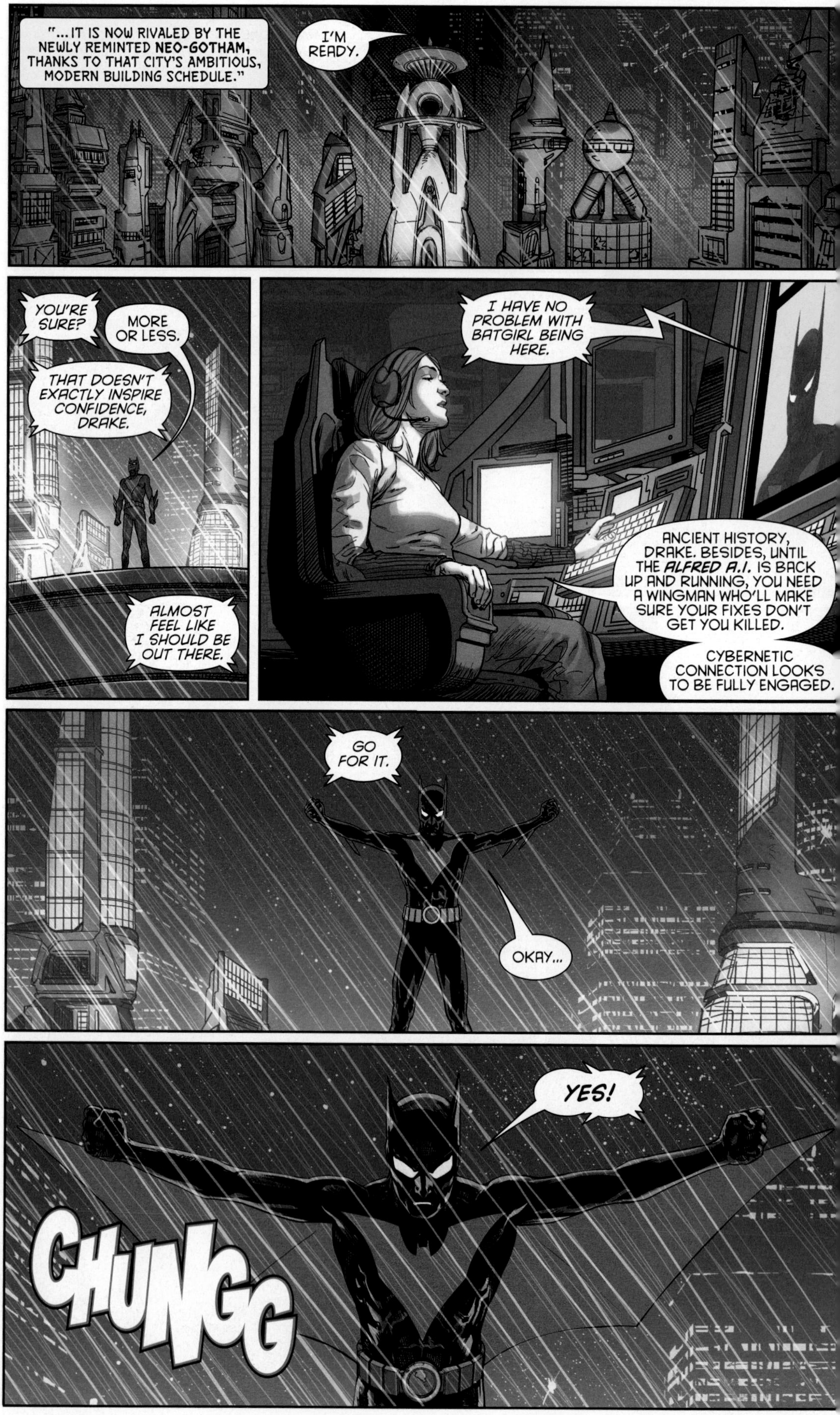

"...IT IS NOW RIVALED BY THE NEWLY REMINTED NEO-GOTHAM, THANKS TO THAT CITY'S AMBITIOUS, MODERN BUILDING SCHEDULE."
I'M READY.
YOU'RE SURE?
MORE OR LESS.
THAT DOESN'T EXACTLY INSPIRE CONFIDENCE, DRAKE.
ALMOST FEEL LIKE I SHOULD BE OUT THERE.
I HAVE NO PROBLEM WITH BATGIRL BEING HERE.
ANCIENT HISTORY, DRAKE. BESIDES, UNTIL THE ALFRED A.I. IS BACK UP AND RUNNING, YOU NEED A WINGMAN WHO'LL MAKE SURE YOUR FIXES DON'T GET YOU KILLED.
CYBERNETIC CONNECTION LOOKS TO BE FULLY ENGAGED.
GO FOR IT.
OKAY...
YES!
CHUNGG

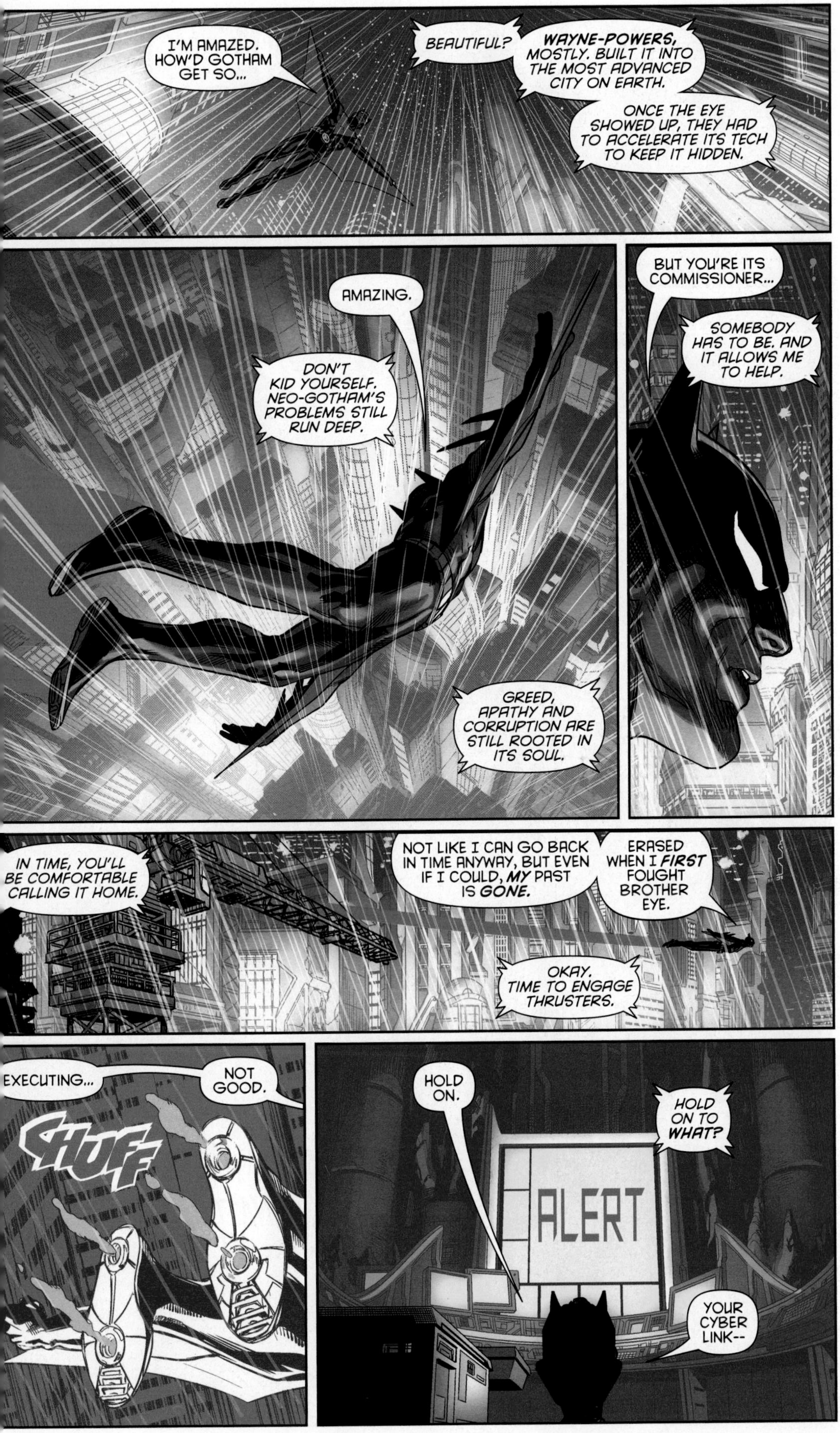
I'M AMAZED. HOW'D GOTHAM GET SO...
BEAUTIFUL?
WAYNE-POWERS, MOSTLY. BUILT IT INTO THE MOST ADVANCED CITY ON EARTH.
ONCE THE EYE SHOWED UP, THEY HAD TO ACCELERATE ITS TECH TO KEEP IT HIDDEN.
AMAZING.
DON'T KID YOURSELF. NEO-GOTHAM'S PROBLEMS STILL RUN DEEP.
GREED, APATHY AND CORRUPTION ARE STILL ROOTED IN ITS SOUL.
BUT YOU'RE ITS COMMISSIONER...
SOMEBODY HAS TO BE. AND IT ALLOWS ME TO HELP.
IN TIME, YOU'LL BE COMFORTABLE CALLING IT HOME.
NOT LIKE I CAN GO BACK IN TIME ANYWAY, BUT EVEN IF I COULD, MY PAST IS GONE.
ERASED WHEN I FIRST FOUGHT BROTHER EYE.
OKAY. TIME TO ENGAGE THRUSTERS.
EXECUTING...
NOT GOOD.
SHUFF
HOLD ON.
HOLD ON TO WHAT?
ALERT
YOUR CYBER LINK--

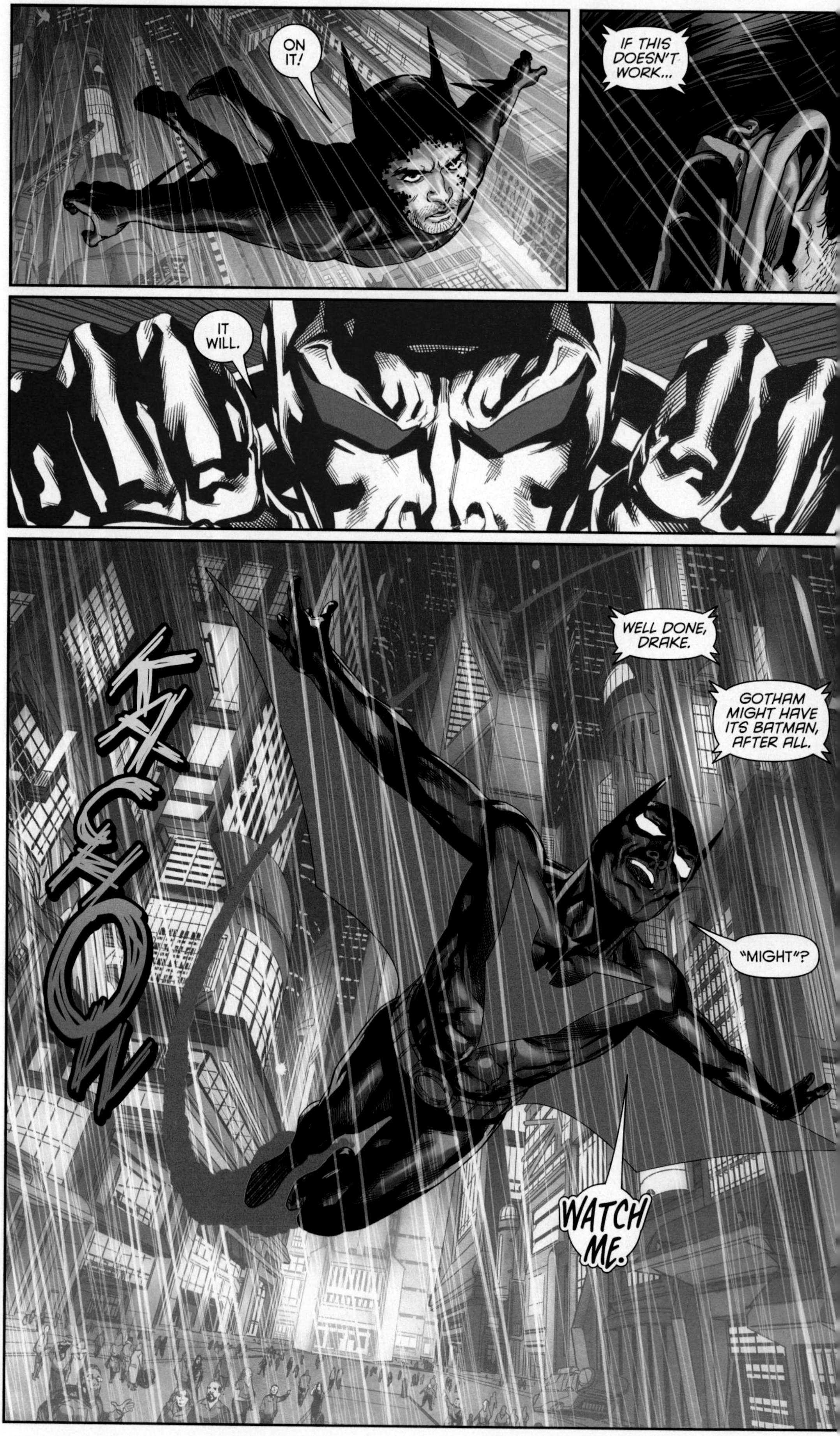
ON IT!
IF THIS DOESN'T WORK...
IT WILL.
KA-CHOOM
WELL DONE, DRAKE.
GOTHAM MIGHT HAVE ITS BATMAN, AFTER ALL.
"MIGHT"?
WATCH ME.

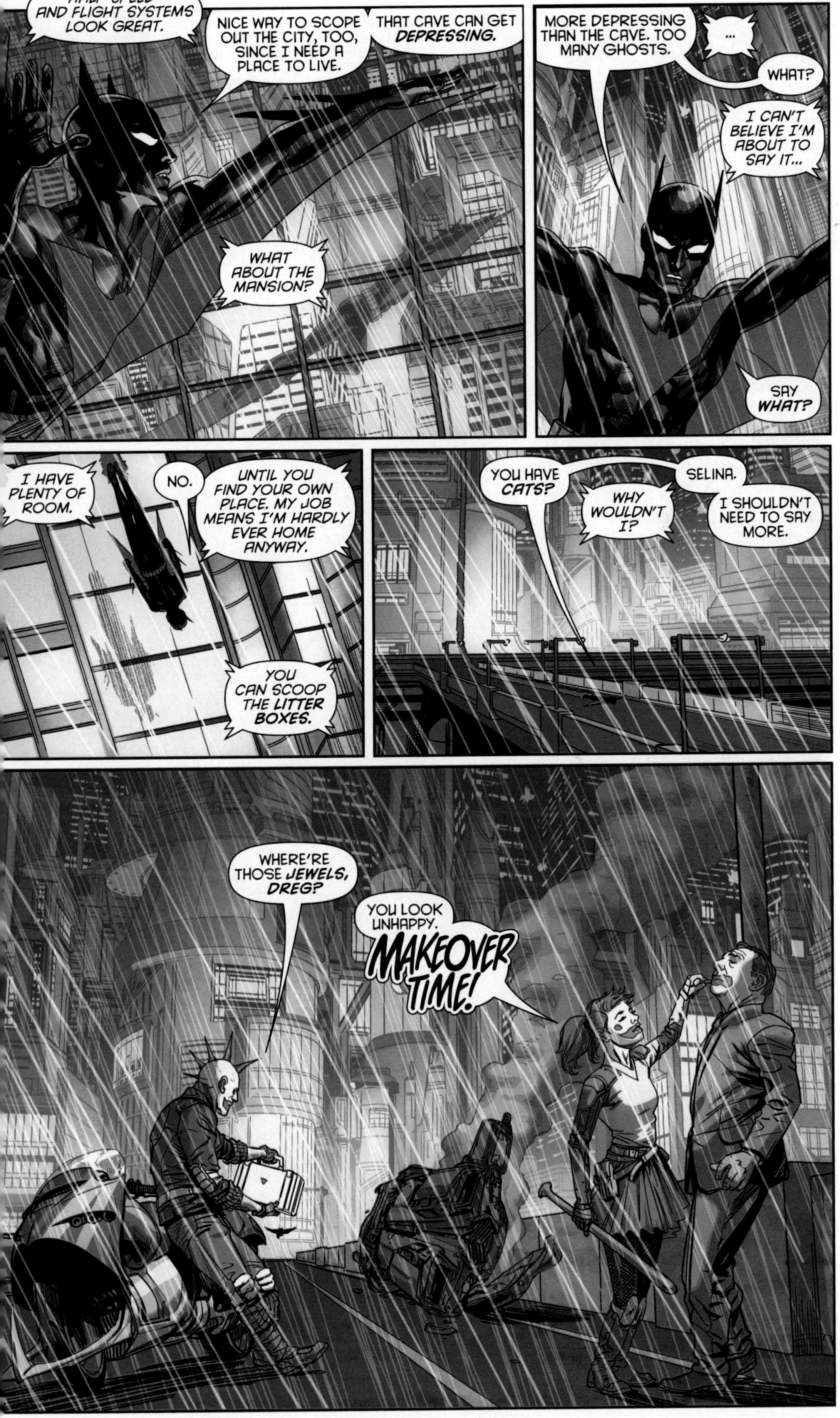
HALF-SPEED AND FLIGHT SYSTEMS LOOK GREAT.
NICE WAY TO SCOPE OUT THE CITY, TOO, SINCE I NEED A PLACE TO LIVE.
THAT CAVE CAN GET DEPRESSING.
WHAT ABOUT THE MANSION?
MORE DEPRESSING THAN THE CAVE. TOO MANY GHOSTS.
...
WHAT?
I CAN'T BELIEVE I'M ABOUT TO SAY IT...
SAY WHAT?
I HAVE PLENTY OF ROOM.
NO.
UNTIL YOU FIND YOUR OWN PLACE. MY JOB MEANS I'M HARDLY EVER HOME ANYWAY.
YOU CAN SCOOP THE LITTER BOXES.
YOU HAVE CATS?
WHY WOULDN'T I?
SELINA.
I SHOULDN'T NEED TO SAY MORE.
WHERE'RE THOSE JEWELS, DREG?
YOU LOOK UNHAPPY.
MAKEOVER TIME!

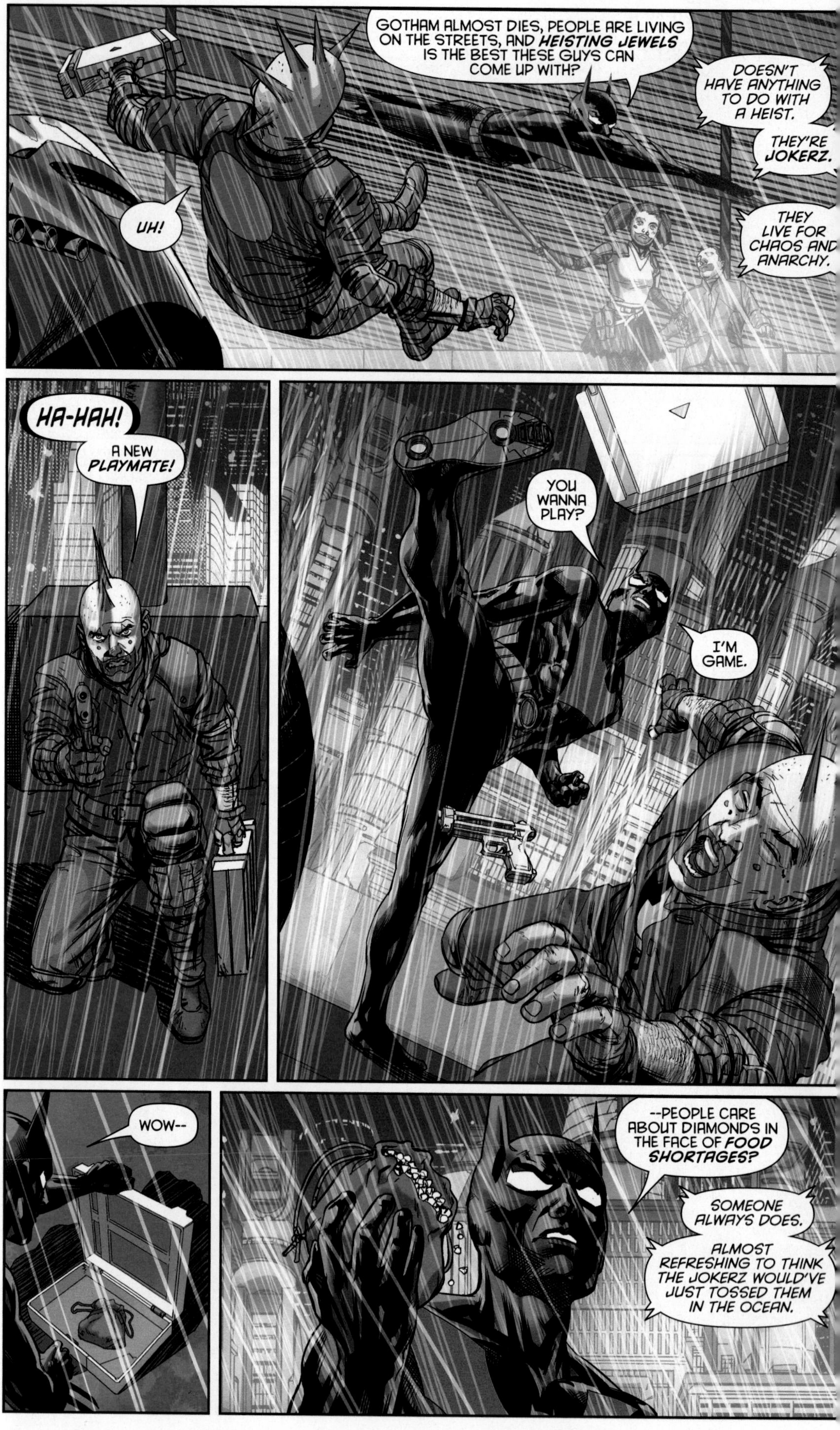
GOTHAM ALMOST DIES, PEOPLE ARE LIVING ON THE STREETS, AND *HEISTING JEWELS* IS THE BEST THESE GUYS CAN COME UP WITH?
DOESN'T HAVE ANYTHING TO DO WITH A HEIST.
THEY'RE *JOKERZ.*
THEY LIVE FOR CHAOS AND ANARCHY.
UH!
HA-HAH!
A NEW *PLAYMATE!*
YOU WANNA PLAY?
I'M GAME.
WOW--
--PEOPLE CARE ABOUT DIAMONDS IN THE FACE OF *FOOD SHORTAGES?*
SOMEONE ALWAYS DOES.
ALMOST REFRESHING TO THINK THE JOKERZ WOULD'VE JUST TOSSED THEM IN THE OCEAN.

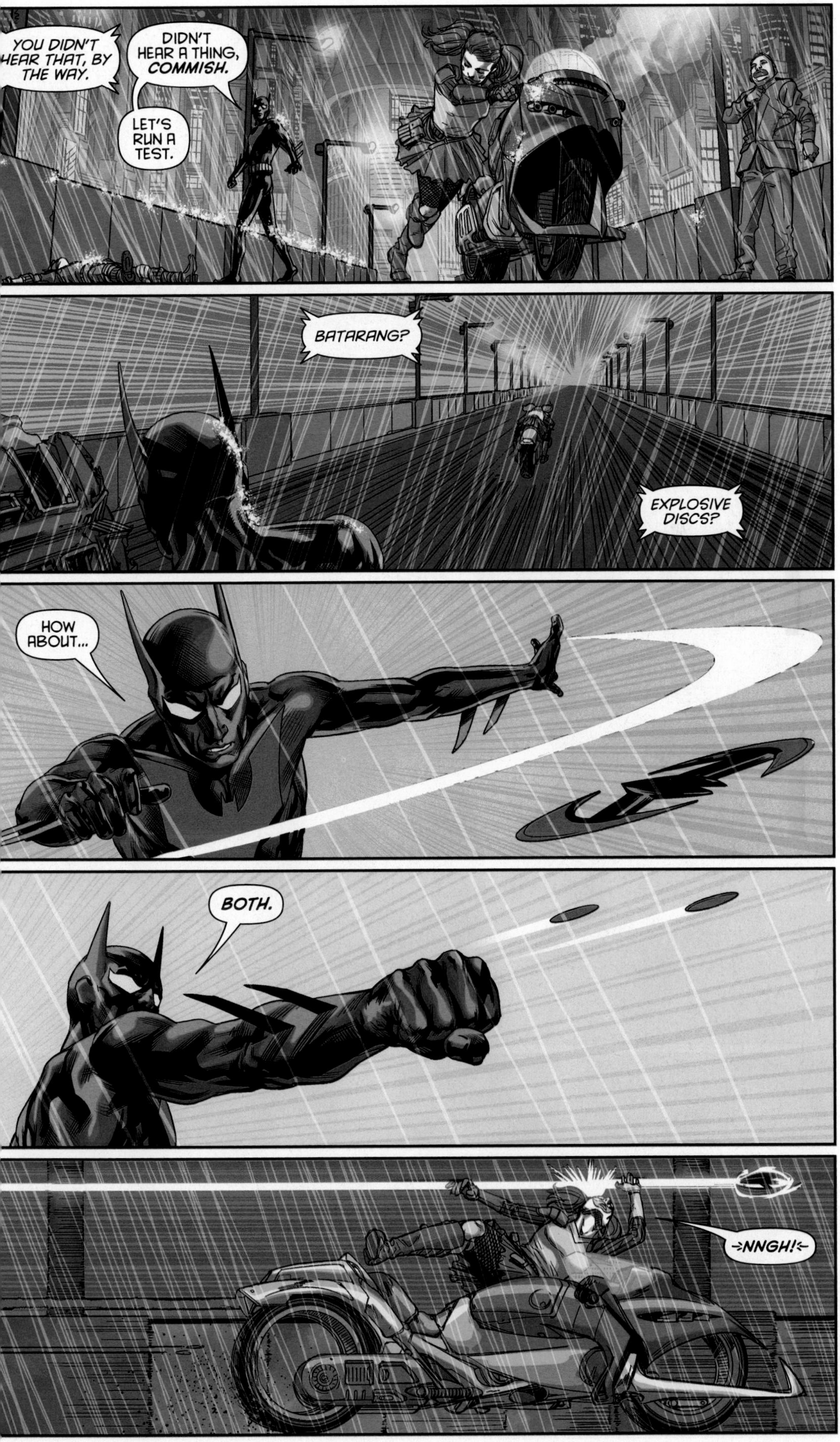
YOU DIDN'T HEAR THAT, BY THE WAY.
DIDN'T HEAR A THING, COMMISH.
LET'S RUN A TEST.
BATARANG?
EXPLOSIVE DISCS?
HOW ABOUT...
BOTH.
NNGH!

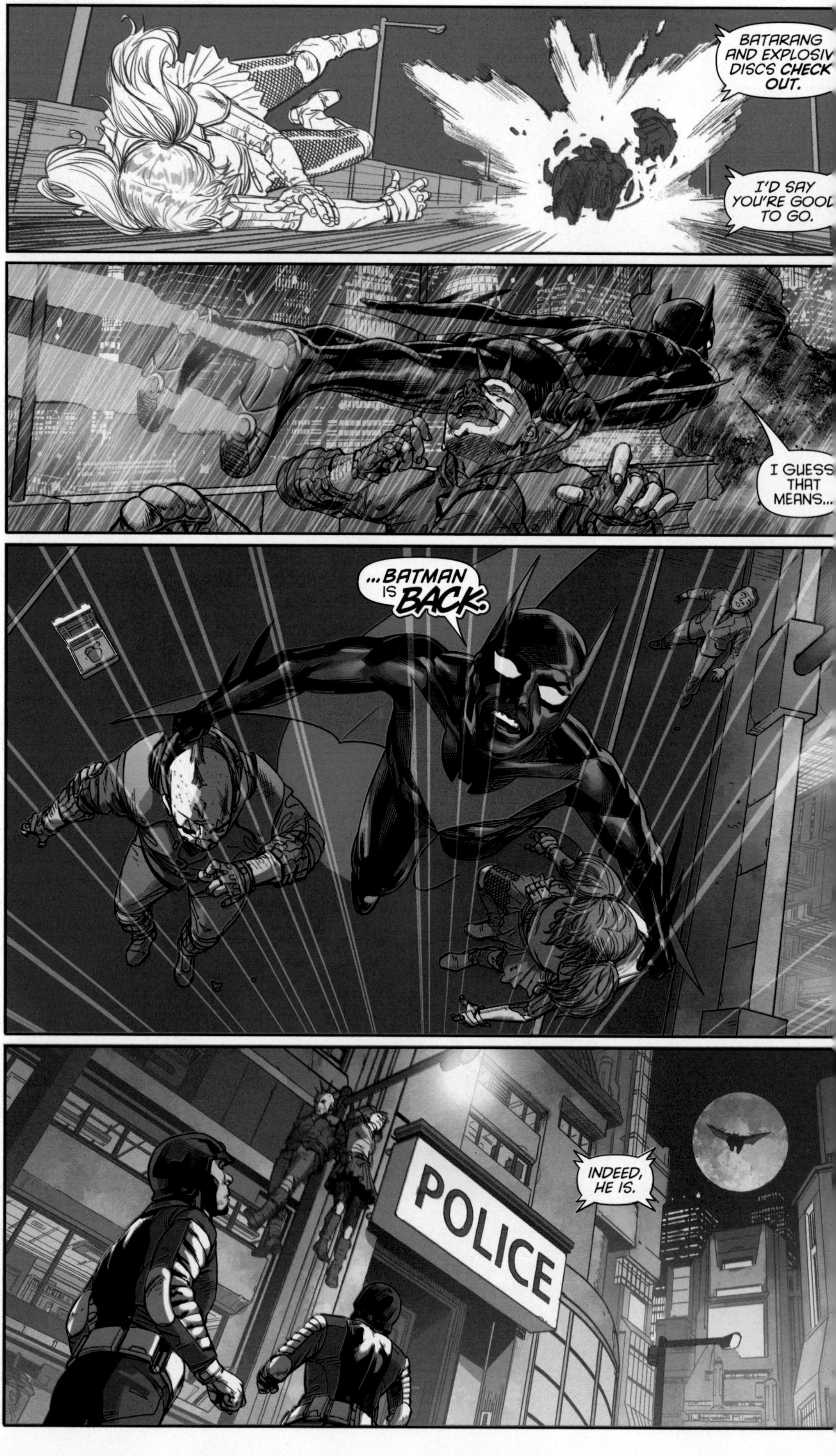
BATARANG AND EXPLOSIV DISCS CHECK OUT.
I'D SAY YOU'RE GOOD TO GO.
I GUESS THAT MEANS...
...BATMAN IS BACK.
INDEED, HE IS.
POLICE

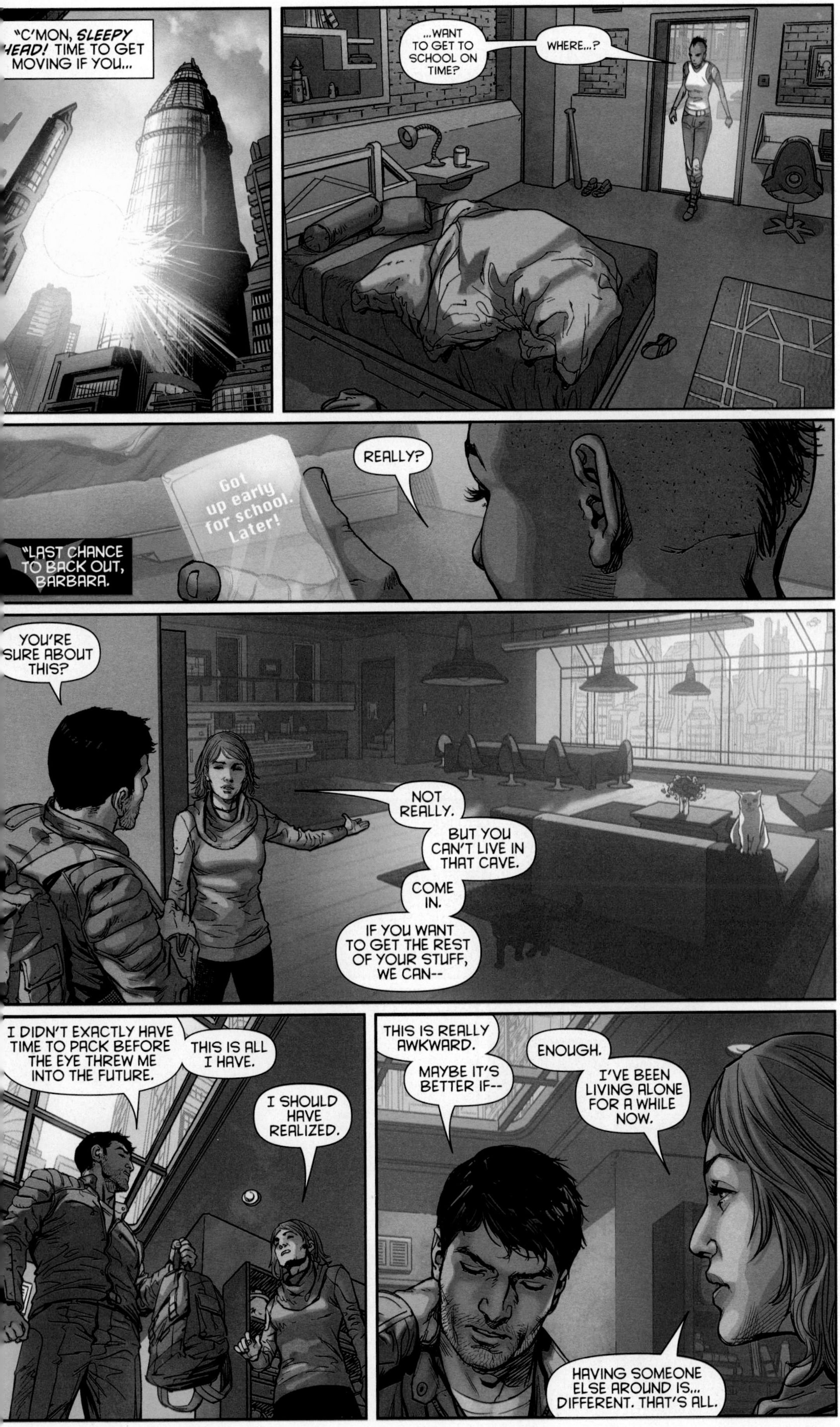
"C'MON, *SLEEPY HEAD!* TIME TO GET MOVING IF YOU...
...WANT TO GET TO SCHOOL ON TIME?
WHERE...?
REALLY?
Got up early for school. Later!
"LAST CHANCE TO BACK OUT, BARBARA.
YOU'RE SURE ABOUT THIS?
NOT REALLY.
BUT YOU CAN'T LIVE IN THAT CAVE.
COME IN.
IF YOU WANT TO GET THE REST OF YOUR STUFF, WE CAN--
I DIDN'T EXACTLY HAVE TIME TO PACK BEFORE THE EYE THREW ME INTO THE FUTURE.
THIS IS ALL I HAVE.
I SHOULD HAVE REALIZED.
THIS IS REALLY AWKWARD.
MAYBE IT'S BETTER IF--
ENOUGH.
I'VE BEEN LIVING ALONE FOR A WHILE NOW.
HAVING SOMEONE ELSE AROUND IS... DIFFERENT. THAT'S ALL.

NEVER MARRIED?

LET'S KEEP PERSONAL LIVES OFF LIMITS, OKAY?

YOU MIGHT FEEL LIKE YOU KNOW ME...

...BUT I HAVEN'T SEEN YOU IN *DECADES*, TIM.

YOU *DISAPPEARED.* I...WE *ALL* THOUGHT YOU WERE *DEAD.*

I LOOK AT YOU AND I GET A LITTLE UNNERVED, YOU KNOW?

YOU HAVEN'T *CHANGED.*

BUT, THE REST OF US...

I SHOULD'VE... DAMN.

THIS ISN'T GOING TO WORK, BARBARA.

I'LL LEAVE.

NO. LIKE I SAID...I'LL ADJUST.

STAY.

WELL, I'M GOING OVER TO NORA'S TONIGHT, ANYWAY.

I HAVE TO TALK TO MATT.

I THINK HE STILL RESENTS ME FOR TAKING HIS BROTHER'S PLACE.

I WANT TO BE GOOD WITH HIM.

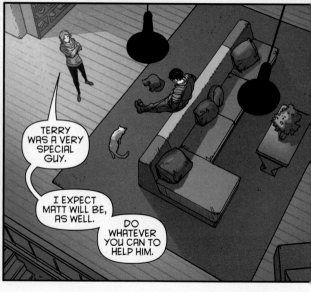

TERRY WAS A VERY SPECIAL GUY.

I EXPECT MATT WILL BE, AS WELL.

DO WHATEVER YOU CAN TO HELP HIM.

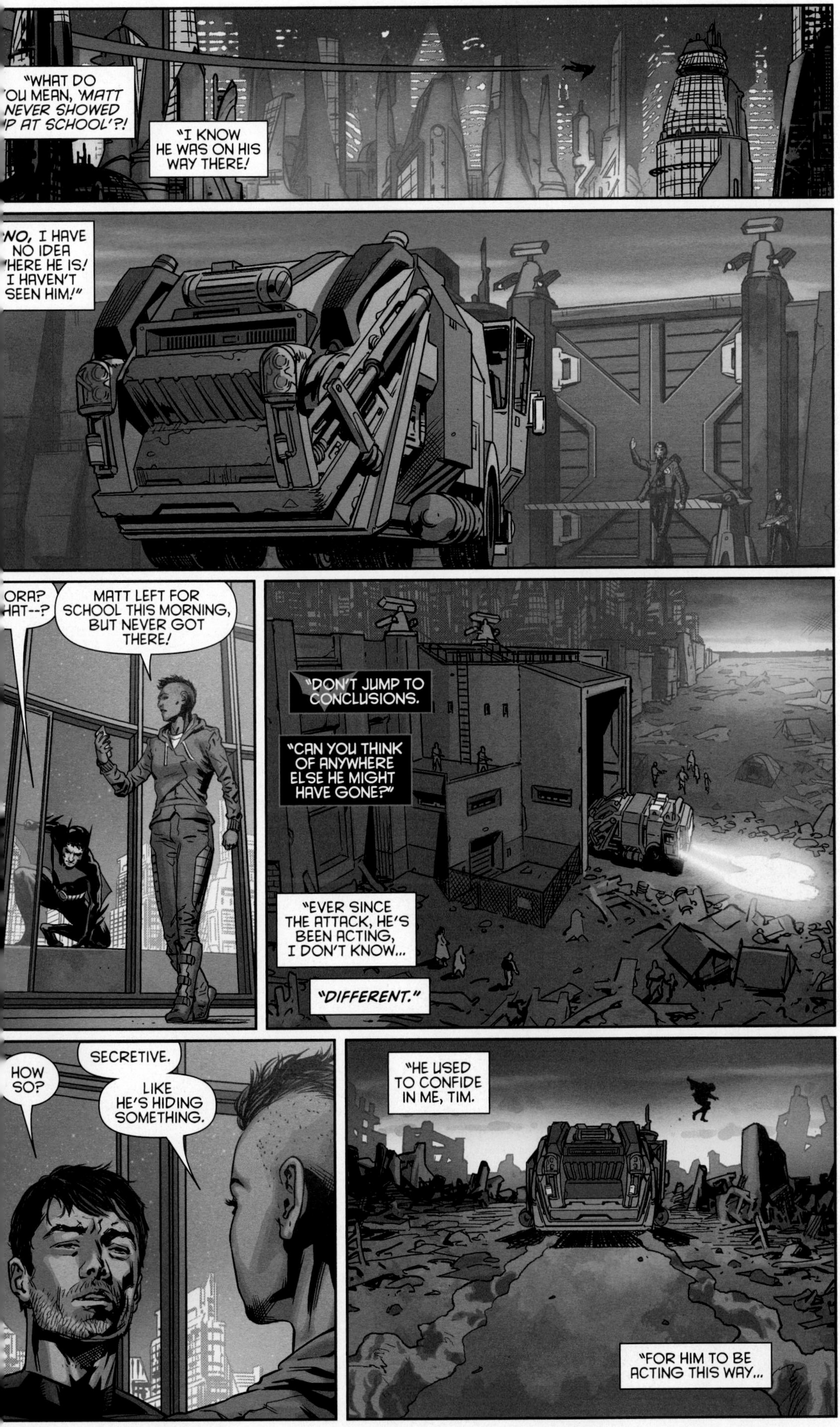
"WHAT DO
'OU MEAN, 'MATT NEVER SHOWED 'P AT SCHOOL'?!
"I KNOW HE WAS ON HIS WAY THERE!
'NO, I HAVE NO IDEA 'HERE HE IS! I HAVEN'T SEEN HIM!"
ORA? HAT--?
MATT LEFT FOR SCHOOL THIS MORNING, BUT NEVER GOT THERE!
"DON'T JUMP TO CONCLUSIONS.
"CAN YOU THINK OF ANYWHERE ELSE HE MIGHT HAVE GONE?"
"EVER SINCE THE ATTACK, HE'S BEEN ACTING, I DON'T KNOW...
"DIFFERENT."
HOW SO?
SECRETIVE.
LIKE HE'S HIDING SOMETHING.
"HE USED TO CONFIDE IN ME, TIM.
"FOR HIM TO BE ACTING THIS WAY...

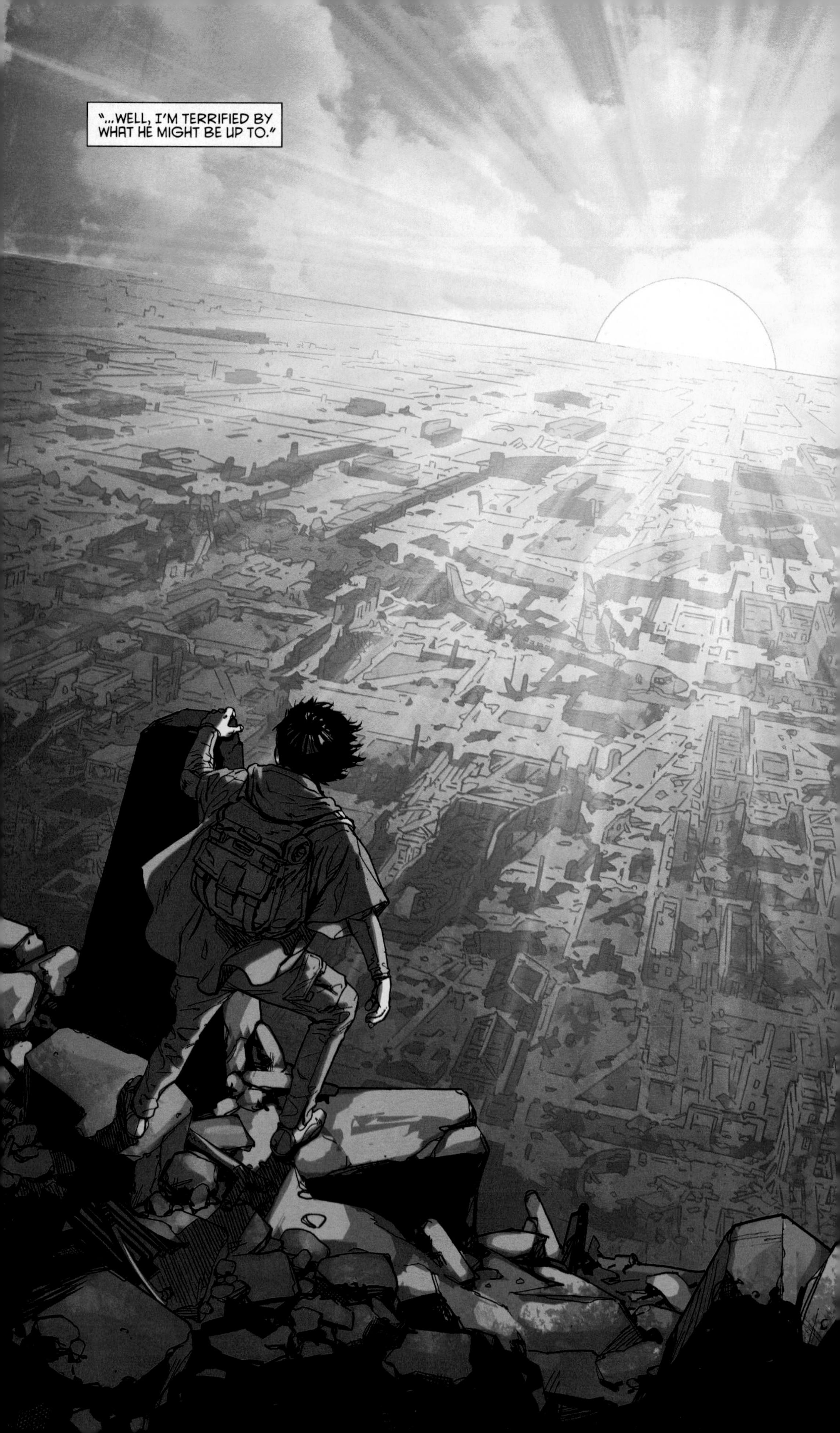
"...WELL, I'M TERRIFIED BY WHAT HE MIGHT BE UP TO."

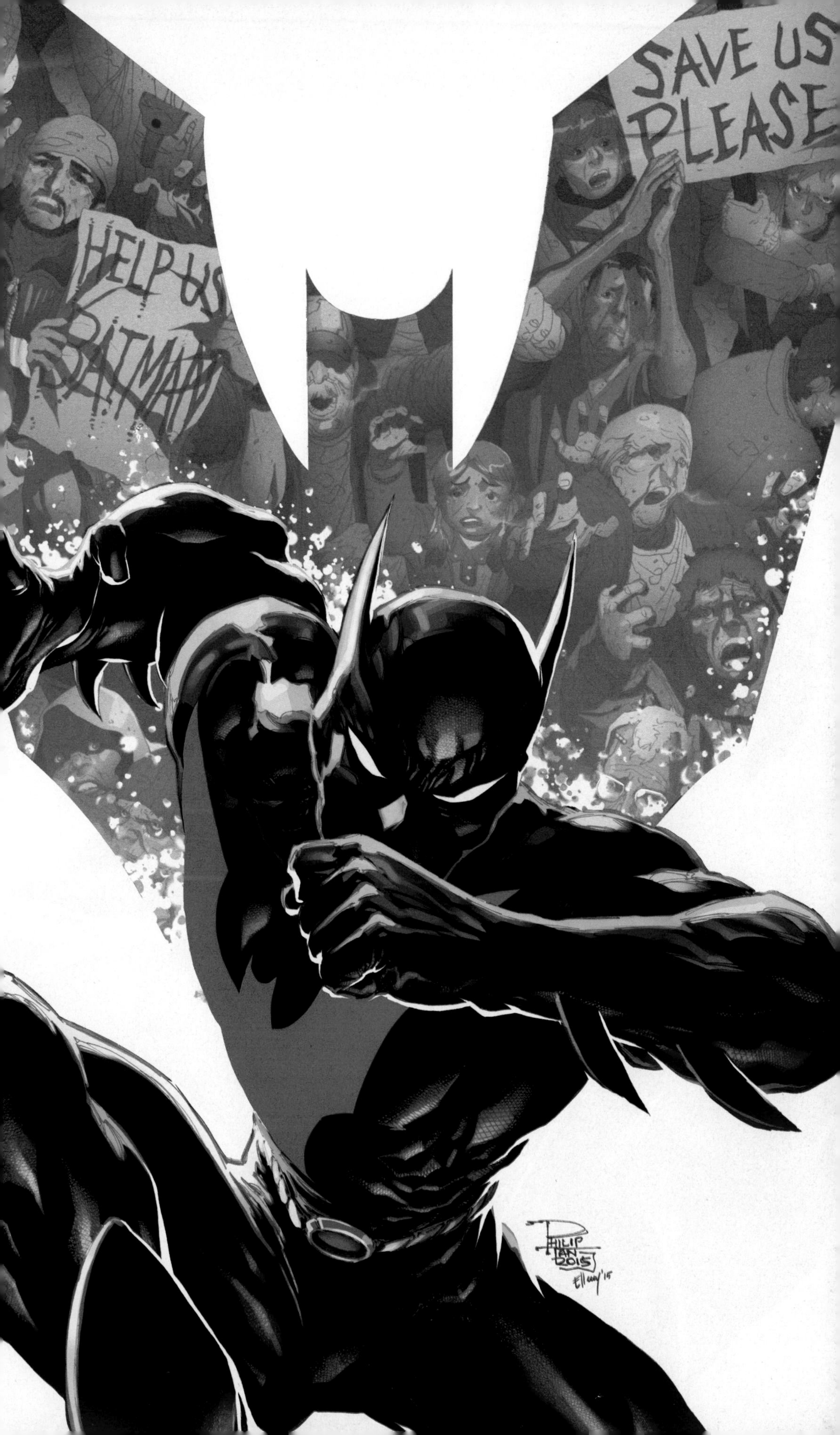
SAVE US
PLEASE
HELP US
BATMAN
PHILIP TAN 2015
Elloy '15

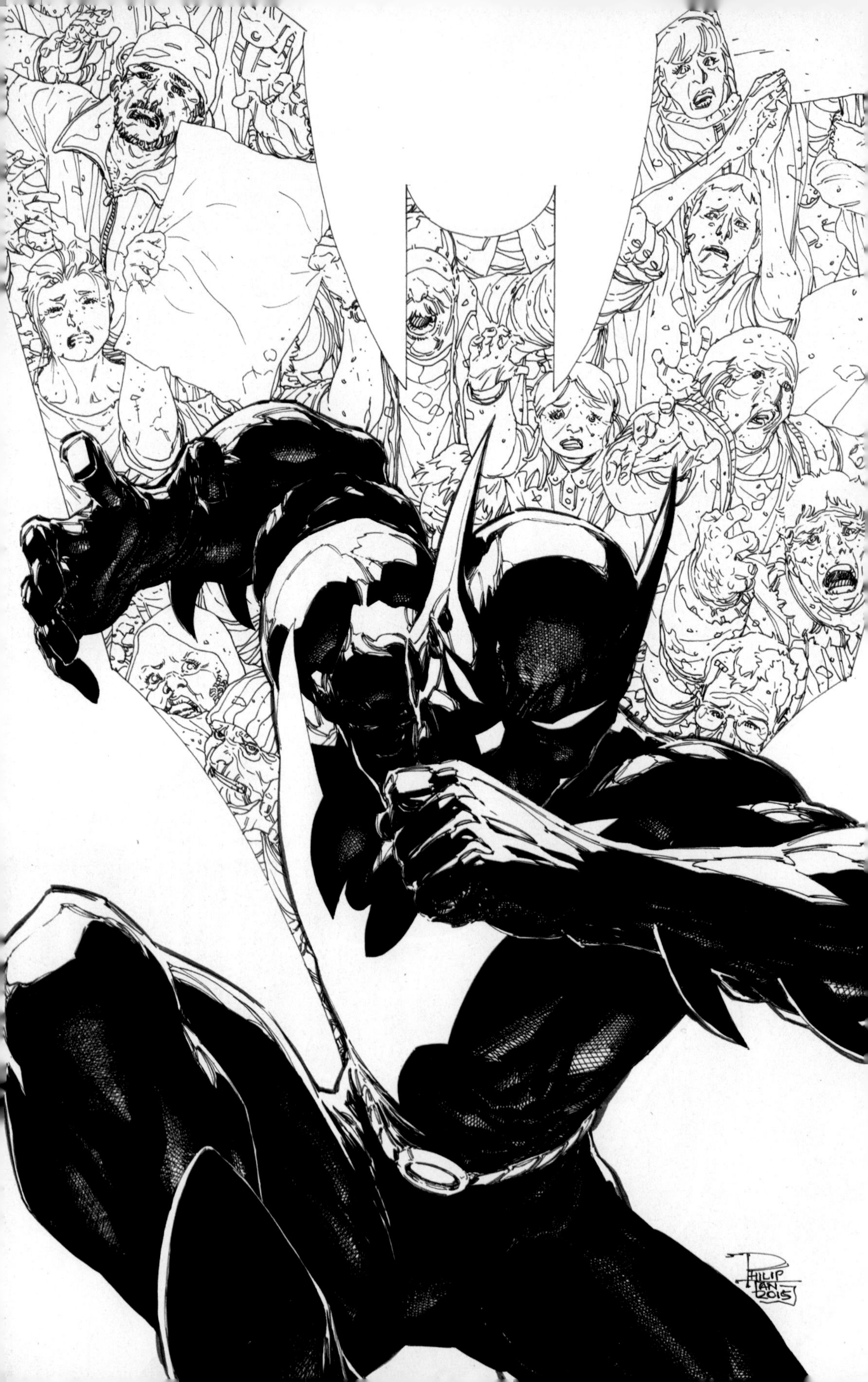
PHILIP TAN 2015

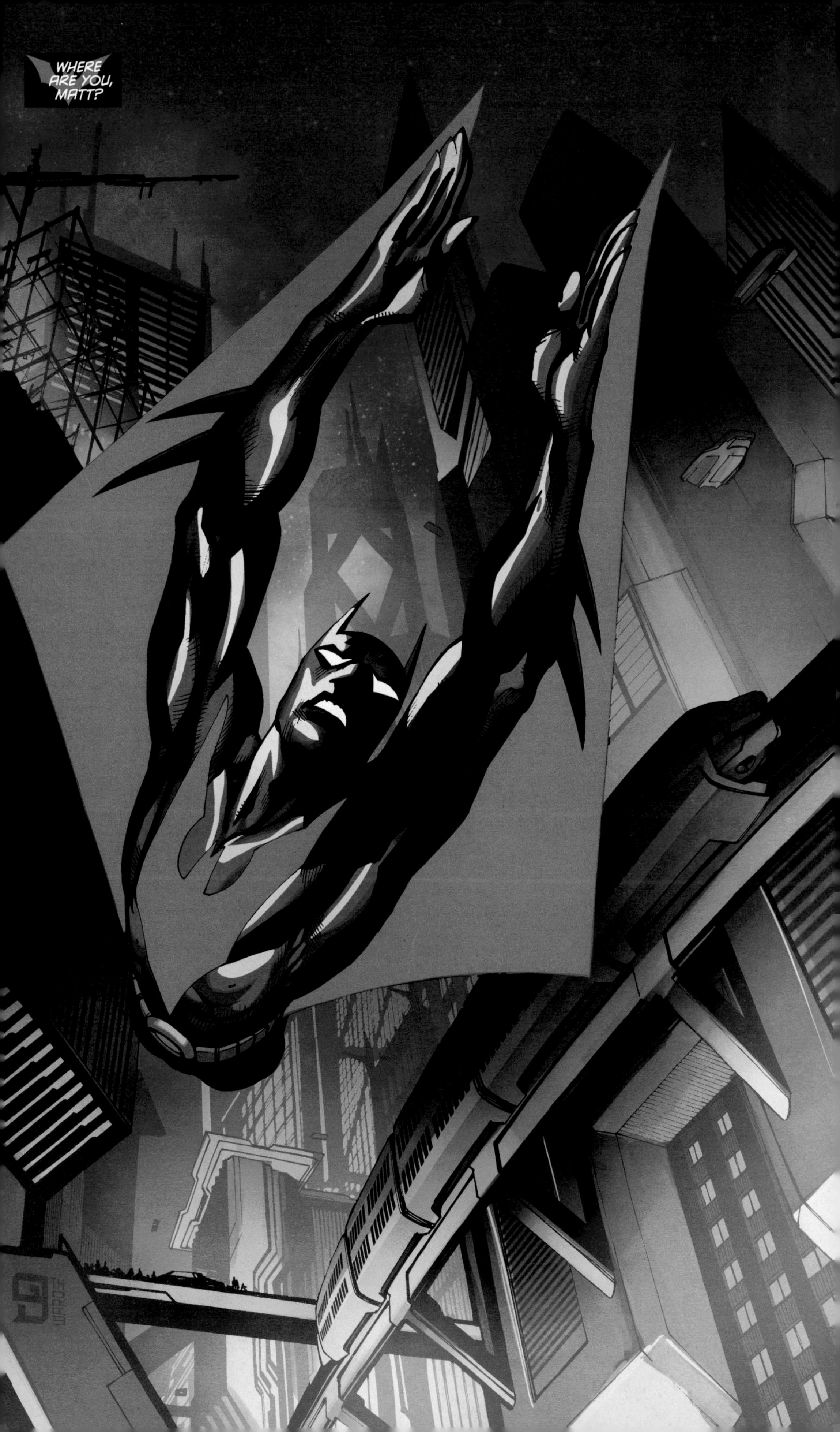
WHERE ARE YOU, MATT?

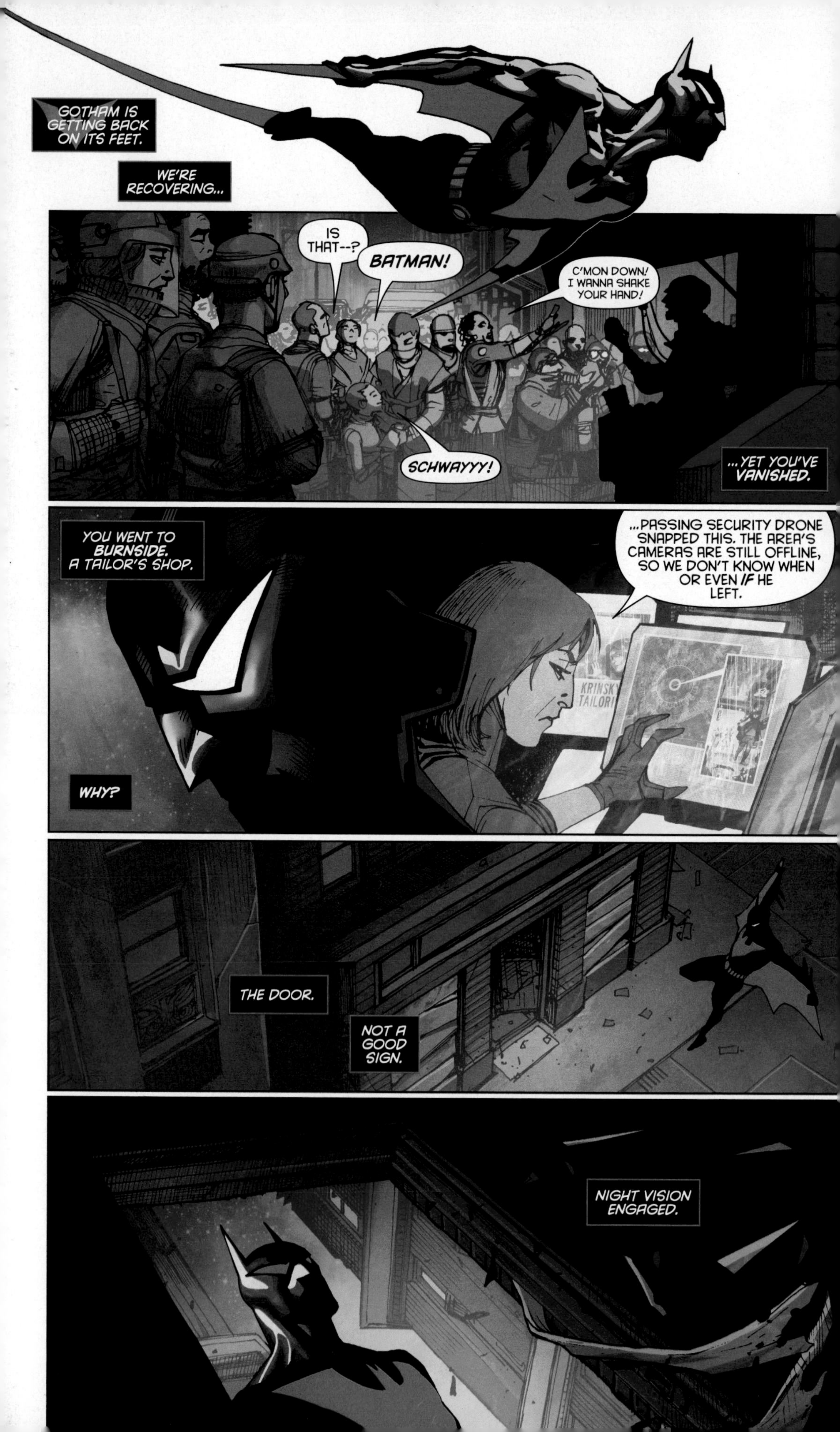

GOTHAM IS GETTING BACK ON ITS FEET.
WE'RE RECOVERING...
IS THAT--?
BATMAN!
C'MON DOWN! I WANNA SHAKE YOUR HAND!
SCHWAYYY!
...YET YOU'VE VANISHED.
YOU WENT TO BURNSIDE. A TAILOR'S SHOP.
...PASSING SECURITY DRONE SNAPPED THIS. THE AREA'S CAMERAS ARE STILL OFFLINE, SO WE DON'T KNOW WHEN OR EVEN IF HE LEFT.
KRINSKY TAILOR
WHY?
THE DOOR.
NOT A GOOD SIGN.
NIGHT VISION ENGAGED.

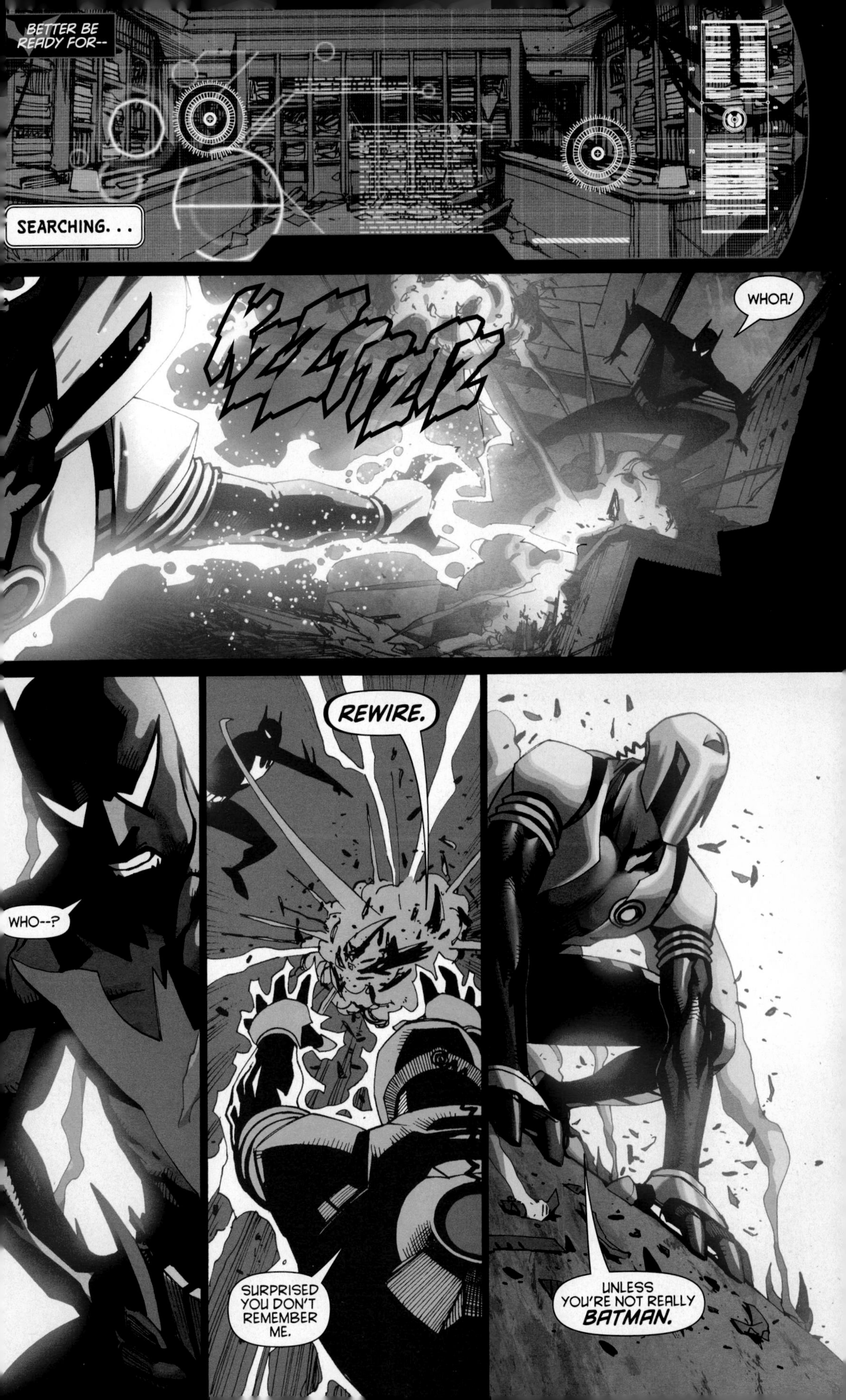
BETTER BE READY FOR--
SEARCHING. . .
WHOA!
WHO--?
REWIRE.
SURPRISED YOU DON'T REMEMBER ME.
UNLESS YOU'RE NOT REALLY BATMAN.

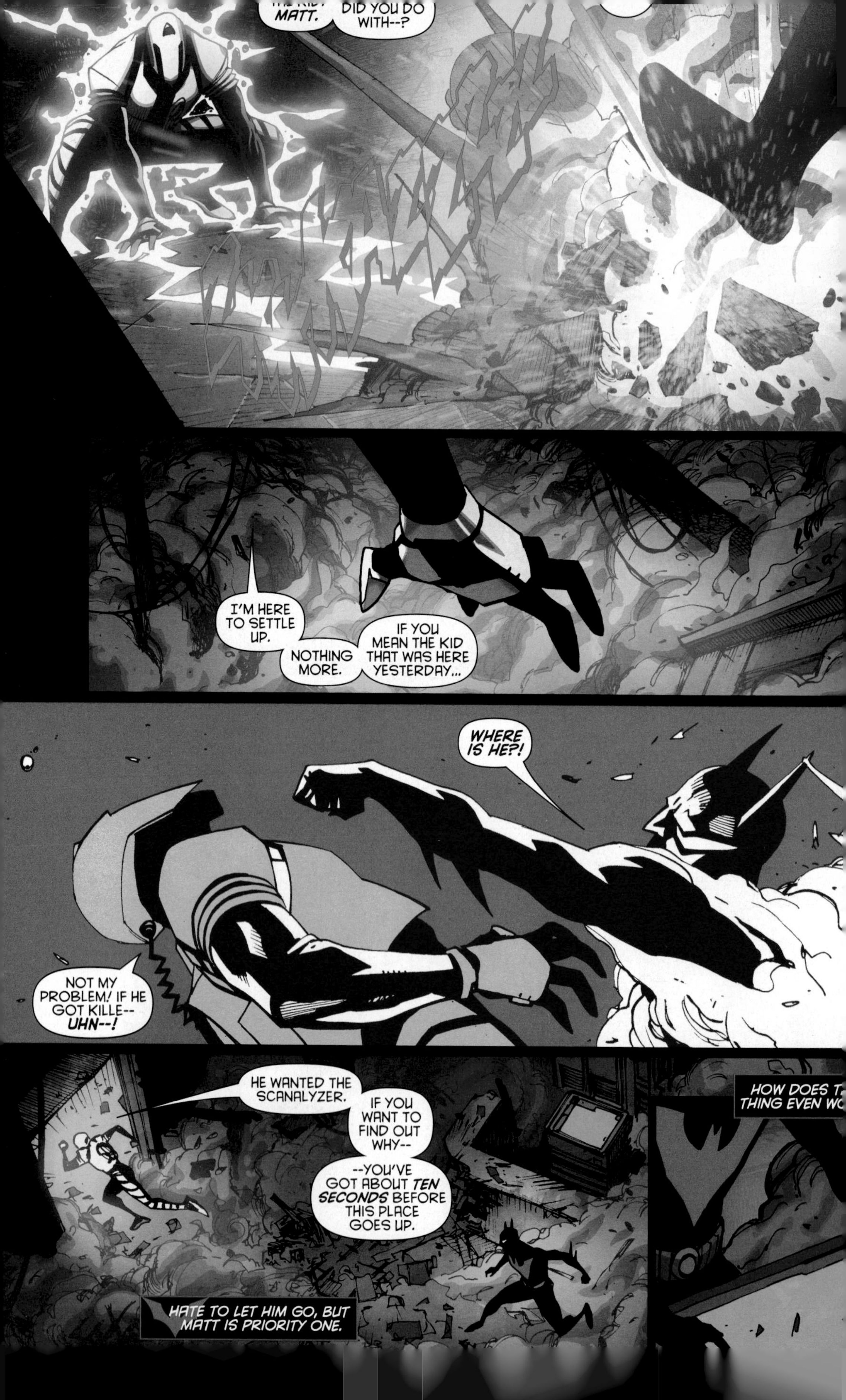

MATT.
DID YOU DO WITH--?
I'M HERE TO SETTLE UP.
NOTHING MORE.
IF YOU MEAN THE KID THAT WAS HERE YESTERDAY...
WHERE IS HE?!
NOT MY PROBLEM! IF HE GOT KILLE-- UHN--!
HE WANTED THE SCANALYZER.
IF YOU WANT TO FIND OUT WHY--
--YOU'VE GOT ABOUT TEN SECONDS BEFORE THIS PLACE GOES UP.
HOW DOES
THING EVEN
HATE TO LET HIM GO, BUT MATT IS PRIORITY ONE.

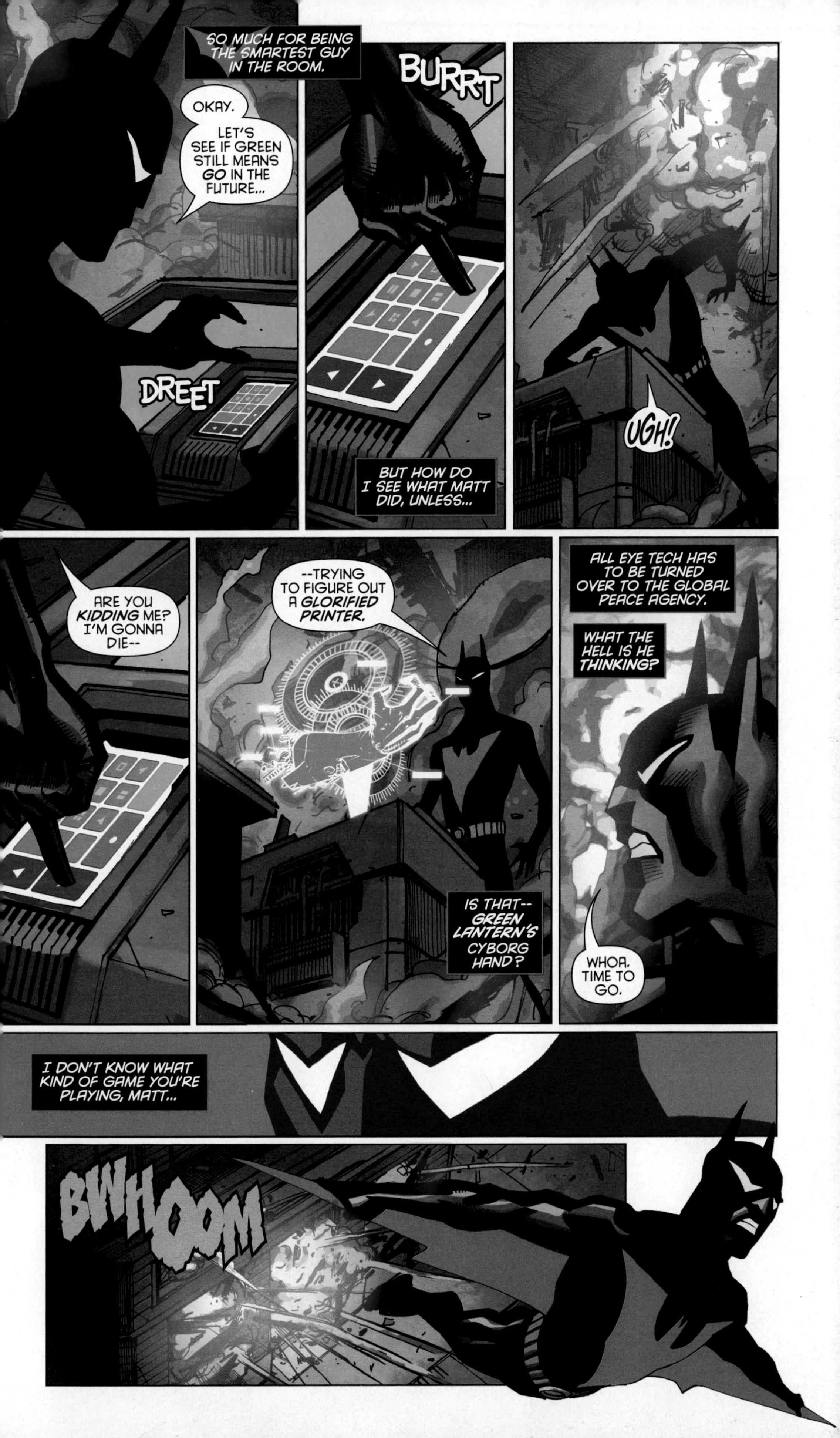
SO MUCH FOR BEING THE SMARTEST GUY IN THE ROOM.
OKAY.
LET'S SEE IF GREEN STILL MEANS GO IN THE FUTURE...
DREET
BURRT
BUT HOW DO I SEE WHAT MATT DID, UNLESS...
UGH!
ARE YOU KIDDING ME? I'M GONNA DIE--
--TRYING TO FIGURE OUT A GLORIFIED PRINTER.
IS THAT-- GREEN LANTERN'S CYBORG HAND?
ALL EYE TECH HAS TO BE TURNED OVER TO THE GLOBAL PEACE AGENCY.
WHAT THE HELL IS HE THINKING?
WHOA. TIME TO GO.
I DON'T KNOW WHAT KIND OF GAME YOU'RE PLAYING, MATT...
BWHOOM

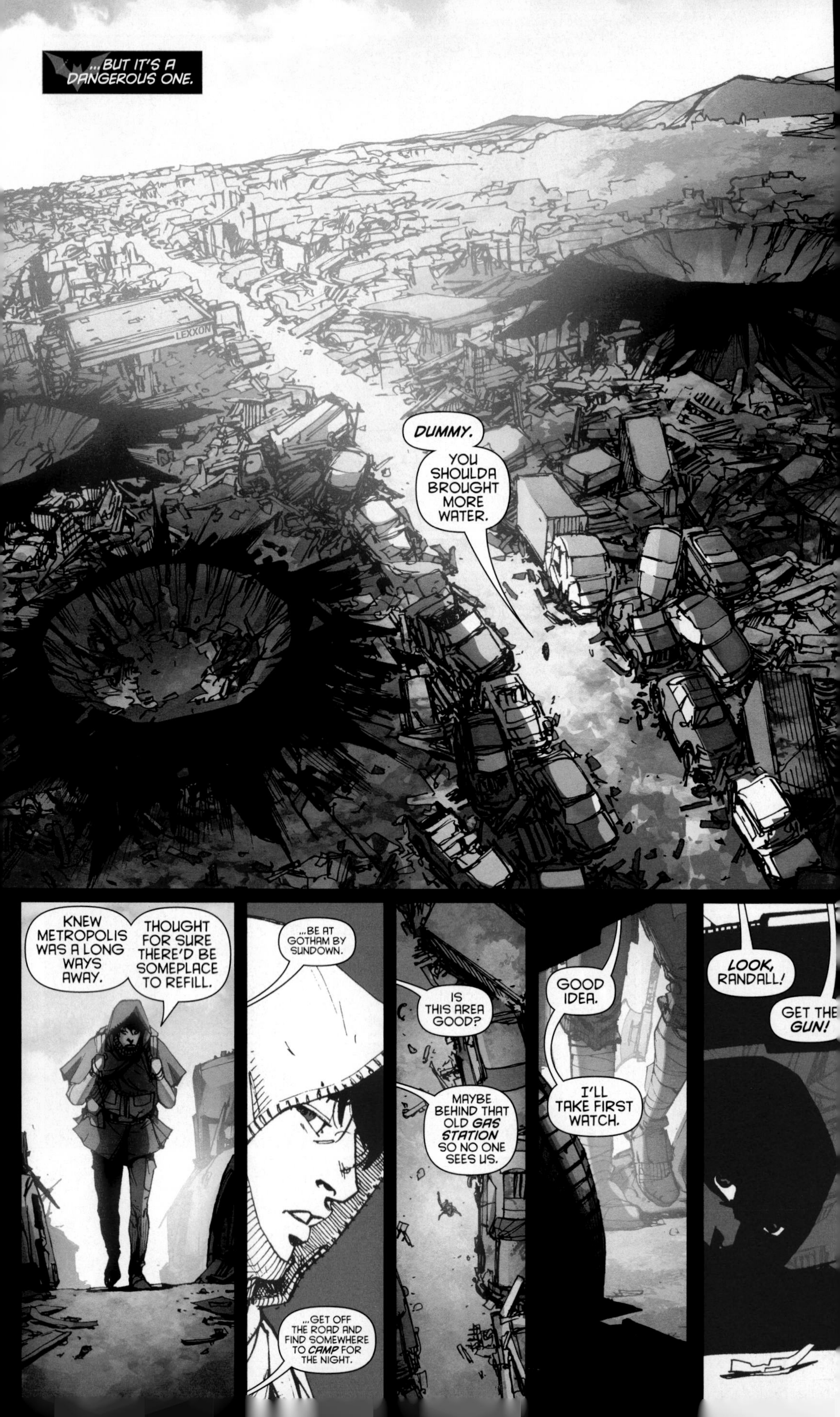
...BUT IT'S A DANGEROUS ONE.
LEXXON
DUMMY.
YOU SHOULDA BROUGHT MORE WATER.
KNEW METROPOLIS WAS A LONG WAYS AWAY.
THOUGHT FOR SURE THERE'D BE SOMEPLACE TO REFILL.
...BE AT GOTHAM BY SUNDOWN.
...GET OFF THE ROAD AND FIND SOMEWHERE TO CAMP FOR THE NIGHT.
IS THIS AREA GOOD?
MAYBE BEHIND THAT OLD GAS STATION SO NO ONE SEES US.
GOOD IDEA.
I'LL TAKE FIRST WATCH.
LOOK, RANDALL!
GET THE GUN!

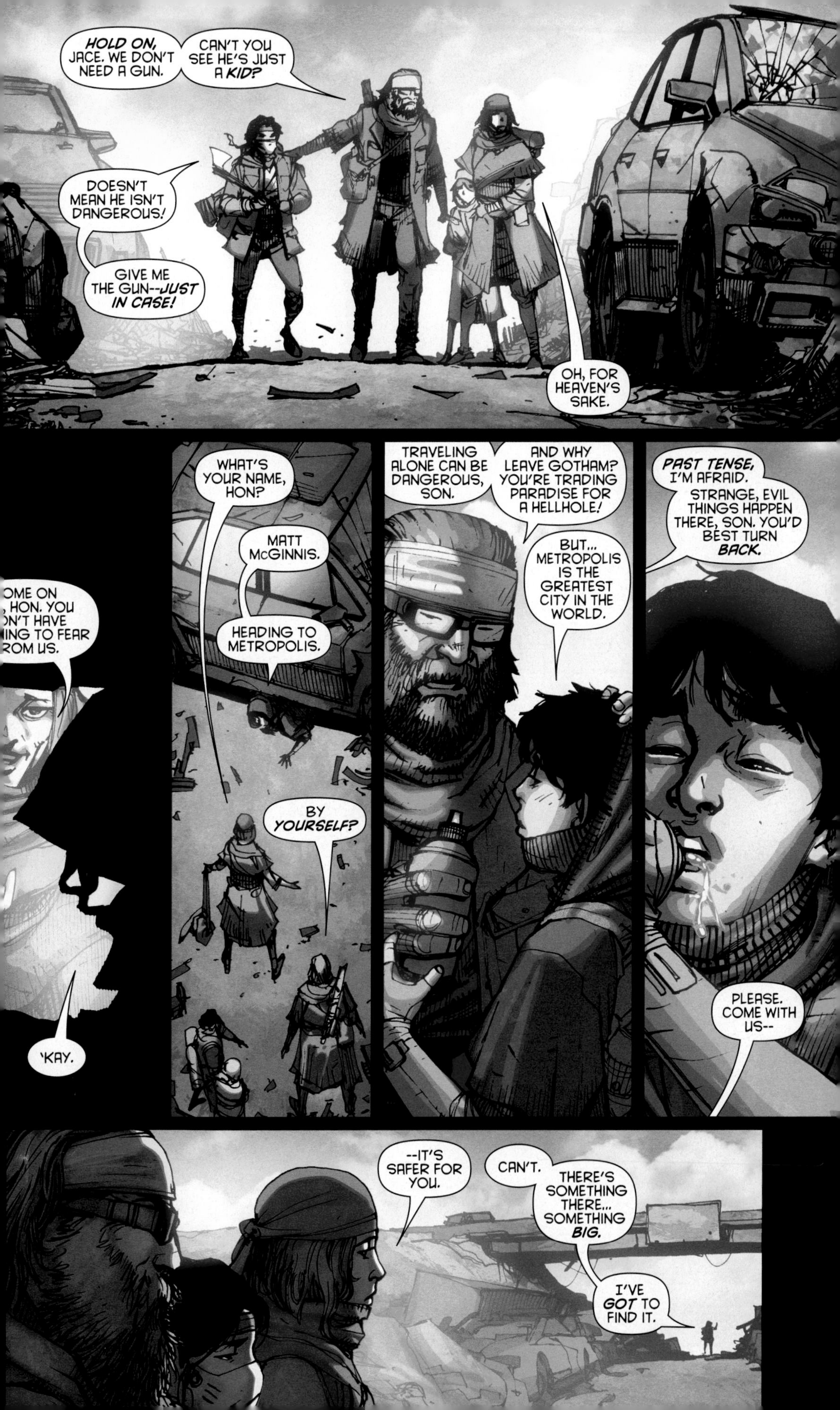
HOLD ON, JACE. WE DON'T NEED A GUN.
CAN'T YOU SEE HE'S JUST A KID?
DOESN'T MEAN HE ISN'T DANGEROUS!
GIVE ME THE GUN--JUST IN CASE!
OH, FOR HEAVEN'S SAKE.
OME ON , HON. YOU N'T HAVE ING TO FEAR ROM US.
'KAY.
WHAT'S YOUR NAME, HON?
MATT McGINNIS.
HEADING TO METROPOLIS.
BY YOURSELF?
TRAVELING ALONE CAN BE DANGEROUS, SON.
AND WHY LEAVE GOTHAM? YOU'RE TRADING PARADISE FOR A HELLHOLE!
BUT... METROPOLIS IS THE GREATEST CITY IN THE WORLD.
PAST TENSE, I'M AFRAID.
STRANGE, EVIL THINGS HAPPEN THERE, SON. YOU'D BEST TURN BACK.
PLEASE. COME WITH US--
--IT'S SAFER FOR YOU.
CAN'T.
THERE'S SOMETHING THERE... SOMETHING BIG.
I'VE GOT TO FIND IT.

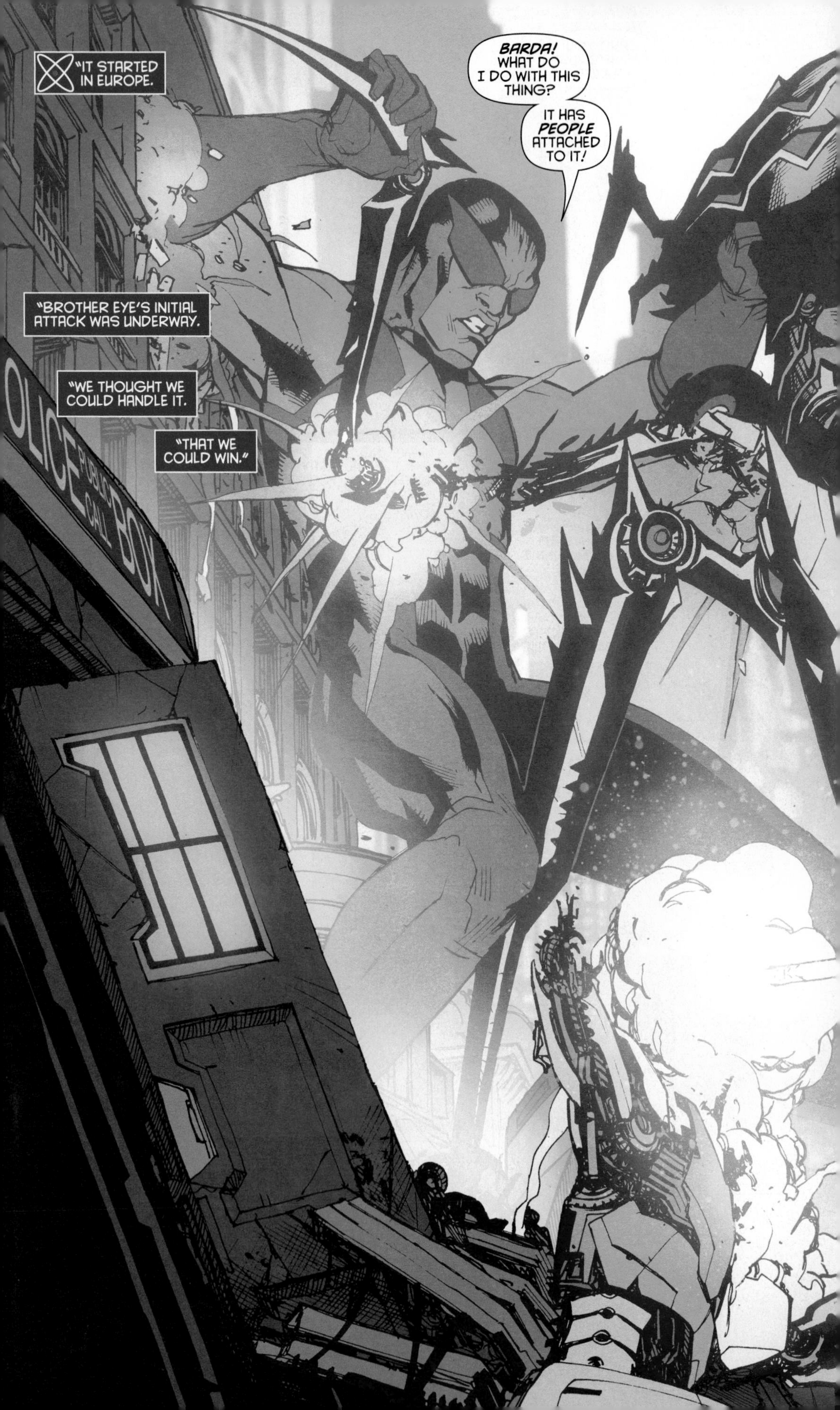
"IT STARTED IN EUROPE.
BARDA! WHAT DO I DO WITH THIS THING?
IT HAS PEOPLE ATTACHED TO IT!
"BROTHER EYE'S INITIAL ATTACK WAS UNDERWAY.
"WE THOUGHT WE COULD HANDLE IT.
"THAT WE COULD WIN."
POLICE PUBLIC CALL BOX

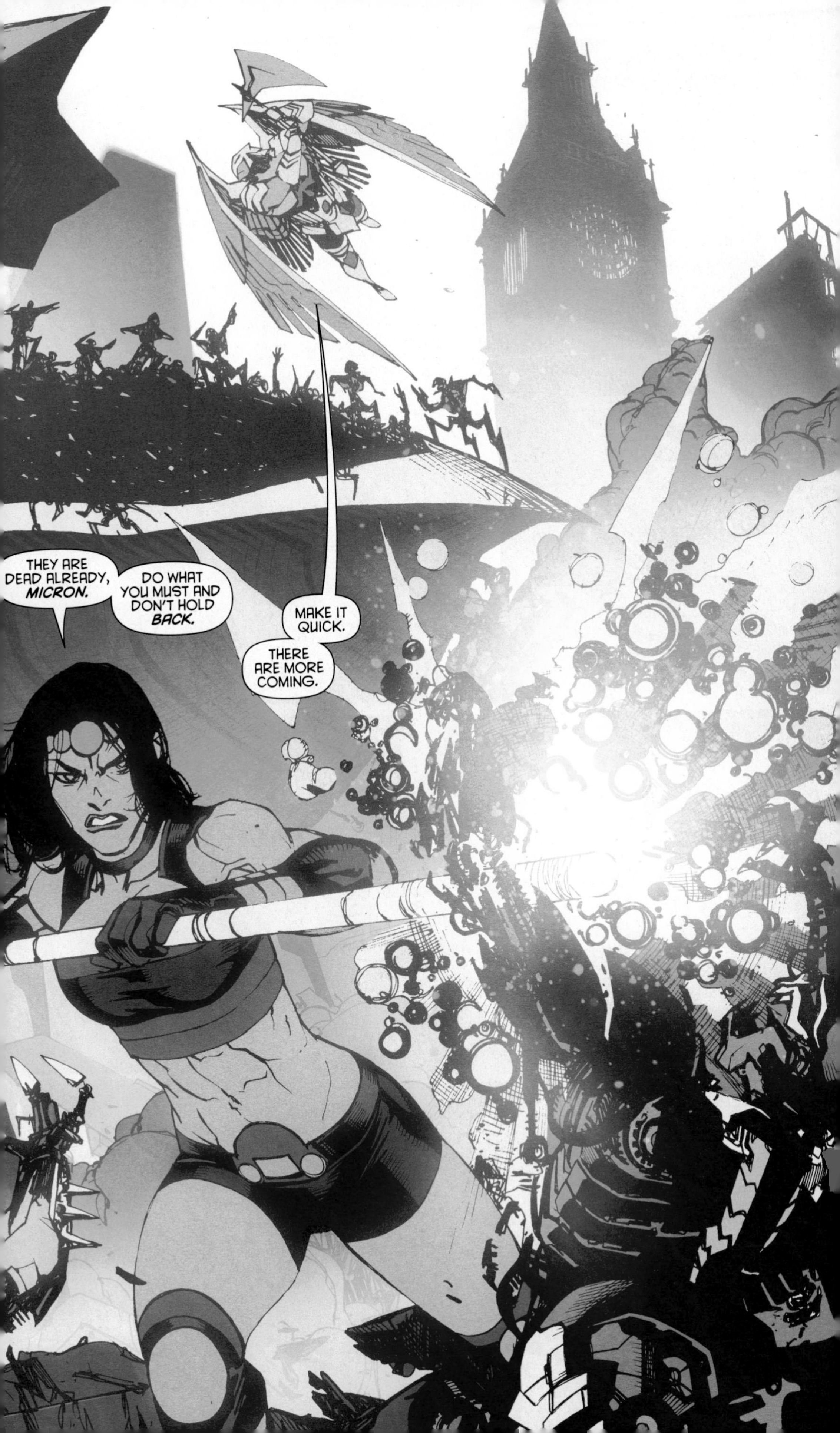
THEY ARE DEAD ALREADY, MICRON.
DO WHAT YOU MUST AND DON'T HOLD BACK.
MAKE IT QUICK.
THERE ARE MORE COMING.

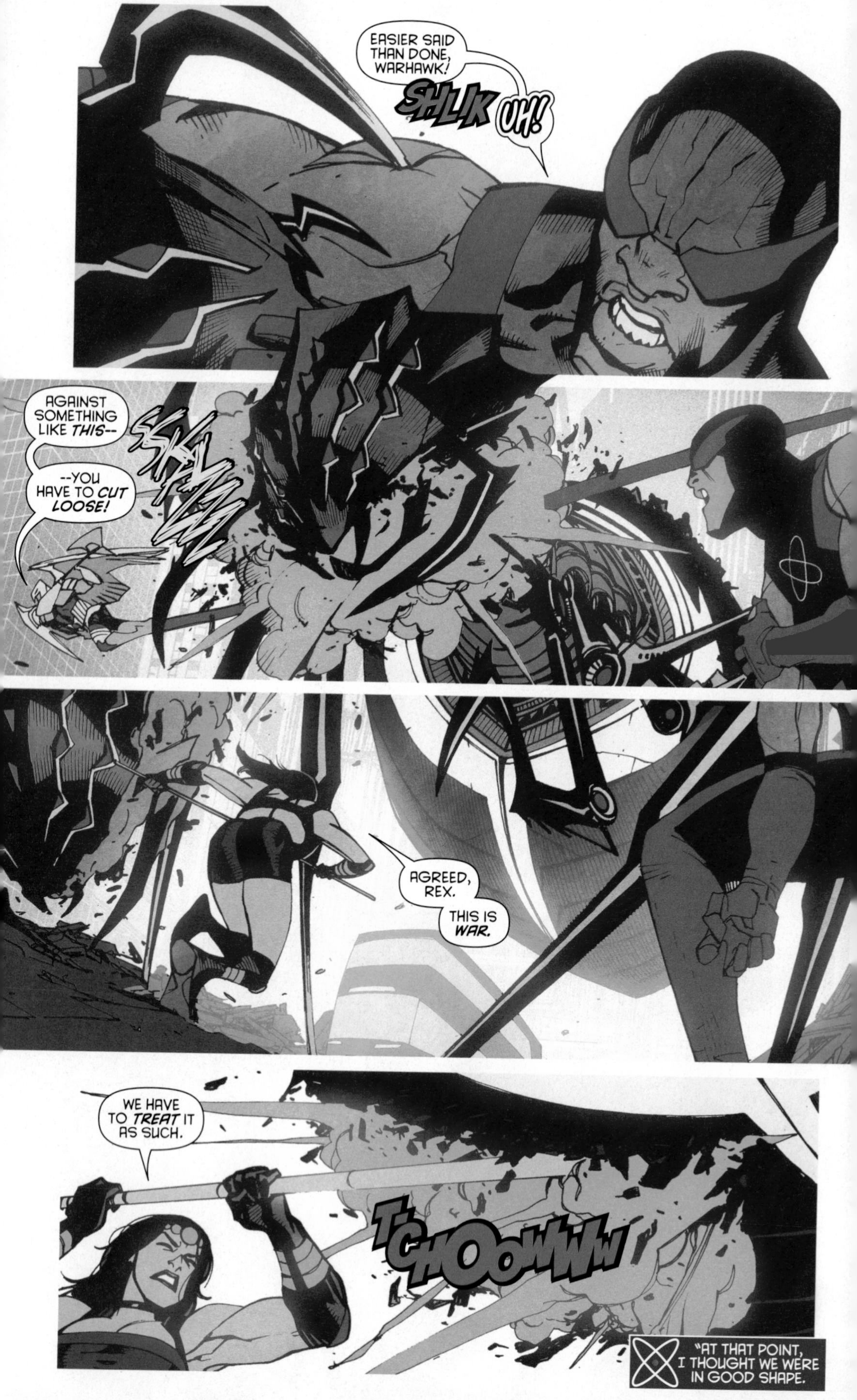
EASIER SAID THAN DONE, WARHAWK!
SHLIK
UH!
AGAINST SOMETHING LIKE *THIS*--
--YOU HAVE TO *CUT LOOSE!*
AGREED, REX.
THIS IS *WAR.*
WE HAVE TO *TREAT* IT AS SUCH.
TCHOOWWW
"AT THAT POINT, I THOUGHT WE WERE IN GOOD SHAPE.

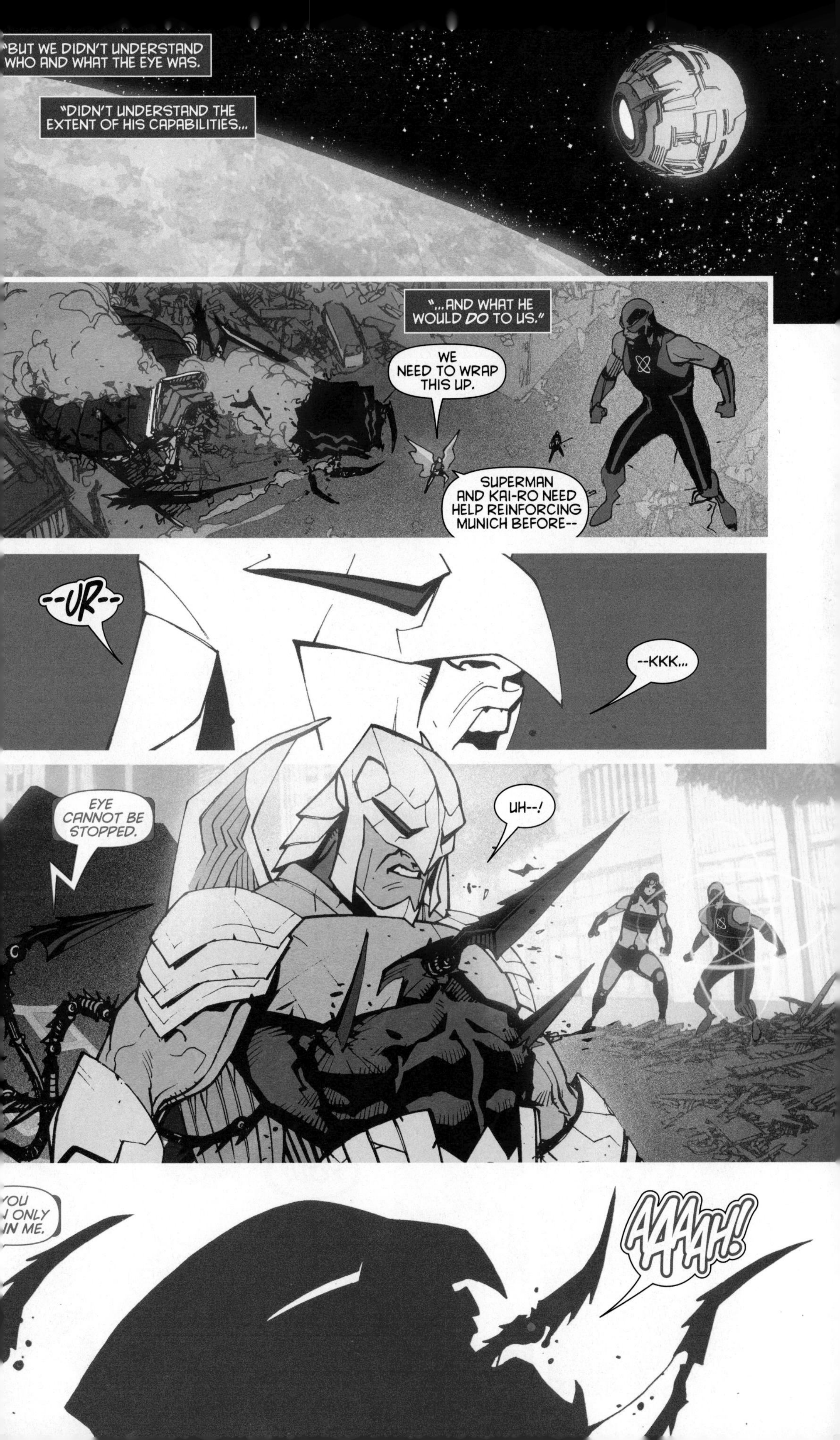
"BUT WE DIDN'T UNDERSTAND WHO AND WHAT THE EYE WAS.
"DIDN'T UNDERSTAND THE EXTENT OF HIS CAPABILITIES...
"...AND WHAT HE WOULD DO TO US."
WE NEED TO WRAP THIS UP.
SUPERMAN AND KAI-RO NEED HELP REINFORCING MUNICH BEFORE--
--UR--
--KKK...
EYE CANNOT BE STOPPED.
UH--!
AAAAH!

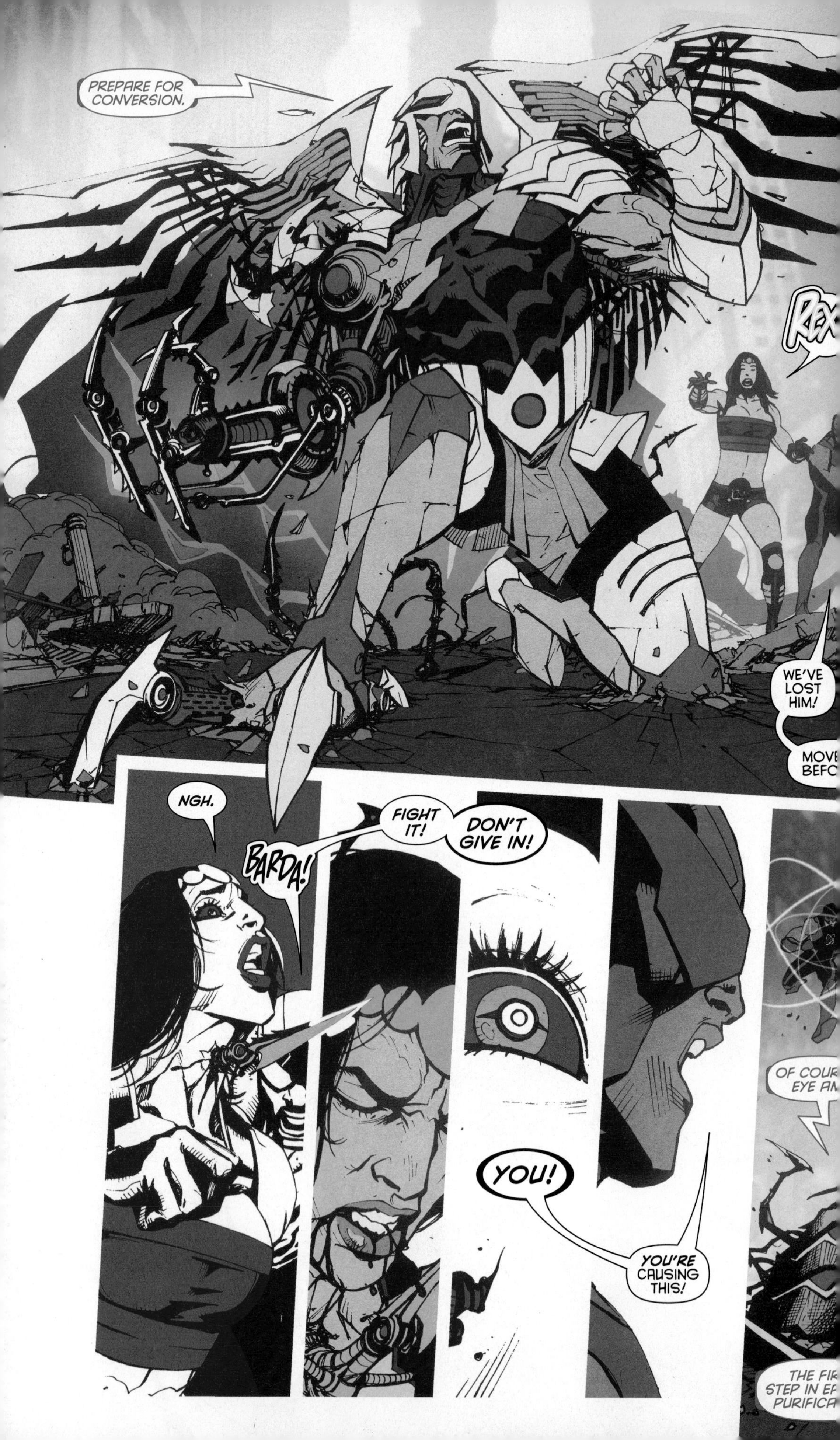
PREPARE FOR CONVERSION.
REX
WE'VE LOST HIM!
MOVE BEFO
NGH.
BARDA!
FIGHT IT!
DON'T GIVE IN!
YOU!
YOU'RE CAUSING THIS!
OF COUR EYE AN
THE FIR STEP IN EP PURIFICA

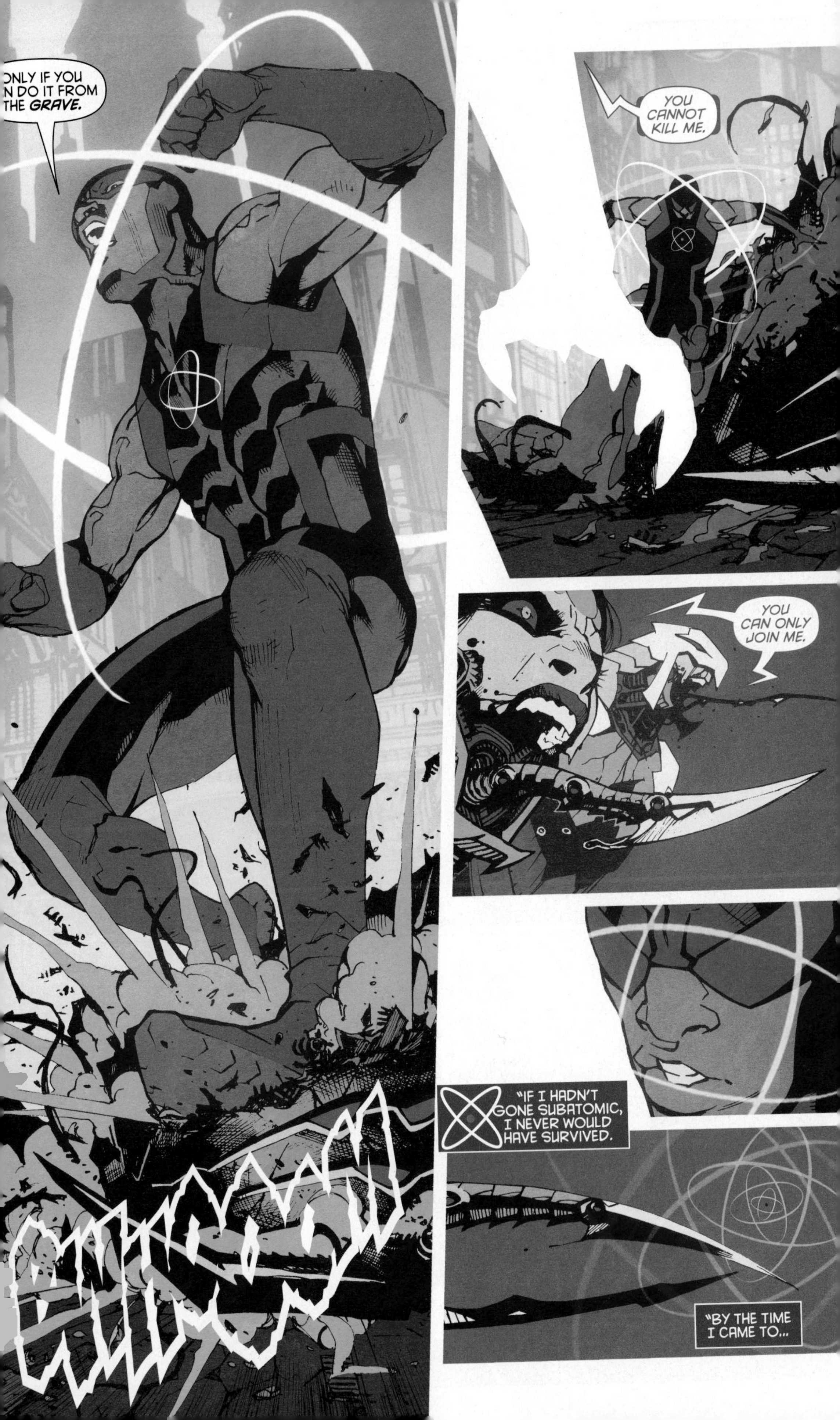
ONLY IF YOU
N DO IT FROM
THE GRAVE.
YOU CANNOT KILL ME.
YOU CAN ONLY JOIN ME.
"IF I HADN'T GONE SUBATOMIC, I NEVER WOULD HAVE SURVIVED.
"BY THE TIME I CAME TO...

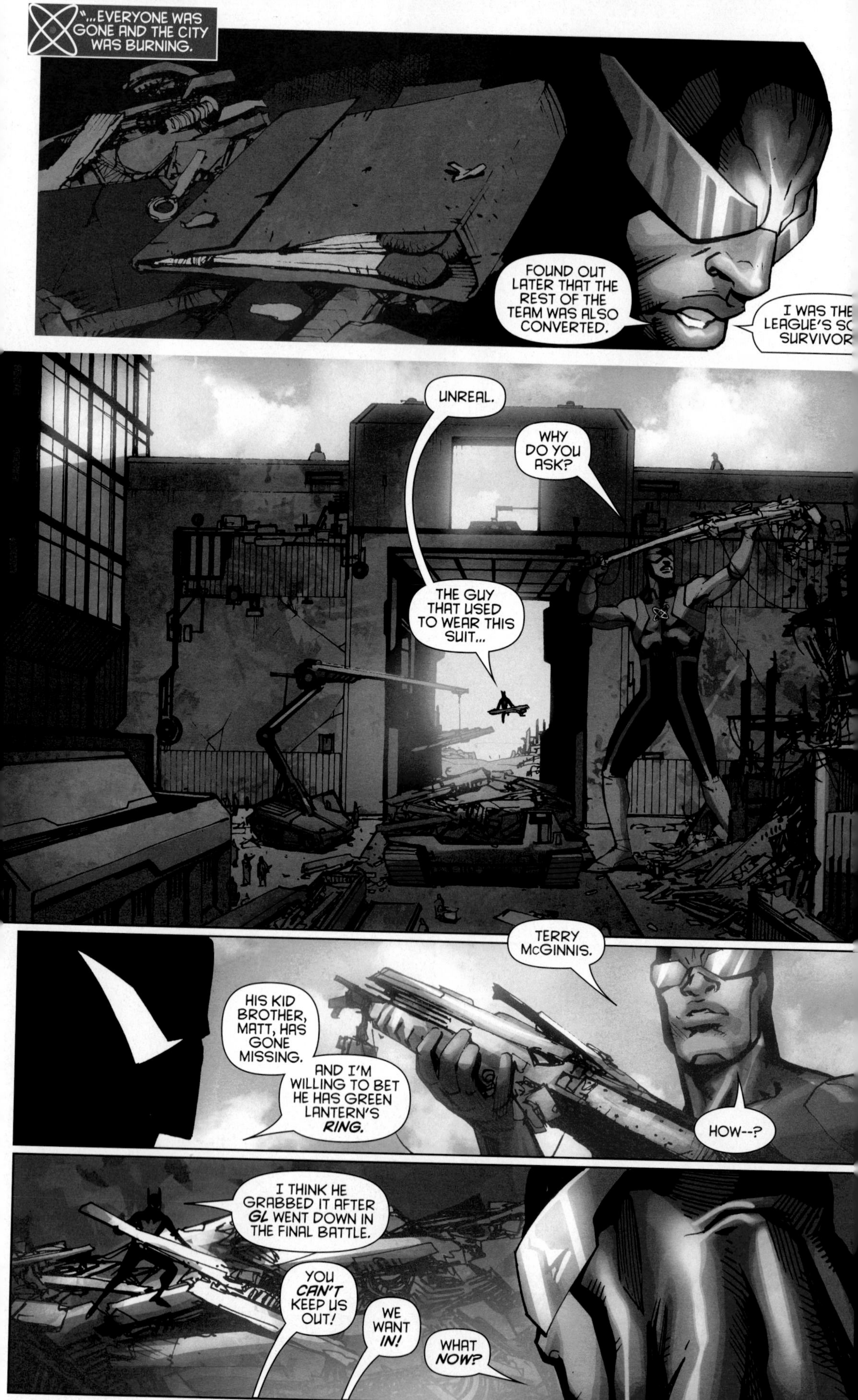
"...EVERYONE WAS GONE AND THE CITY WAS BURNING.
FOUND OUT LATER THAT THE REST OF THE TEAM WAS ALSO CONVERTED.
I WAS THE LEAGUE'S SO SURVIVOR
UNREAL.
WHY DO YOU ASK?
THE GUY THAT USED TO WEAR THIS SUIT...
TERRY McGINNIS.
HIS KID BROTHER, MATT, HAS GONE MISSING.
AND I'M WILLING TO BET HE HAS GREEN LANTERN'S *RING.*
HOW--?
I THINK HE GRABBED IT AFTER *GL* WENT DOWN IN THE FINAL BATTLE.
YOU *CAN'T* KEEP US OUT!
WE WANT *IN!*
WHAT *NOW?*

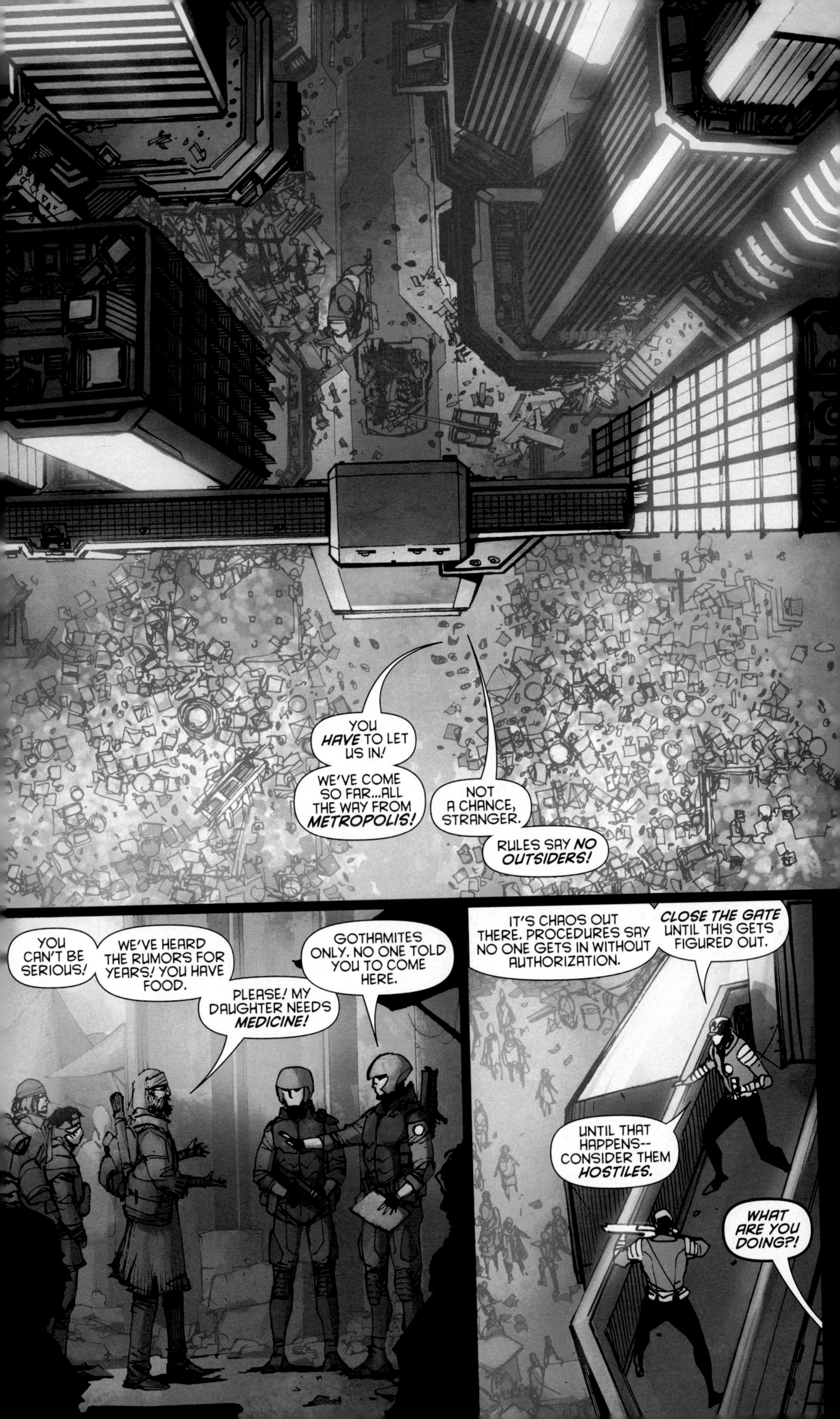
YOU HAVE TO LET US IN!
WE'VE COME SO FAR...ALL THE WAY FROM METROPOLIS!
NOT A CHANCE, STRANGER.
RULES SAY NO OUTSIDERS!
YOU CAN'T BE SERIOUS!
WE'VE HEARD THE RUMORS FOR YEARS! YOU HAVE FOOD.
PLEASE! MY DAUGHTER NEEDS MEDICINE!
GOTHAMITES ONLY. NO ONE TOLD YOU TO COME HERE.
IT'S CHAOS OUT THERE. PROCEDURES SAY NO ONE GETS IN WITHOUT AUTHORIZATION.
CLOSE THE GATE UNTIL THIS GETS FIGURED OUT.
UNTIL THAT HAPPENS-- CONSIDER THEM HOSTILES.
WHAT ARE YOU DOING?!

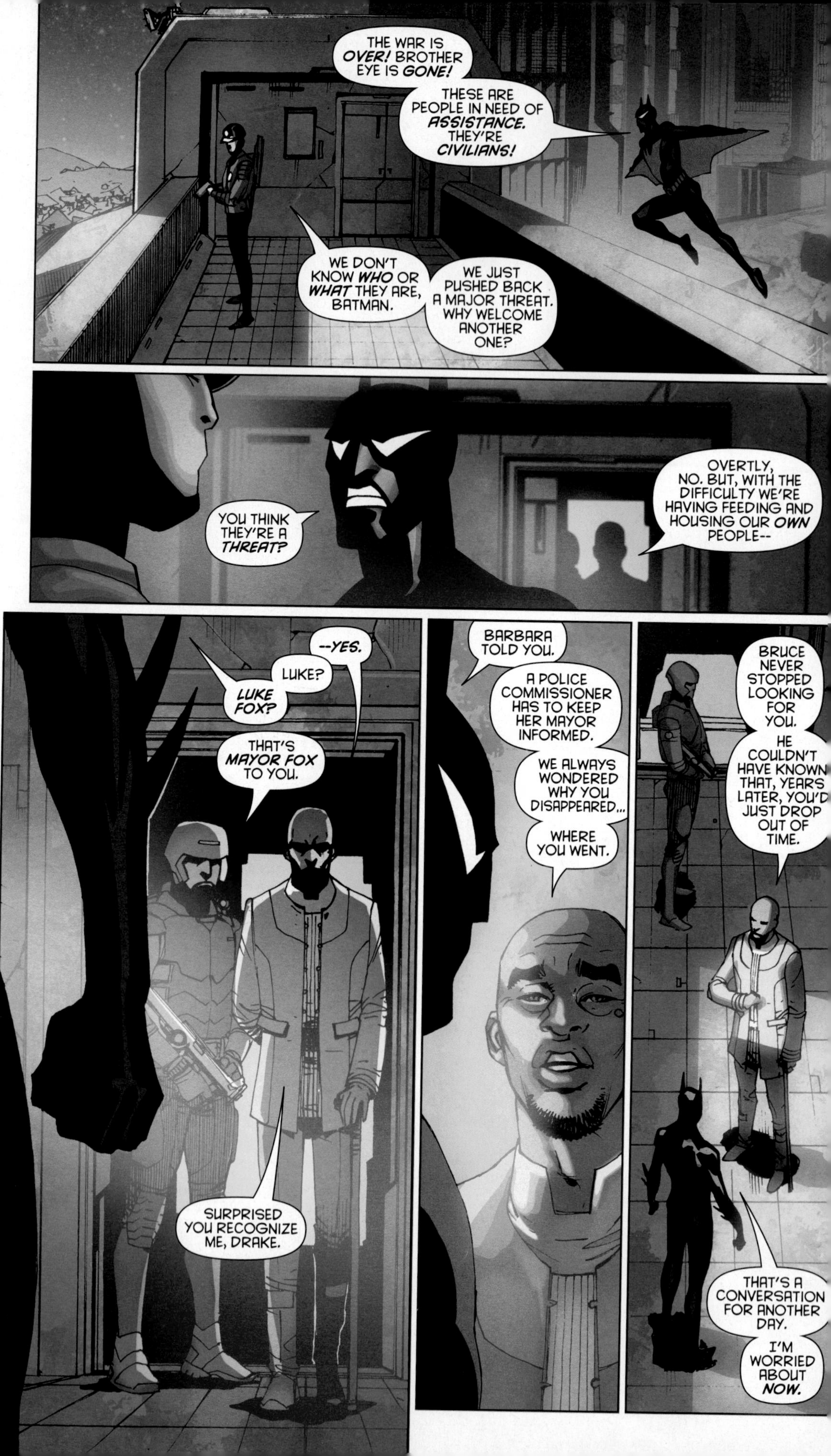
THE WAR IS OVER! BROTHER EYE IS GONE!
THESE ARE PEOPLE IN NEED OF ASSISTANCE. THEY'RE CIVILIANS!
WE DON'T KNOW WHO OR WHAT THEY ARE, BATMAN.
WE JUST PUSHED BACK A MAJOR THREAT. WHY WELCOME ANOTHER ONE?
YOU THINK THEY'RE A THREAT?
OVERTLY, NO. BUT, WITH THE DIFFICULTY WE'RE HAVING FEEDING AND HOUSING OUR OWN PEOPLE--
--YES.
LUKE?
LUKE FOX?
THAT'S MAYOR FOX TO YOU.
SURPRISED YOU RECOGNIZE ME, DRAKE.
BARBARA TOLD YOU.
A POLICE COMMISSIONER HAS TO KEEP HER MAYOR INFORMED.
WE ALWAYS WONDERED WHY YOU DISAPPEARED...
WHERE YOU WENT.
BRUCE NEVER STOPPED LOOKING FOR YOU.
HE COULDN'T HAVE KNOWN THAT, YEARS LATER, YOU'D JUST DROP OUT OF TIME.
THAT'S A CONVERSATION FOR ANOTHER DAY.
I'M WORRIED ABOUT NOW.

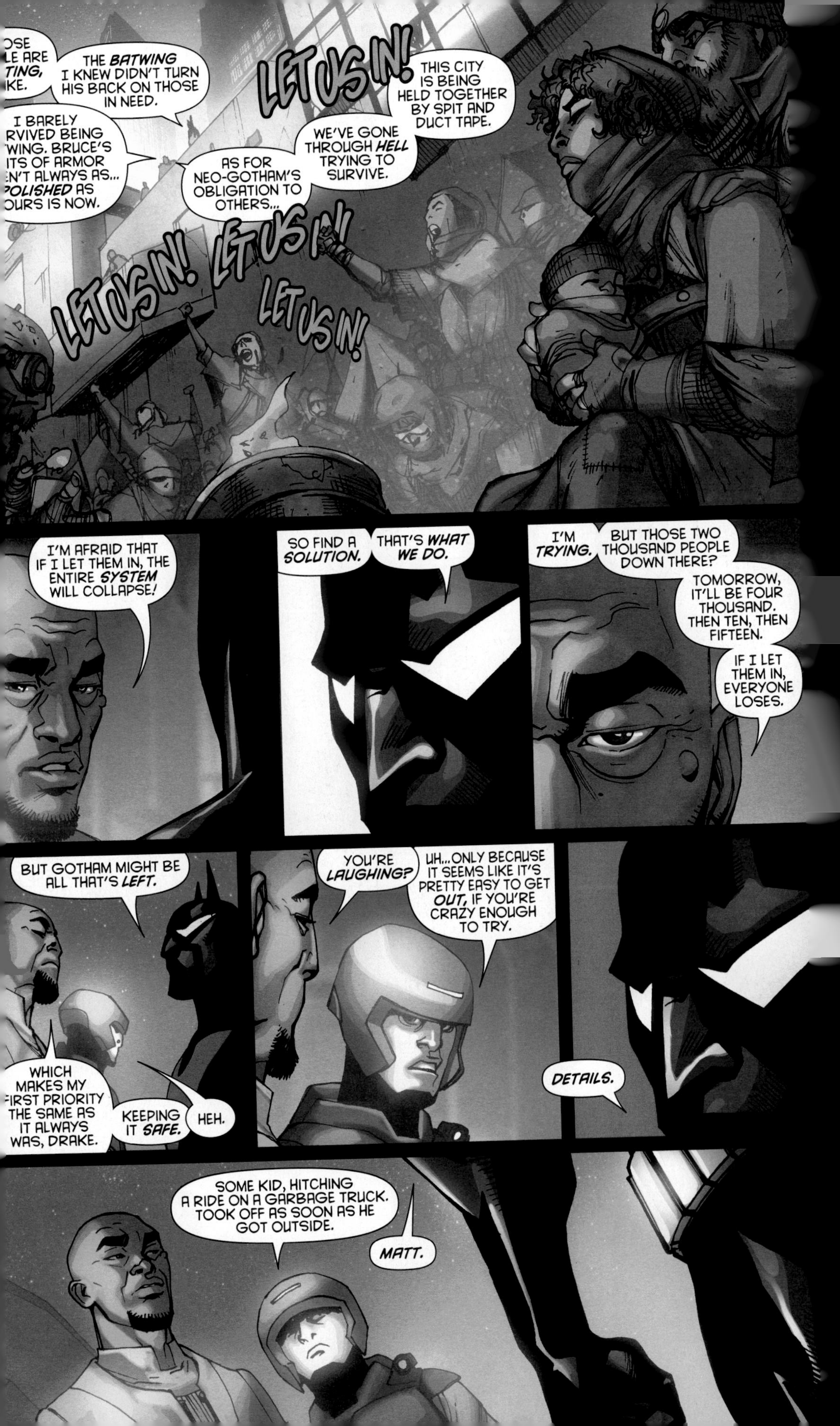
OSE LE ARE TING, KE.
THE BATWING I KNEW DIDN'T TURN HIS BACK ON THOSE IN NEED.
I BARELY RVIVED BEING TWING. BRUCE'S ITS OF ARMOR N'T ALWAYS AS... POLISHED AS OURS IS NOW.
LET US IN!
THIS CITY IS BEING HELD TOGETHER BY SPIT AND DUCT TAPE.
WE'VE GONE THROUGH HELL TRYING TO SURVIVE.
AS FOR NEO-GOTHAM'S OBLIGATION TO OTHERS...
LET US IN! LET US IN! LET US IN!
I'M AFRAID THAT IF I LET THEM IN, THE ENTIRE SYSTEM WILL COLLAPSE!
SO FIND A SOLUTION.
THAT'S WHAT WE DO.
I'M TRYING.
BUT THOSE TWO THOUSAND PEOPLE DOWN THERE?
TOMORROW, IT'LL BE FOUR THOUSAND. THEN TEN, THEN FIFTEEN.
IF I LET THEM IN, EVERYONE LOSES.
BUT GOTHAM MIGHT BE ALL THAT'S LEFT.
WHICH MAKES MY FIRST PRIORITY THE SAME AS IT ALWAYS WAS, DRAKE.
KEEPING IT SAFE.
HEH.
YOU'RE LAUGHING?
UH...ONLY BECAUSE IT SEEMS LIKE IT'S PRETTY EASY TO GET OUT, IF YOU'RE CRAZY ENOUGH TO TRY.
DETAILS.
SOME KID, HITCHING A RIDE ON A GARBAGE TRUCK. TOOK OFF AS SOON AS HE GOT OUTSIDE.
MATT.

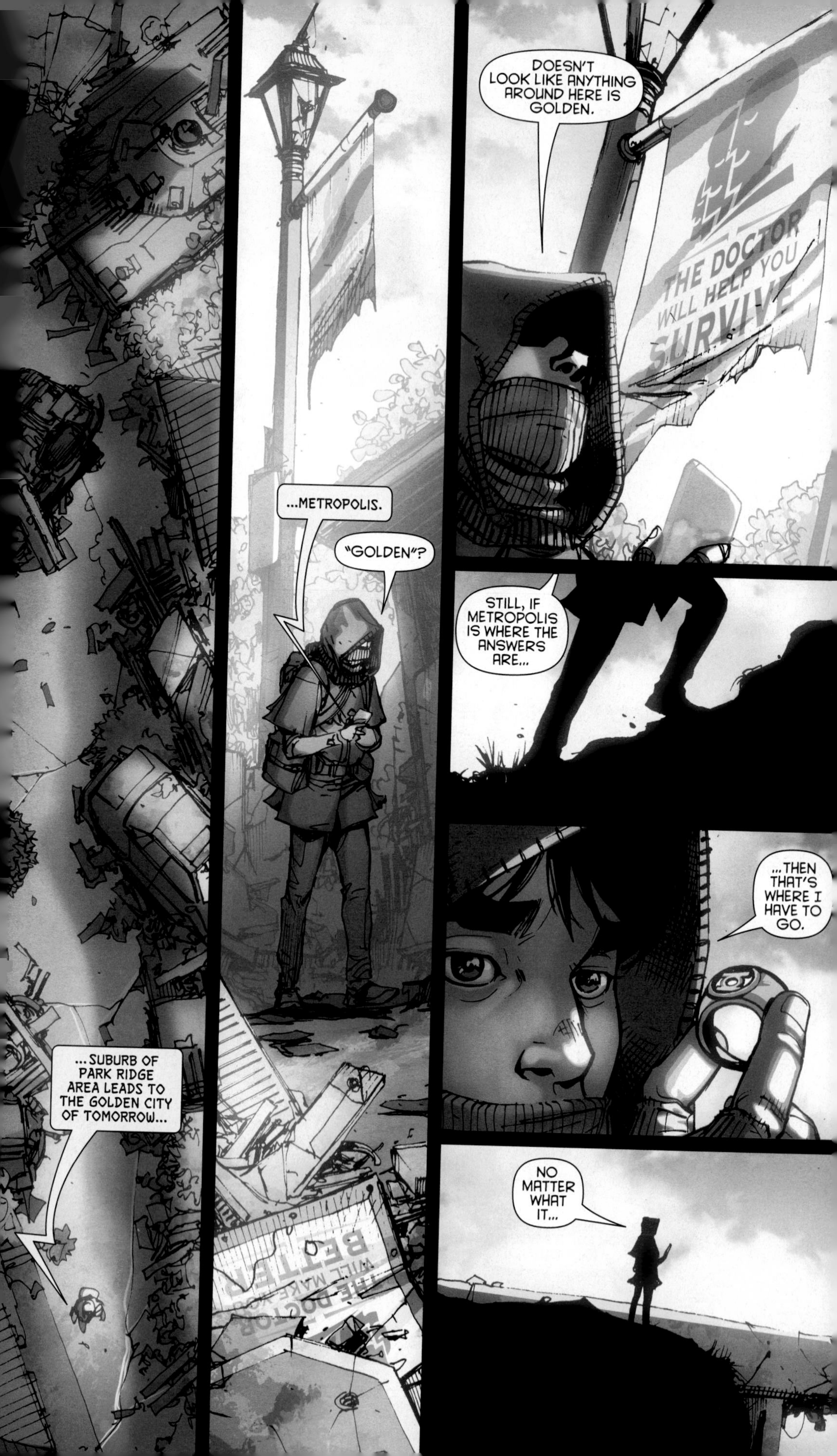
...SUBURB OF PARK RIDGE AREA LEADS TO THE GOLDEN CITY OF TOMORROW...
...METROPOLIS.
"GOLDEN"?
DOESN'T LOOK LIKE ANYTHING AROUND HERE IS GOLDEN.
THE DOCTOR WILL HELP YOU SURVIVE
STILL, IF METROPOLIS IS WHERE THE ANSWERS ARE...
...THEN THAT'S WHERE I HAVE TO GO.
NO MATTER WHAT IT...

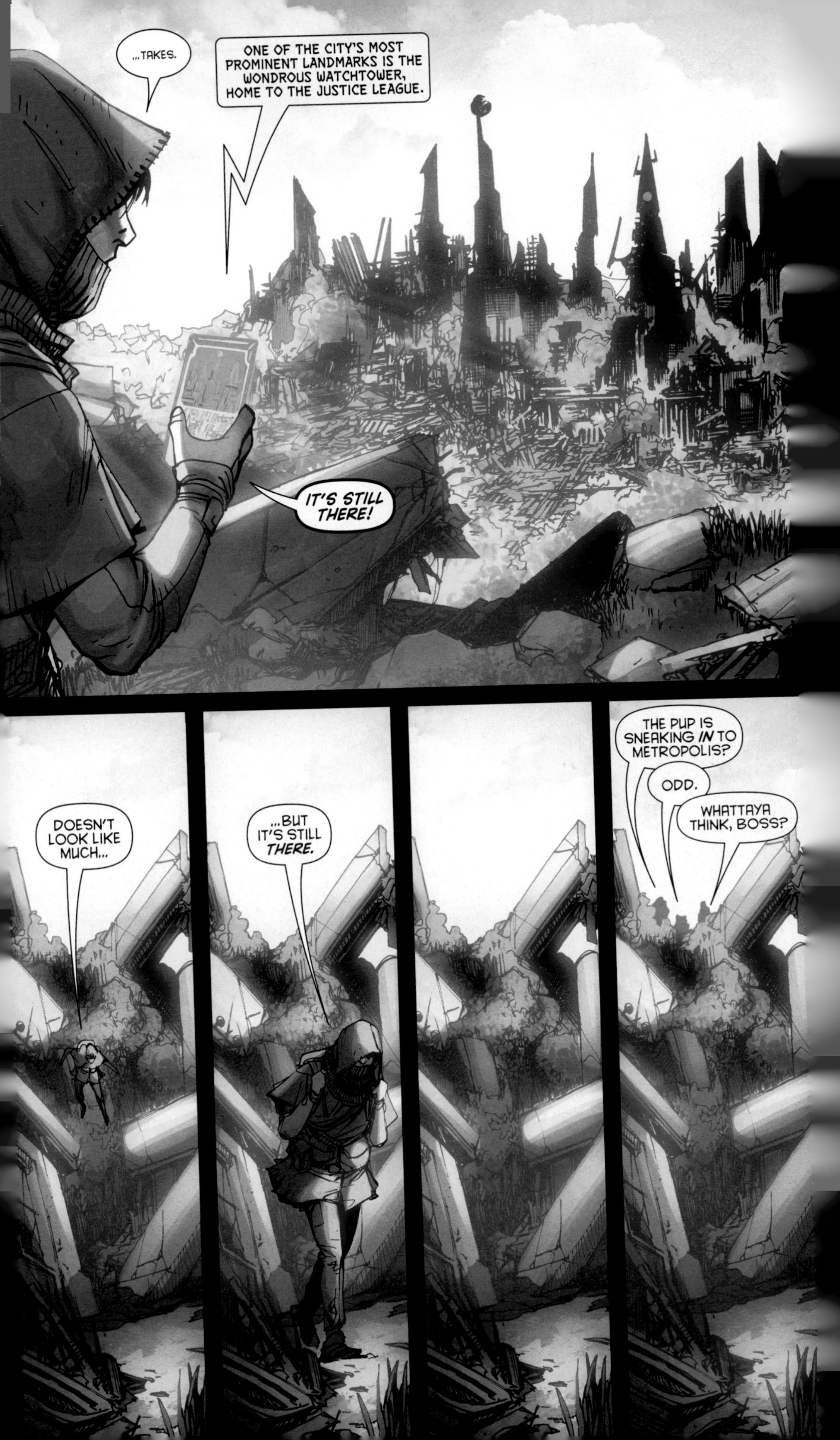
...TAKES.
ONE OF THE CITY'S MOST PROMINENT LANDMARKS IS THE WONDROUS WATCHTOWER, HOME TO THE JUSTICE LEAGUE.
IT'S STILL THERE!
DOESN'T LOOK LIKE MUCH...
...BUT IT'S STILL THERE.
THE PUP IS SNEAKING IN TO METROPOLIS?
ODD.
WHATTAYA THINK, BOSS?

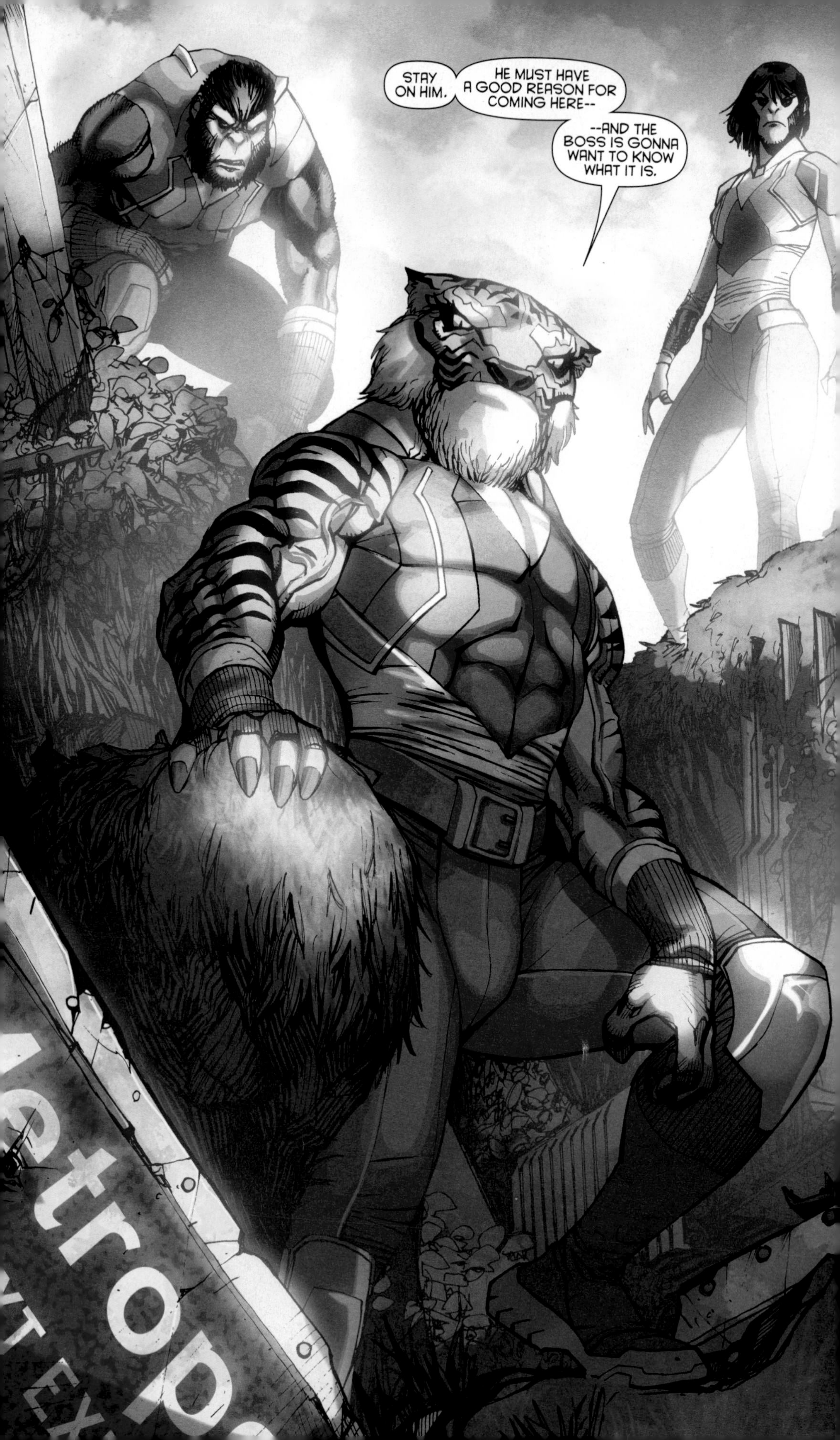
STAY ON HIM.
HE MUST HAVE A GOOD REASON FOR COMING HERE--
--AND THE BOSS IS GONNA WANT TO KNOW WHAT IT IS.

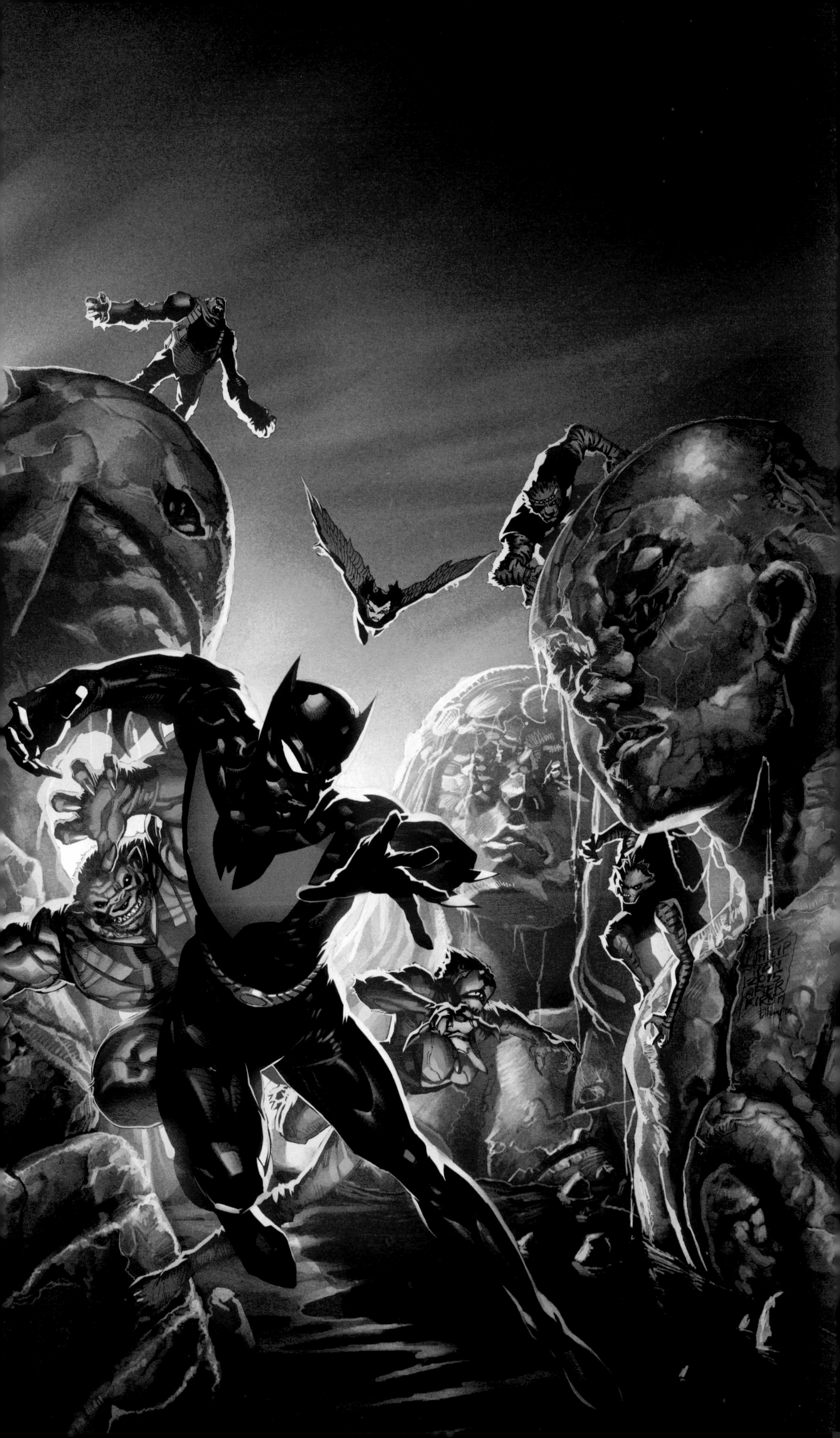

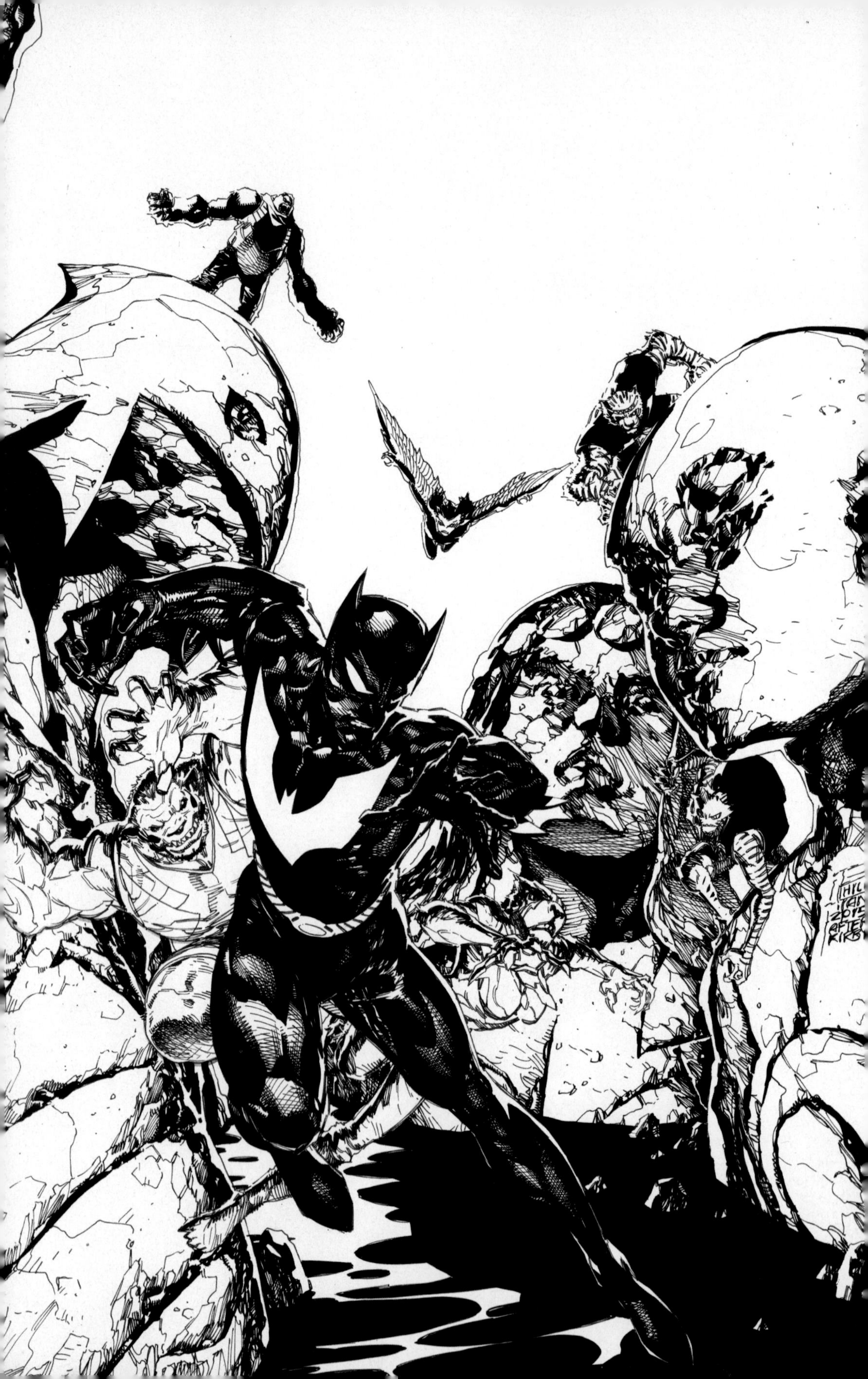

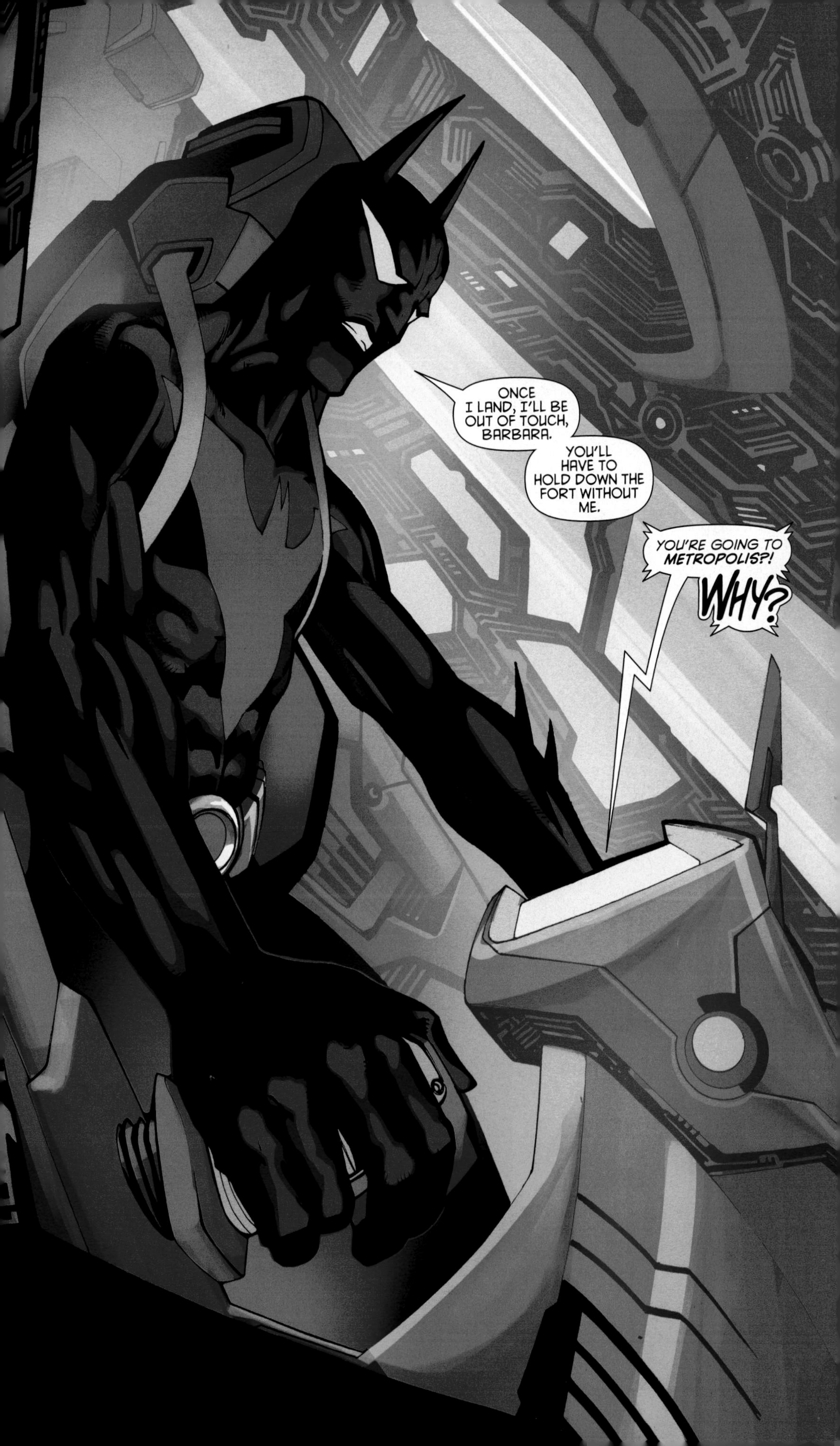
ONCE I LAND, I'LL BE OUT OF TOUCH, BARBARA.
YOU'LL HAVE TO HOLD DOWN THE FORT WITHOUT ME.
YOU'RE GOING TO METROPOLIS?!
WHY?

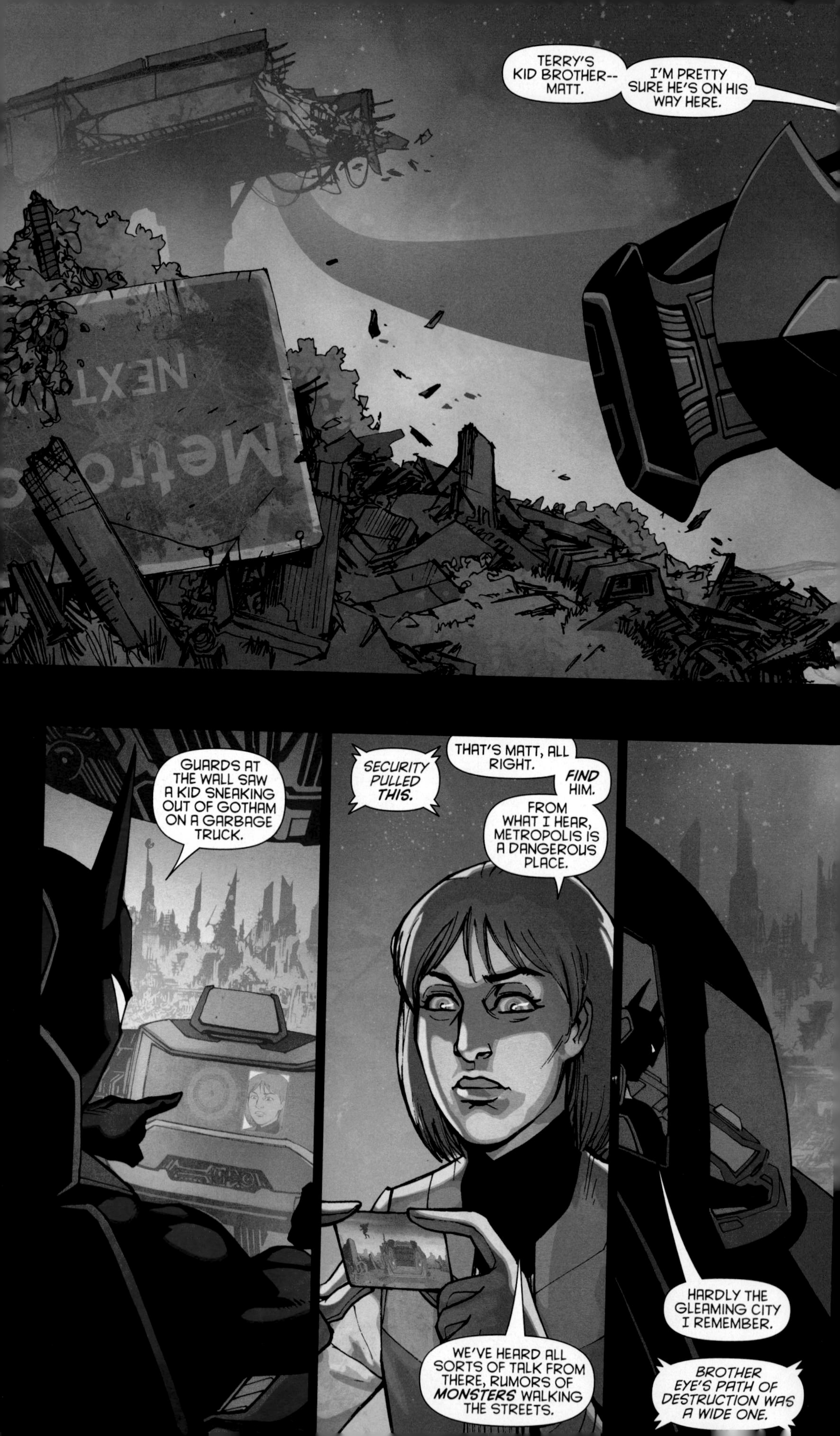

NEXT
Metro
TERRY'S KID BROTHER-- MATT.
I'M PRETTY SURE HE'S ON HIS WAY HERE.
GUARDS AT THE WALL SAW A KID SNEAKING OUT OF GOTHAM ON A GARBAGE TRUCK.
SECURITY PULLED *THIS.*
THAT'S MATT, ALL RIGHT.
FIND HIM.
FROM WHAT I HEAR, METROPOLIS IS A DANGEROUS PLACE.
WE'VE HEARD ALL SORTS OF TALK FROM THERE, RUMORS OF ***MONSTERS*** WALKING THE STREETS.
HARDLY THE GLEAMING CITY I REMEMBER.
BROTHER EYE'S PATH OF DESTRUCTION WAS A WIDE ONE.

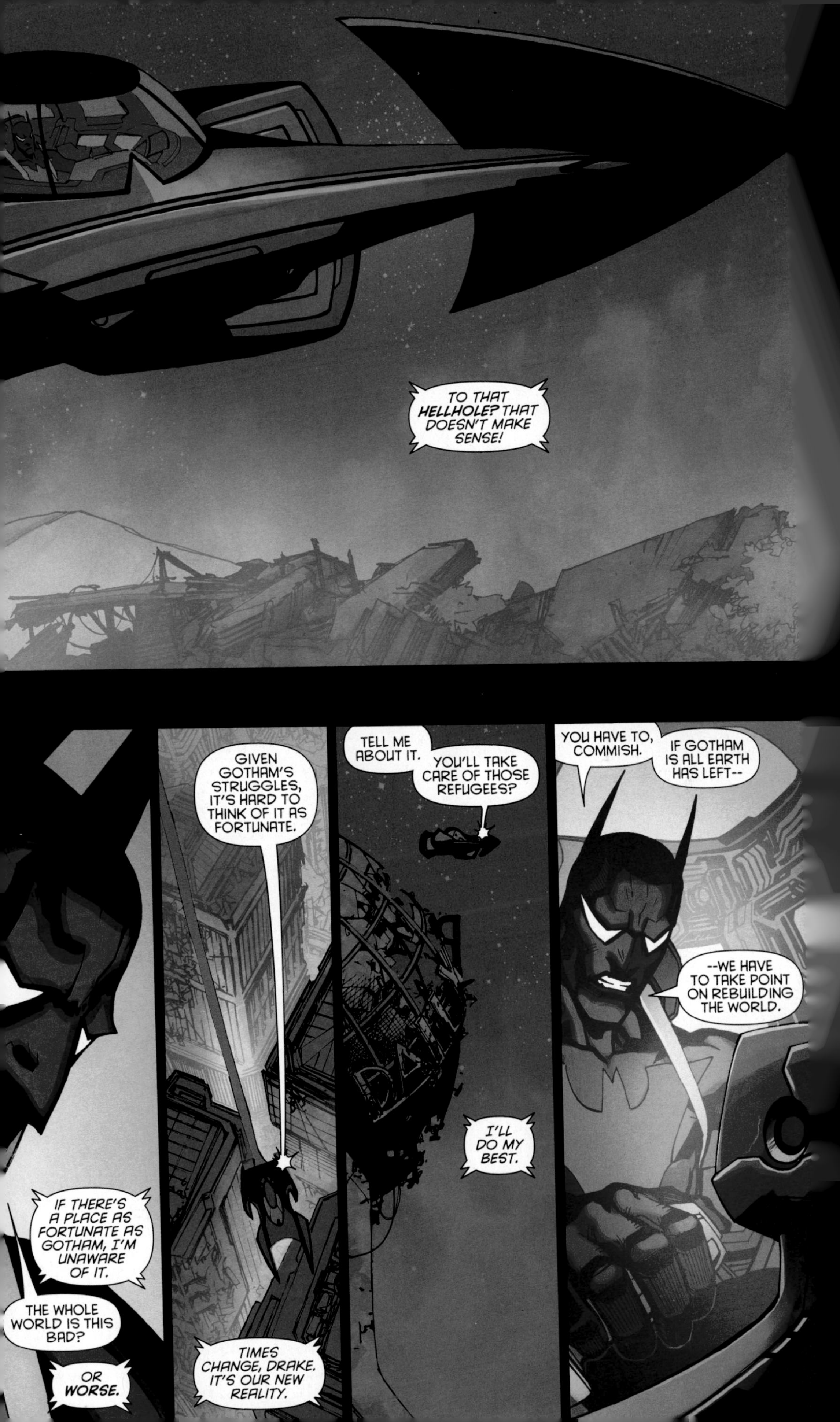
TO THAT **HELLHOLE?** THAT DOESN'T MAKE SENSE!
IF THERE'S A PLACE AS FORTUNATE AS GOTHAM, I'M UNAWARE OF IT.
THE WHOLE WORLD IS THIS BAD?
OR **WORSE.**
GIVEN GOTHAM'S STRUGGLES, IT'S HARD TO THINK OF IT AS FORTUNATE.
TIMES CHANGE, DRAKE. IT'S OUR NEW REALITY.
TELL ME ABOUT IT.
YOU'LL TAKE CARE OF THOSE REFUGEES?
I'LL DO MY BEST.
YOU HAVE TO, COMMISH.
IF GOTHAM IS ALL EARTH HAS LEFT--
--WE HAVE TO TAKE POINT ON REBUILDING THE WORLD.

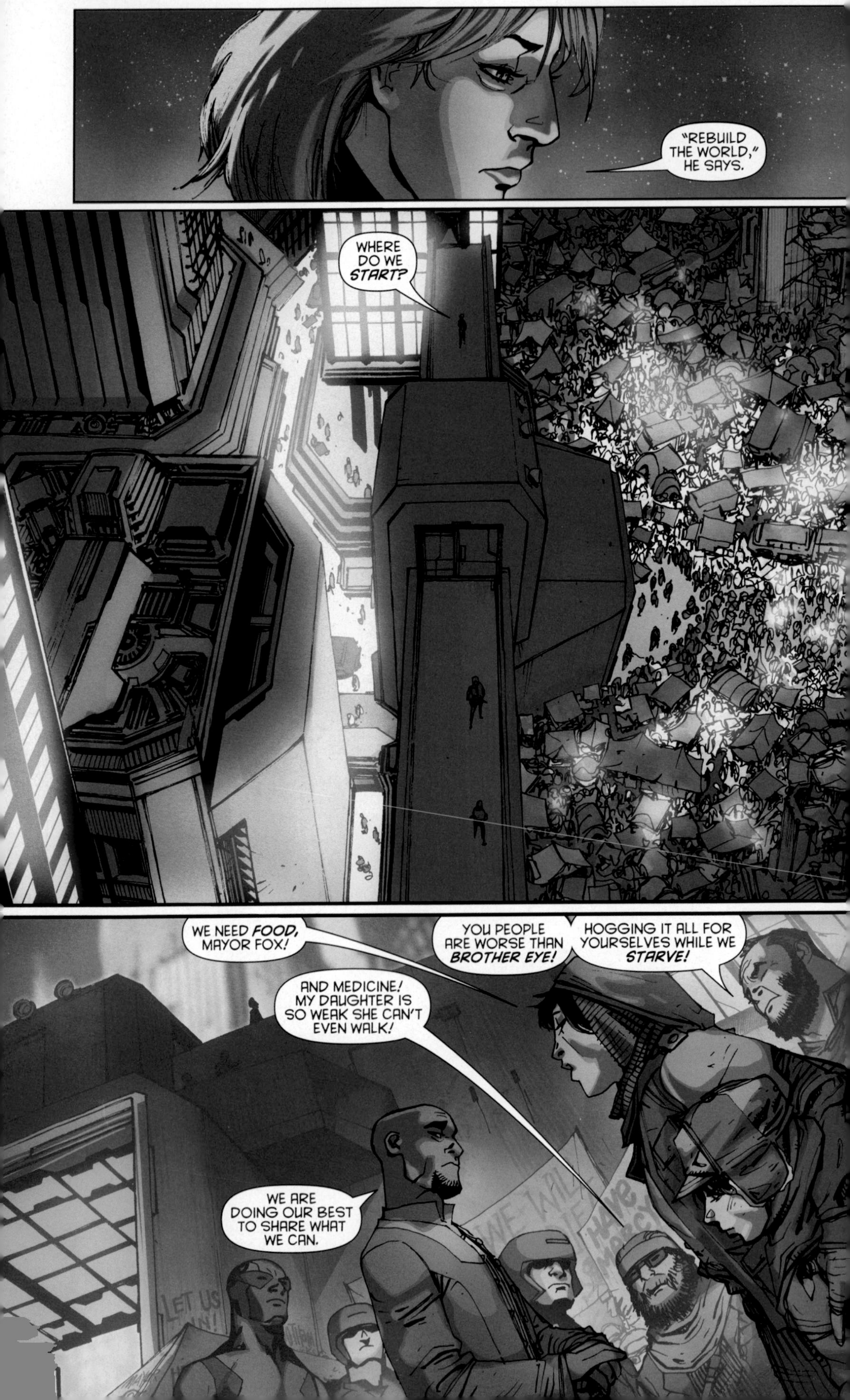
"REBUILD THE WORLD," HE SAYS.
WHERE DO WE *START?*
WE NEED *FOOD,* MAYOR FOX!
YOU PEOPLE ARE WORSE THAN *BROTHER EYE!*
HOGGING IT ALL FOR YOURSELVES WHILE WE *STARVE!*
AND MEDICINE! MY DAUGHTER IS SO WEAK SHE CAN'T EVEN WALK!
WE ARE DOING OUR BEST TO SHARE WHAT WE CAN.
LET US IN!

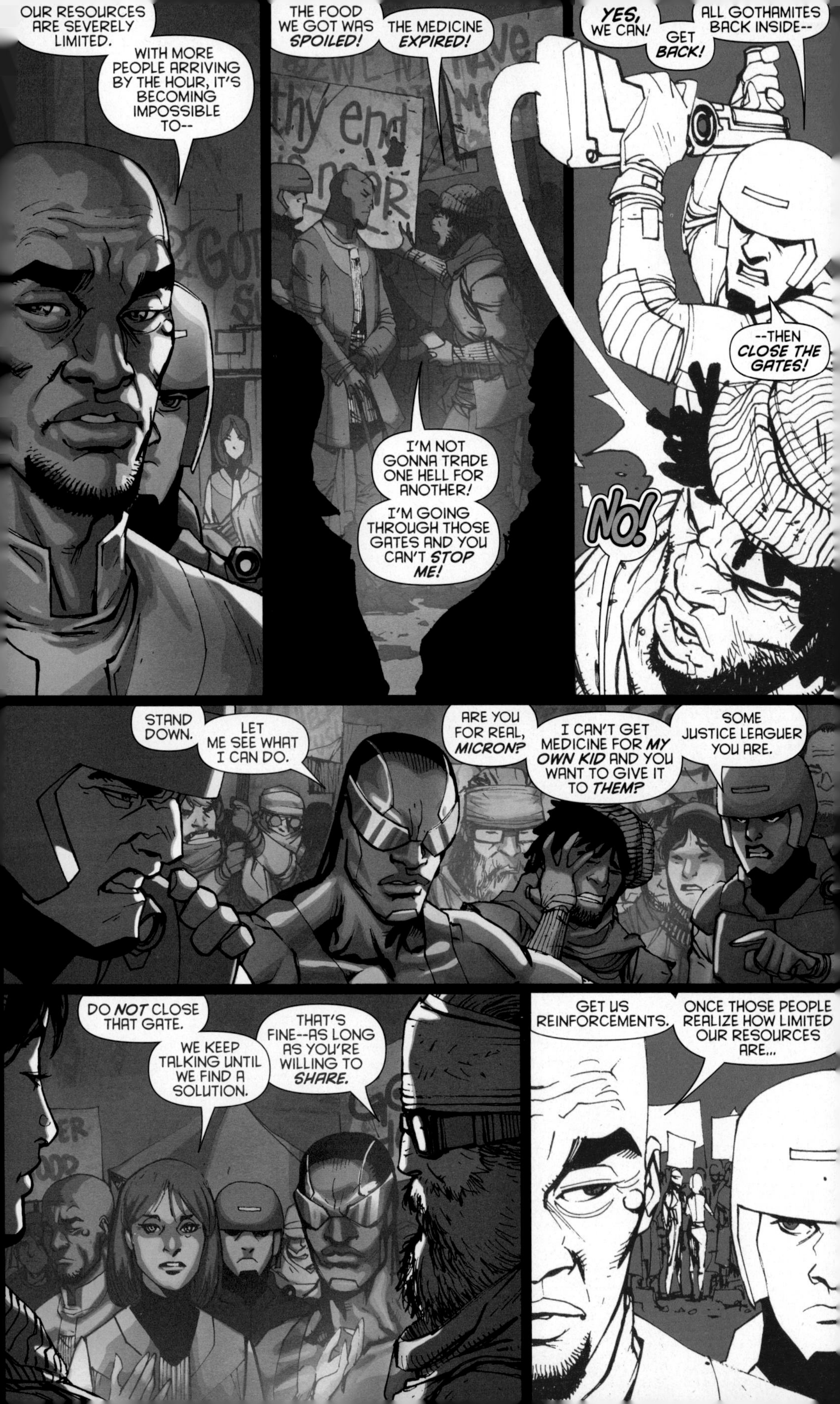

OUR RESOURCES ARE SEVERELY LIMITED.
WITH MORE PEOPLE ARRIVING BY THE HOUR, IT'S BECOMING IMPOSSIBLE TO--
THE FOOD WE GOT WAS *SPOILED!*
THE MEDICINE *EXPIRED!*
I'M NOT GONNA TRADE ONE HELL FOR ANOTHER!
I'M GOING THROUGH THOSE GATES AND YOU CAN'T *STOP ME!*
YES, WE CAN!
GET *BACK!*
ALL GOTHAMITES BACK INSIDE--
--THEN *CLOSE THE GATES!*
NO!
STAND DOWN.
LET ME SEE WHAT I CAN DO.
ARE YOU FOR REAL, *MICRON?*
I CAN'T GET MEDICINE FOR *MY OWN KID* AND YOU WANT TO GIVE IT TO *THEM?*
SOME JUSTICE LEAGUER YOU ARE.
DO *NOT* CLOSE THAT GATE.
WE KEEP TALKING UNTIL WE FIND A SOLUTION.
THAT'S FINE--AS LONG AS YOU'RE WILLING TO *SHARE.*
GET US REINFORCEMENTS.
ONCE THOSE PEOPLE REALIZE HOW LIMITED OUR RESOURCES ARE...

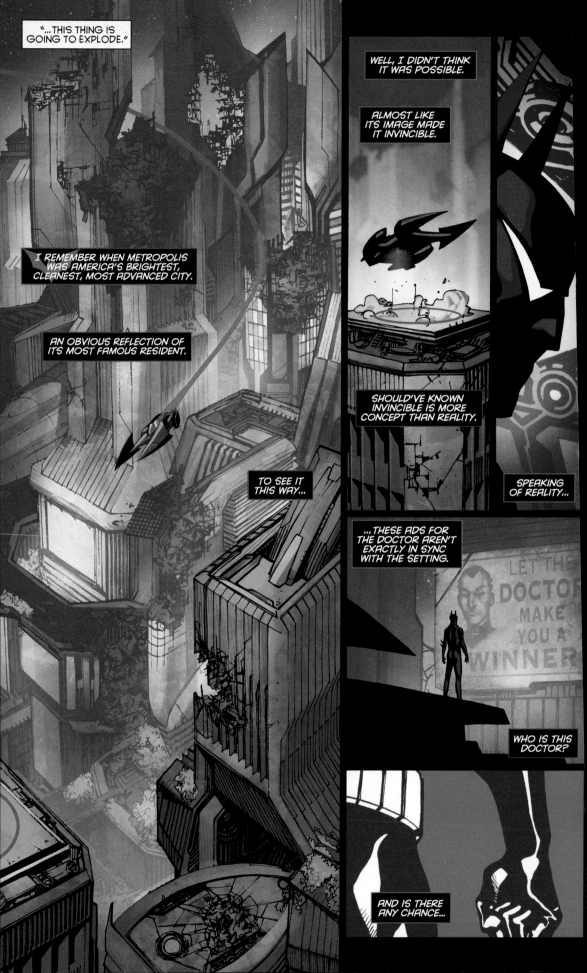

"...THIS THING IS GOING TO EXPLODE."

I REMEMBER WHEN METROPOLIS WAS AMERICA'S BRIGHTEST, CLEANEST, MOST ADVANCED CITY.

AN OBVIOUS REFLECTION OF ITS MOST FAMOUS RESIDENT.

TO SEE IT THIS WAY...

WELL, I DIDN'T THINK IT WAS POSSIBLE.

ALMOST LIKE ITS IMAGE MADE IT INVINCIBLE.

SHOULD'VE KNOWN INVINCIBLE IS MORE CONCEPT THAN REALITY.

SPEAKING OF REALITY...

...THESE ADS FOR THE DOCTOR AREN'T EXACTLY IN SYNC WITH THE SETTING.

LET THE DOCTOR MAKE YOU A WINNER

WHO IS THIS DOCTOR?

AND IS THERE ANY CHANCE...

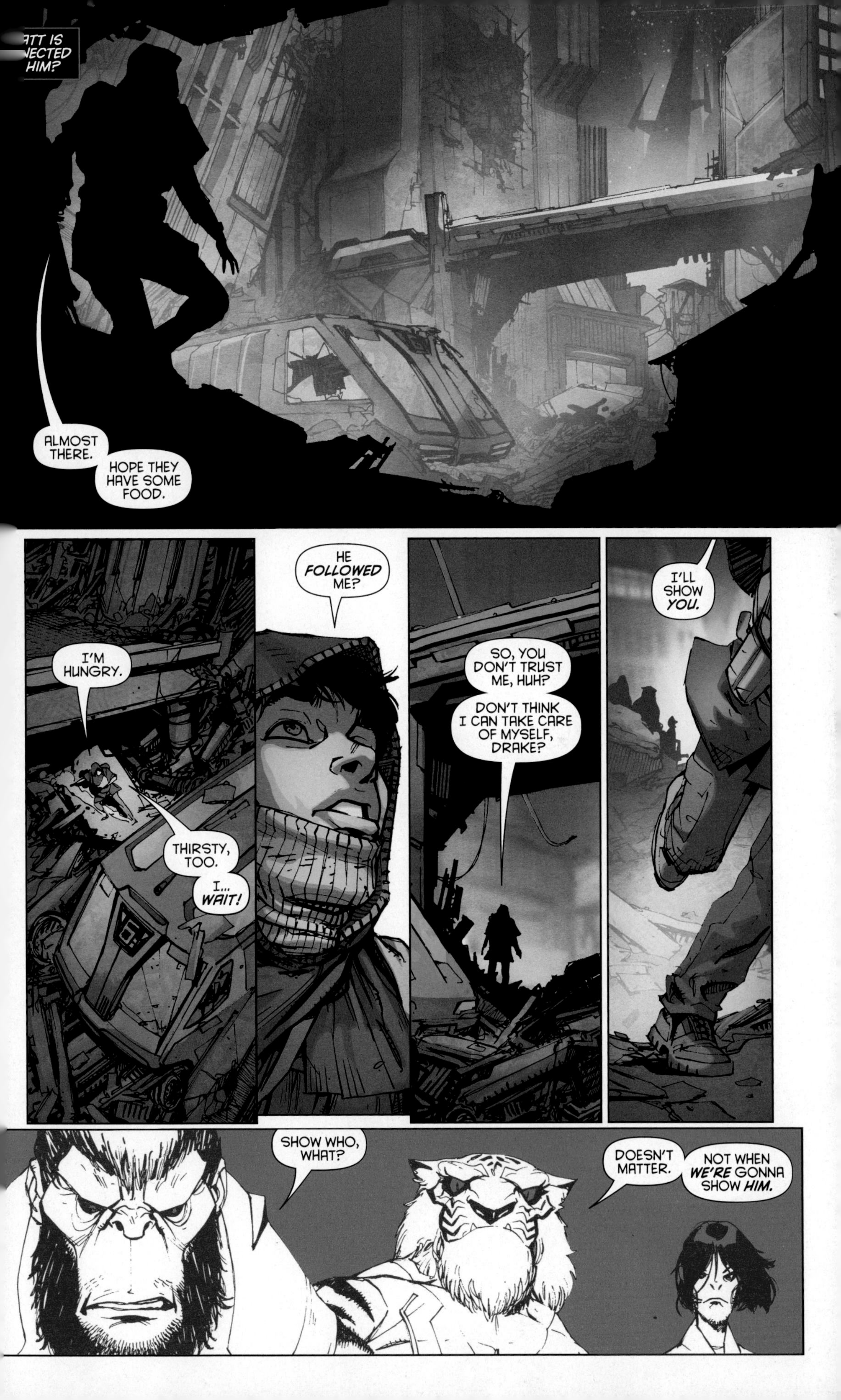
ATT IS
NECTED
HIM?
ALMOST THERE.
HOPE THEY HAVE SOME FOOD.
I'M HUNGRY.
THIRSTY, TOO.
I... WAIT!
HE FOLLOWED ME?
SO, YOU DON'T TRUST ME, HUH?
DON'T THINK I CAN TAKE CARE OF MYSELF, DRAKE?
I'LL SHOW YOU.
SHOW WHO, WHAT?
DOESN'T MATTER.
NOT WHEN WE'RE GONNA SHOW HIM.

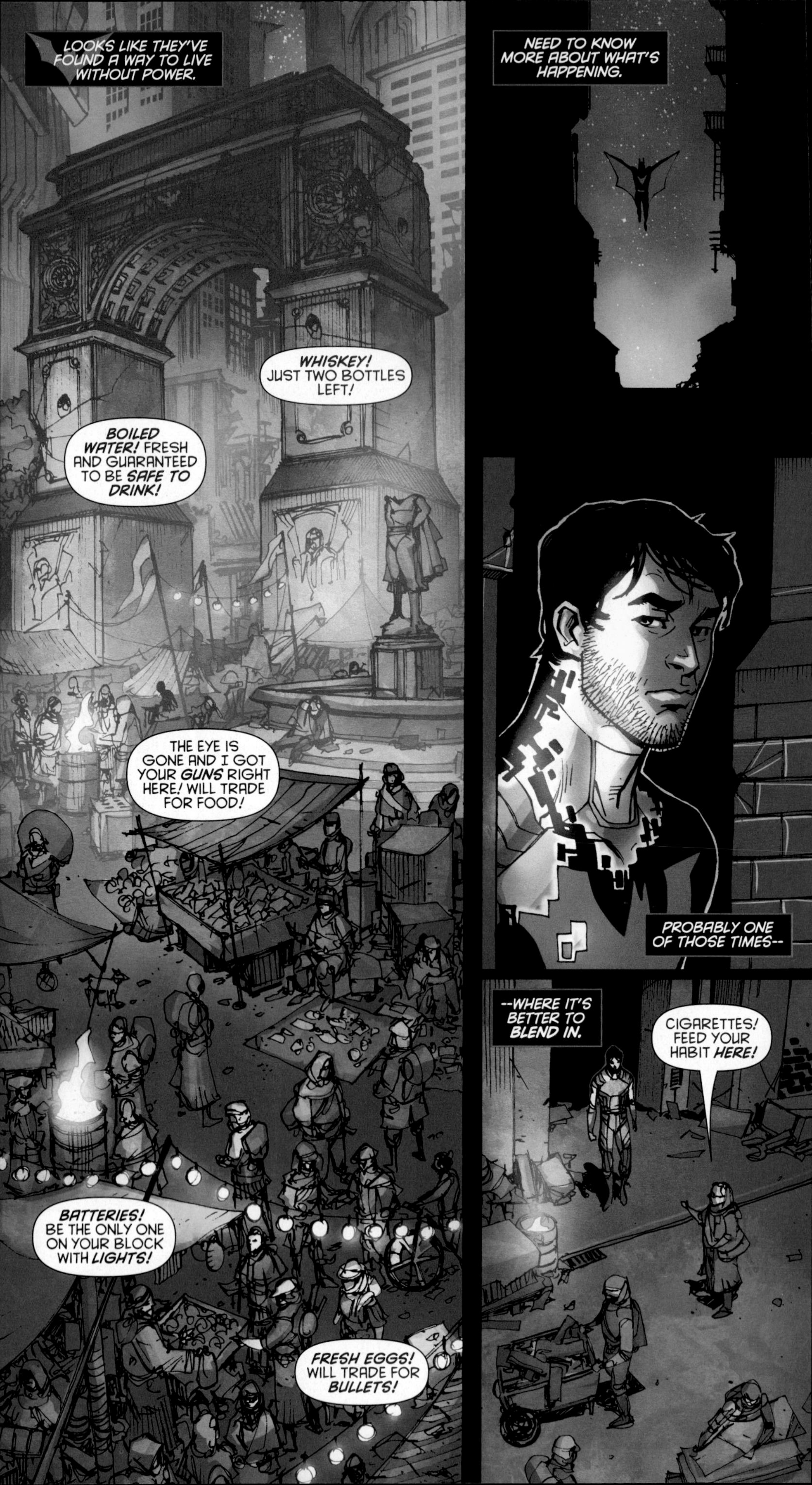
LOOKS LIKE THEY'VE FOUND A WAY TO LIVE WITHOUT POWER.
WHISKEY! JUST TWO BOTTLES LEFT!
BOILED WATER! FRESH AND GUARANTEED TO BE SAFE TO DRINK!
THE EYE IS GONE AND I GOT YOUR GUNS RIGHT HERE! WILL TRADE FOR FOOD!
BATTERIES! BE THE ONLY ONE ON YOUR BLOCK WITH LIGHTS!
FRESH EGGS! WILL TRADE FOR BULLETS!
NEED TO KNOW MORE ABOUT WHAT'S HAPPENING.
PROBABLY ONE OF THOSE TIMES--
--WHERE IT'S BETTER TO BLEND IN.
CIGARETTES! FEED YOUR HABIT HERE!

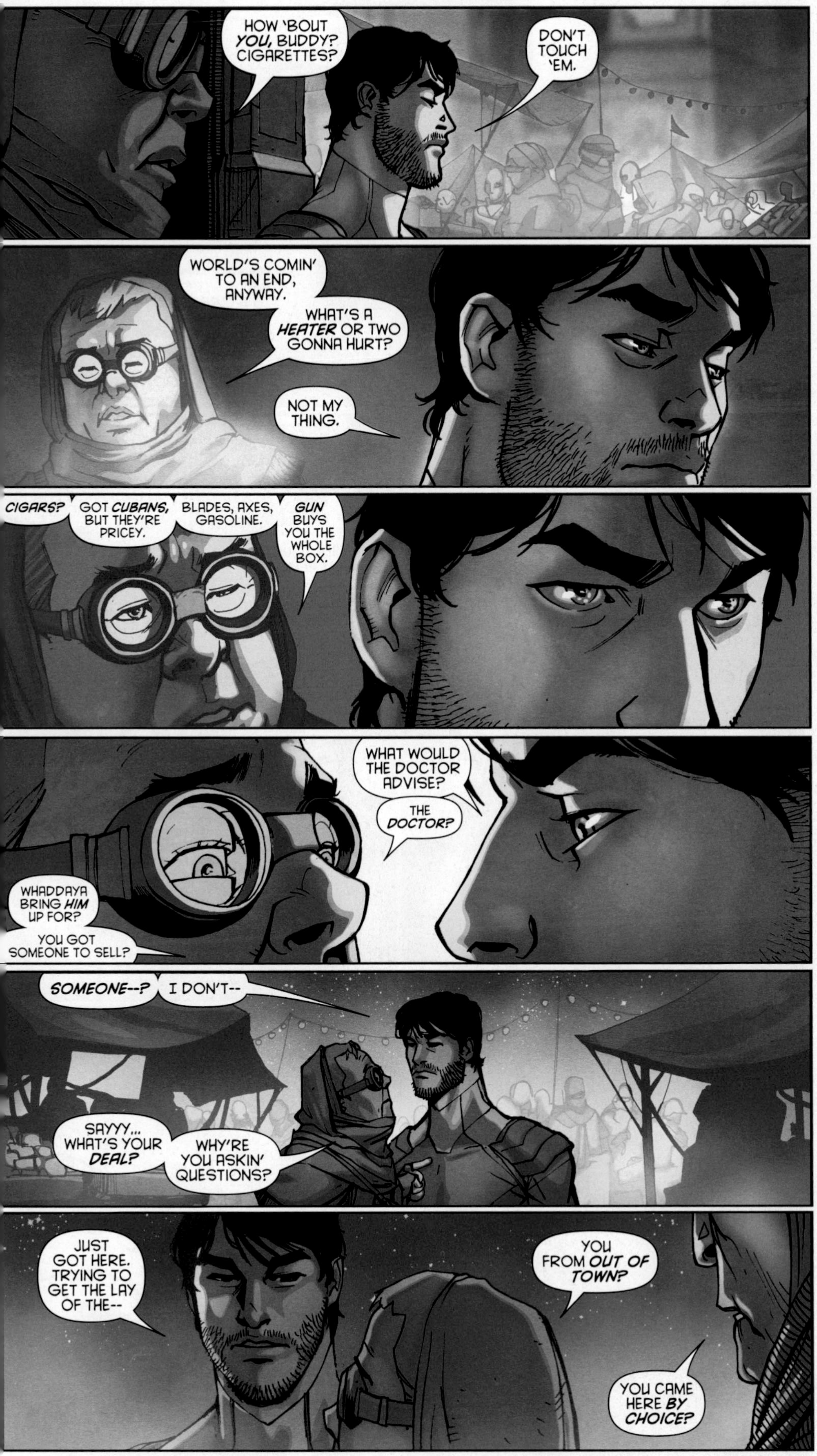
HOW 'BOUT YOU, BUDDY? CIGARETTES?
DON'T TOUCH 'EM.
WORLD'S COMIN' TO AN END, ANYWAY.
WHAT'S A HEATER OR TWO GONNA HURT?
NOT MY THING.
CIGARS?
GOT CUBANS, BUT THEY'RE PRICEY.
BLADES, AXES, GASOLINE.
GUN BUYS YOU THE WHOLE BOX.
WHAT WOULD THE DOCTOR ADVISE?
THE DOCTOR?
WHADDAYA BRING HIM UP FOR?
YOU GOT SOMEONE TO SELL?
SOMEONE--?
I DON'T--
SAYYY... WHAT'S YOUR DEAL?
WHY'RE YOU ASKIN' QUESTIONS?
JUST GOT HERE. TRYING TO GET THE LAY OF THE--
YOU FROM OUT OF TOWN?
YOU CAME HERE BY CHOICE?

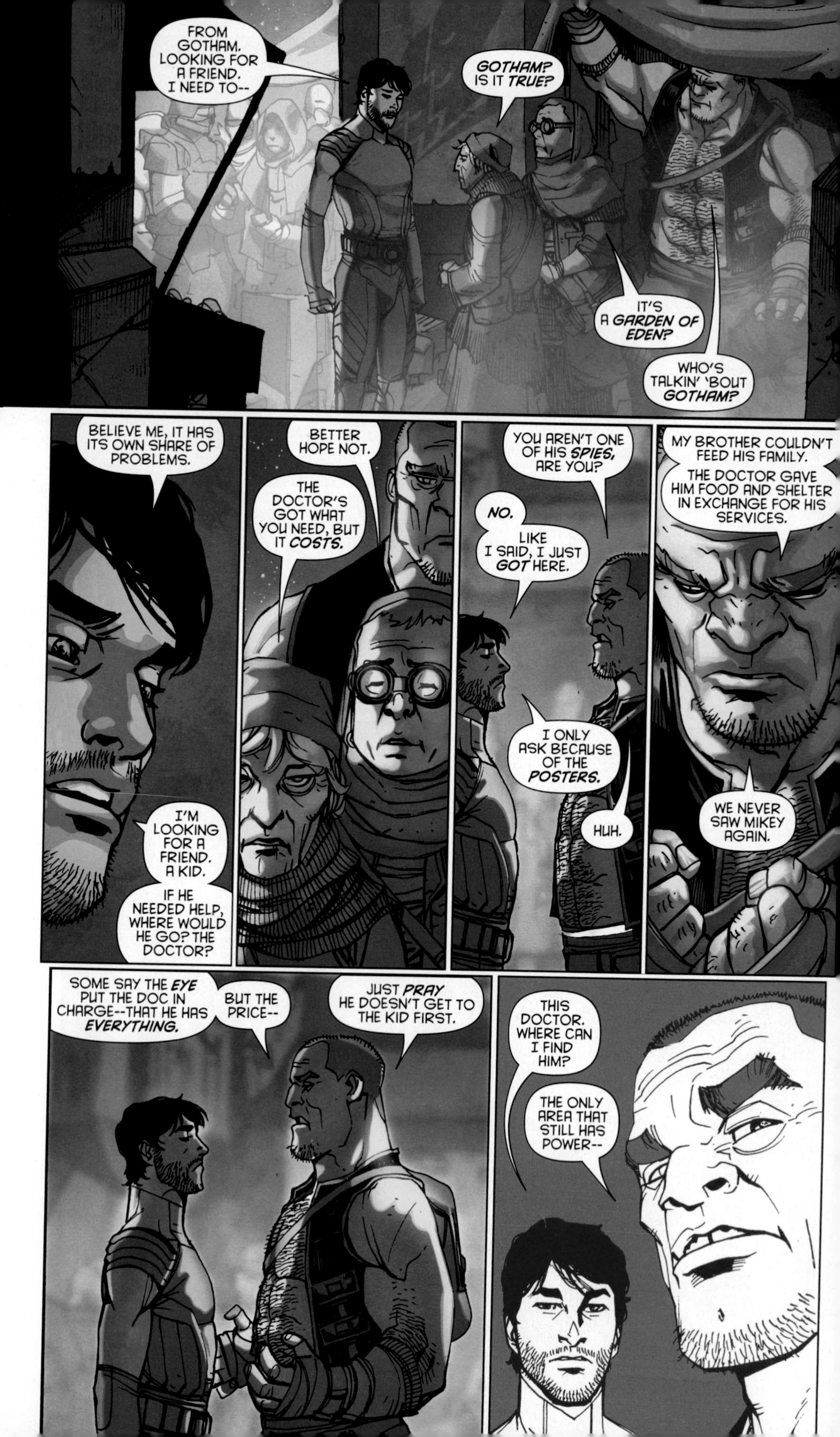
FROM GOTHAM. LOOKING FOR A FRIEND. I NEED TO--
GOTHAM? IS IT TRUE?
IT'S A GARDEN OF EDEN?
WHO'S TALKIN' 'BOUT GOTHAM?
BELIEVE ME, IT HAS ITS OWN SHARE OF PROBLEMS.
I'M LOOKING FOR A FRIEND. A KID.
IF HE NEEDED HELP, WHERE WOULD HE GO? THE DOCTOR?
BETTER HOPE NOT.
THE DOCTOR'S GOT WHAT YOU NEED, BUT IT COSTS.
YOU AREN'T ONE OF HIS SPIES, ARE YOU?
NO.
LIKE I SAID, I JUST GOT HERE.
I ONLY ASK BECAUSE OF THE POSTERS.
HUH.
MY BROTHER COULDN'T FEED HIS FAMILY.
THE DOCTOR GAVE HIM FOOD AND SHELTER IN EXCHANGE FOR HIS SERVICES.
WE NEVER SAW MIKEY AGAIN.
SOME SAY THE EYE PUT THE DOC IN CHARGE--THAT HE HAS EVERYTHING.
BUT THE PRICE--
JUST PRAY HE DOESN'T GET TO THE KID FIRST.
THIS DOCTOR. WHERE CAN I FIND HIM?
THE ONLY AREA THAT STILL HAS POWER--

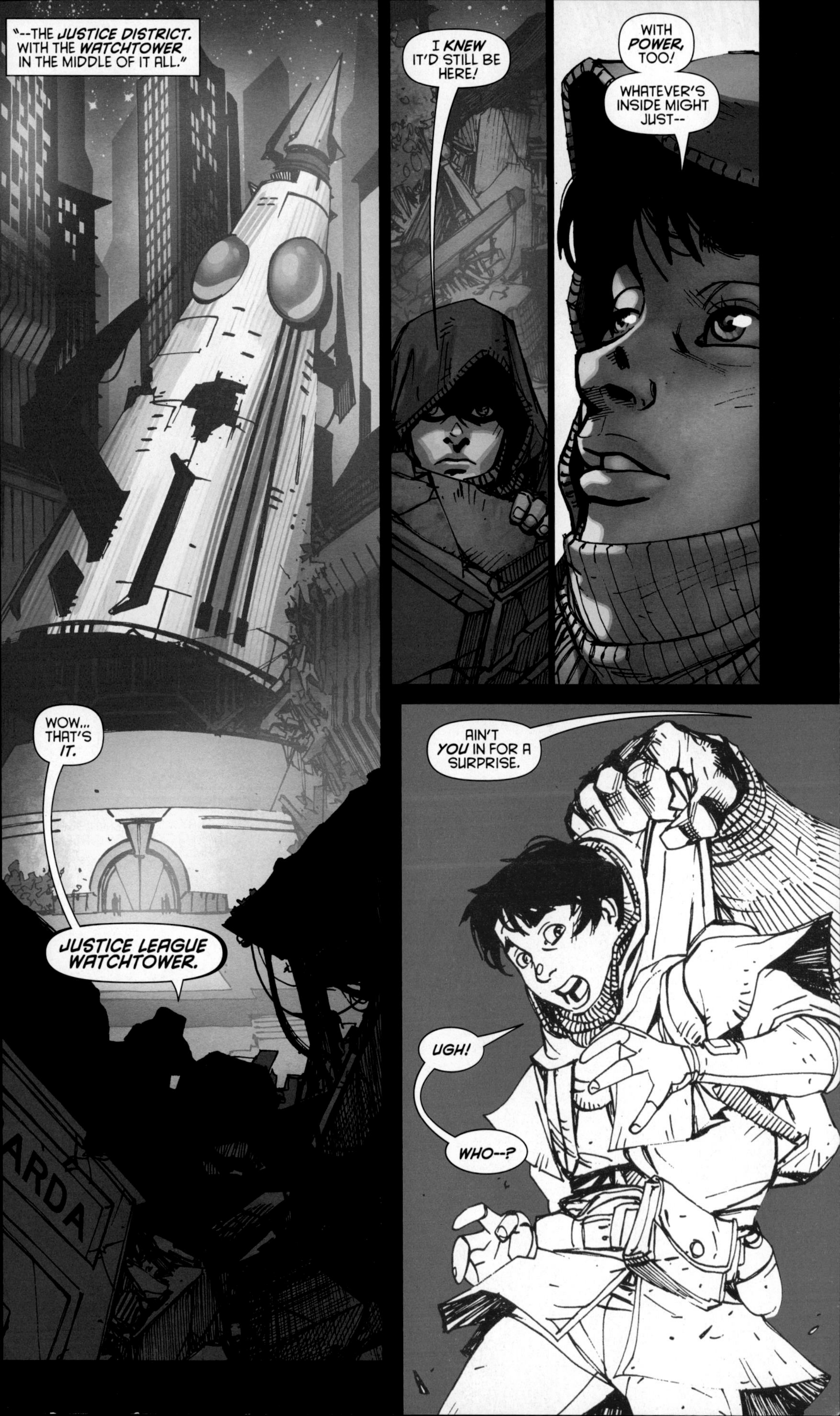
"--THE JUSTICE DISTRICT. WITH THE WATCHTOWER IN THE MIDDLE OF IT ALL."
I KNEW IT'D STILL BE HERE!
WITH POWER, TOO!
WHATEVER'S INSIDE MIGHT JUST--
WOW... THAT'S IT.
JUSTICE LEAGUE WATCHTOWER.
ARDA
AIN'T YOU IN FOR A SURPRISE.
UGH!
WHO--?

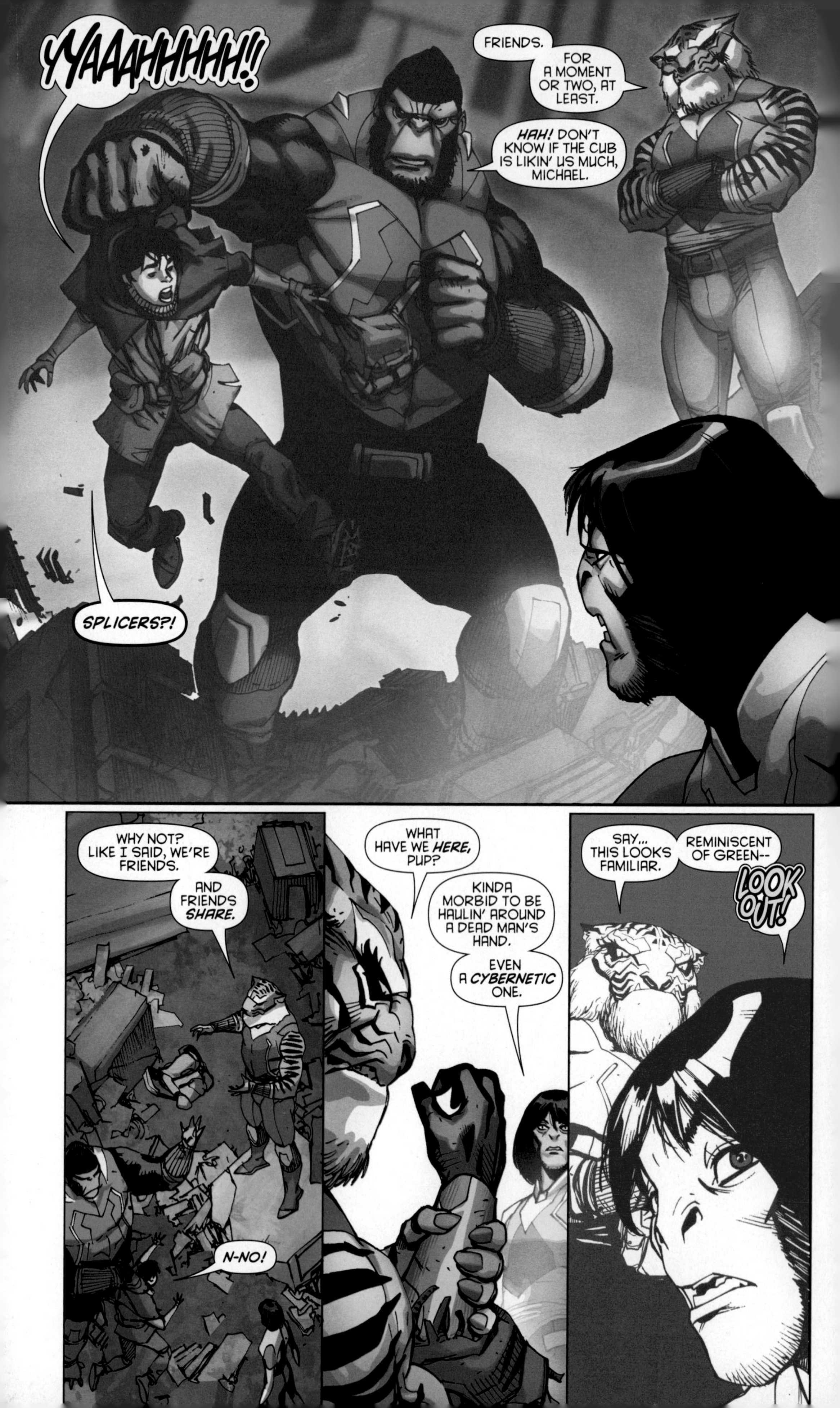
YYAAAHHHHH!!
SPLICERS?!
FRIENDS.
FOR A MOMENT OR TWO, AT LEAST.
HAH! DON'T KNOW IF THE CUB IS LIKIN' US MUCH, MICHAEL.
WHY NOT? LIKE I SAID, WE'RE FRIENDS.
AND FRIENDS SHARE.
N-NO!
WHAT HAVE WE HERE, PUP?
KINDA MORBID TO BE HAULIN' AROUND A DEAD MAN'S HAND.
EVEN A CYBERNETIC ONE.
SAY... THIS LOOKS FAMILIAR.
REMINISCENT OF GREEN--
LOOK OUT!

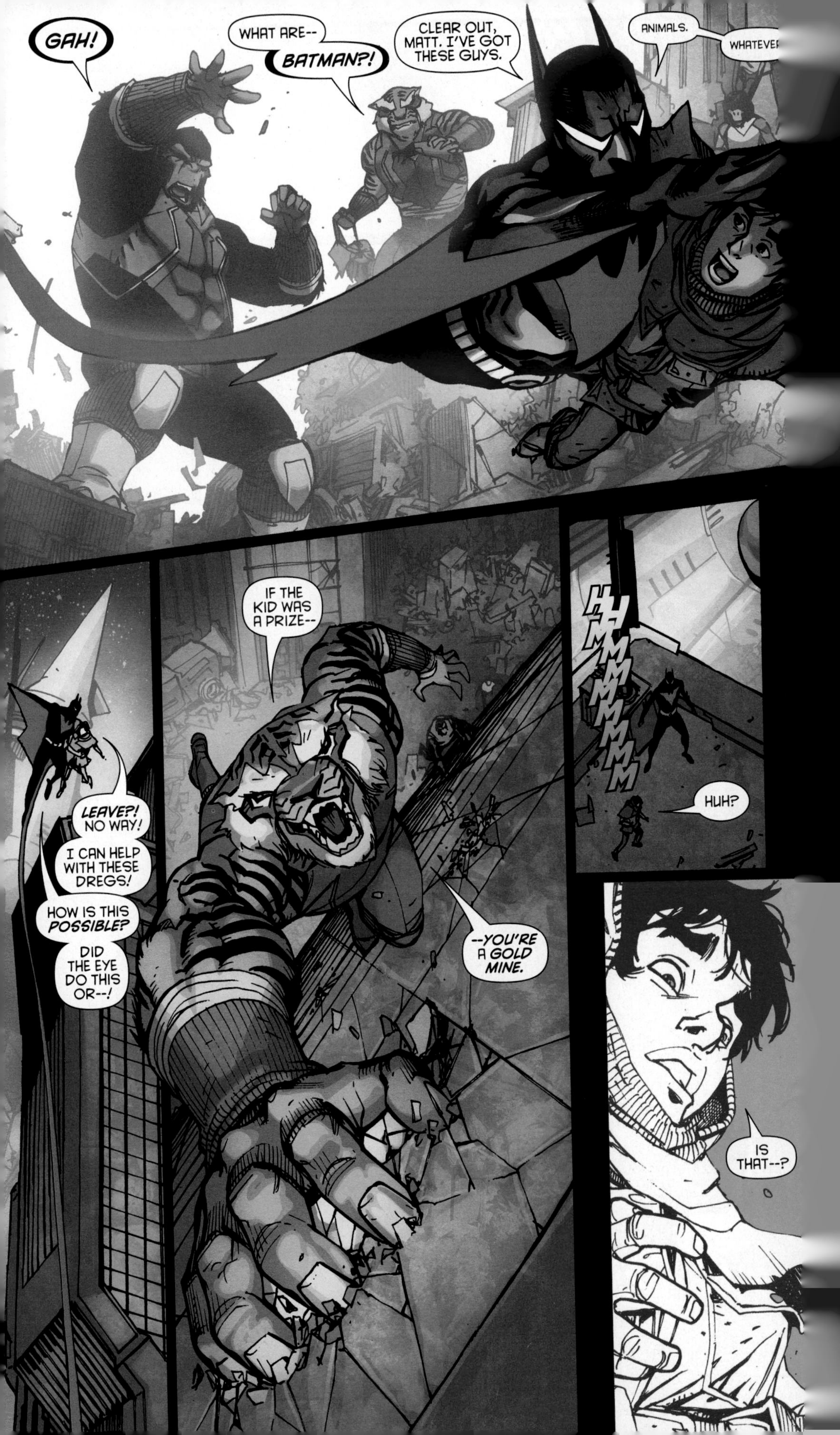
GAH!
WHAT ARE--
BATMAN?!
CLEAR OUT, MATT. I'VE GOT THESE GUYS.
ANIMALS.
WHATEVER
LEAVE?! NO WAY!
I CAN HELP WITH THESE DREGS!
HOW IS THIS POSSIBLE?
DID THE EYE DO THIS OR--!
IF THE KID WAS A PRIZE--
--YOU'RE A GOLD MINE.
HMMMMMMMMM
HUH?
IS THAT--?

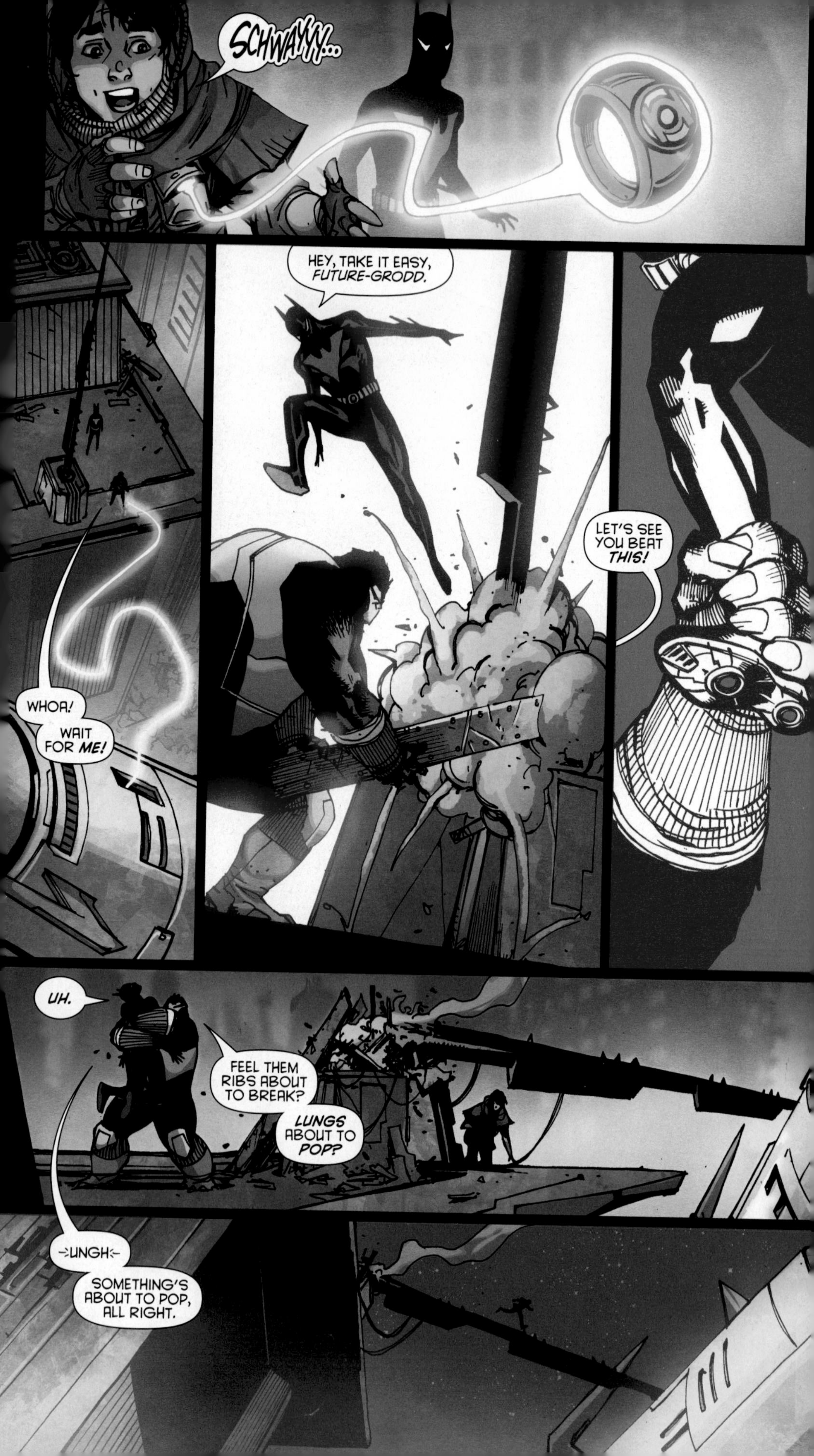
SCHWAYYY...
HEY, TAKE IT EASY, FUTURE-GRODD.
LET'S SEE YOU BEAT THIS!
WHOA!
WAIT FOR ME!
UH.
FEEL THEM RIBS ABOUT TO BREAK?
LUNGS ABOUT TO POP?
UNGH
SOMETHING'S ABOUT TO POP, ALL RIGHT.

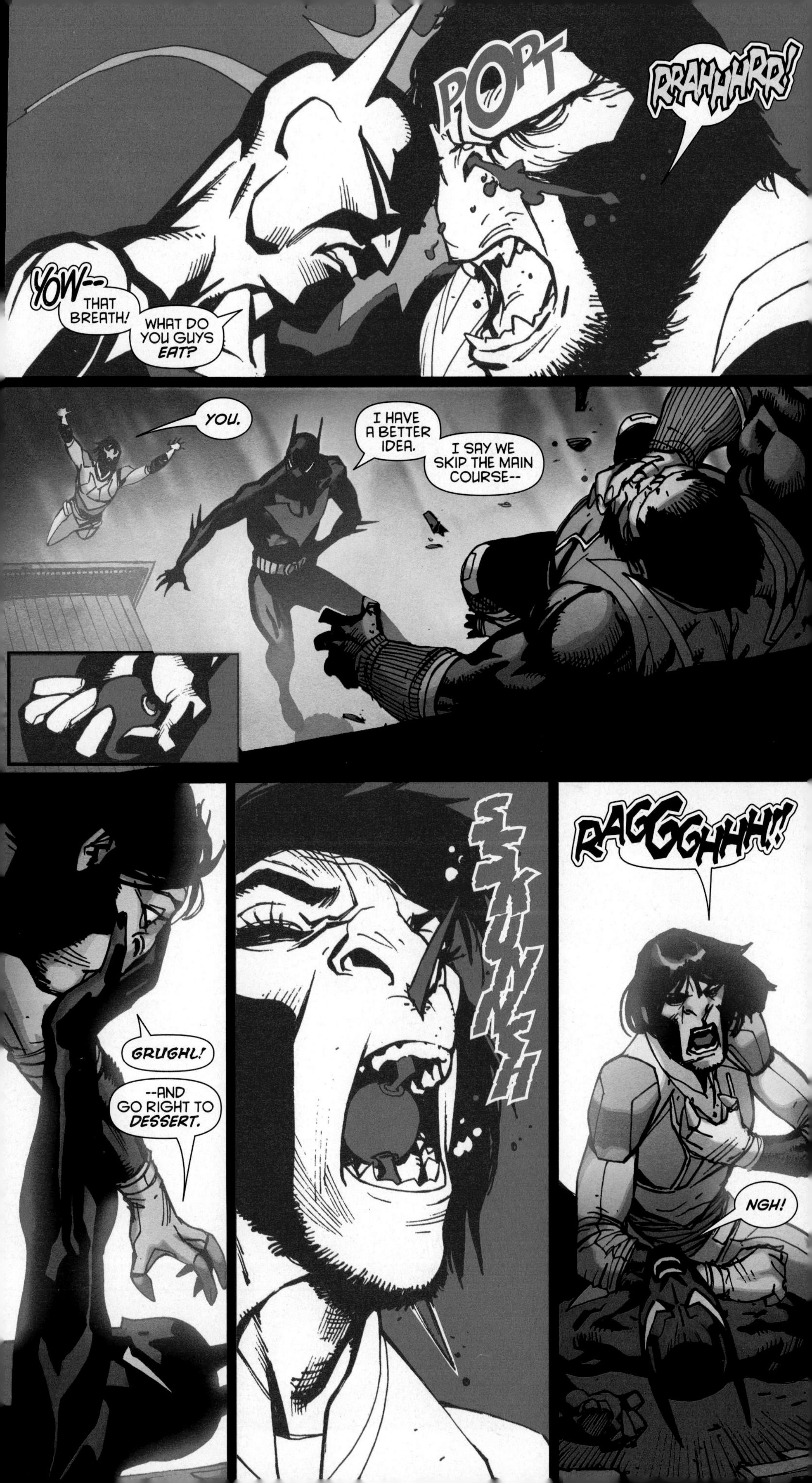
POP
RRAHHHRR!
YOW--
THAT BREATH!
WHAT DO YOU GUYS EAT?
YOU.
I HAVE A BETTER IDEA.
I SAY WE SKIP THE MAIN COURSE--
GRUGHL!
--AND GO RIGHT TO DESSERT.
RAGGGHHH!!
NGH!

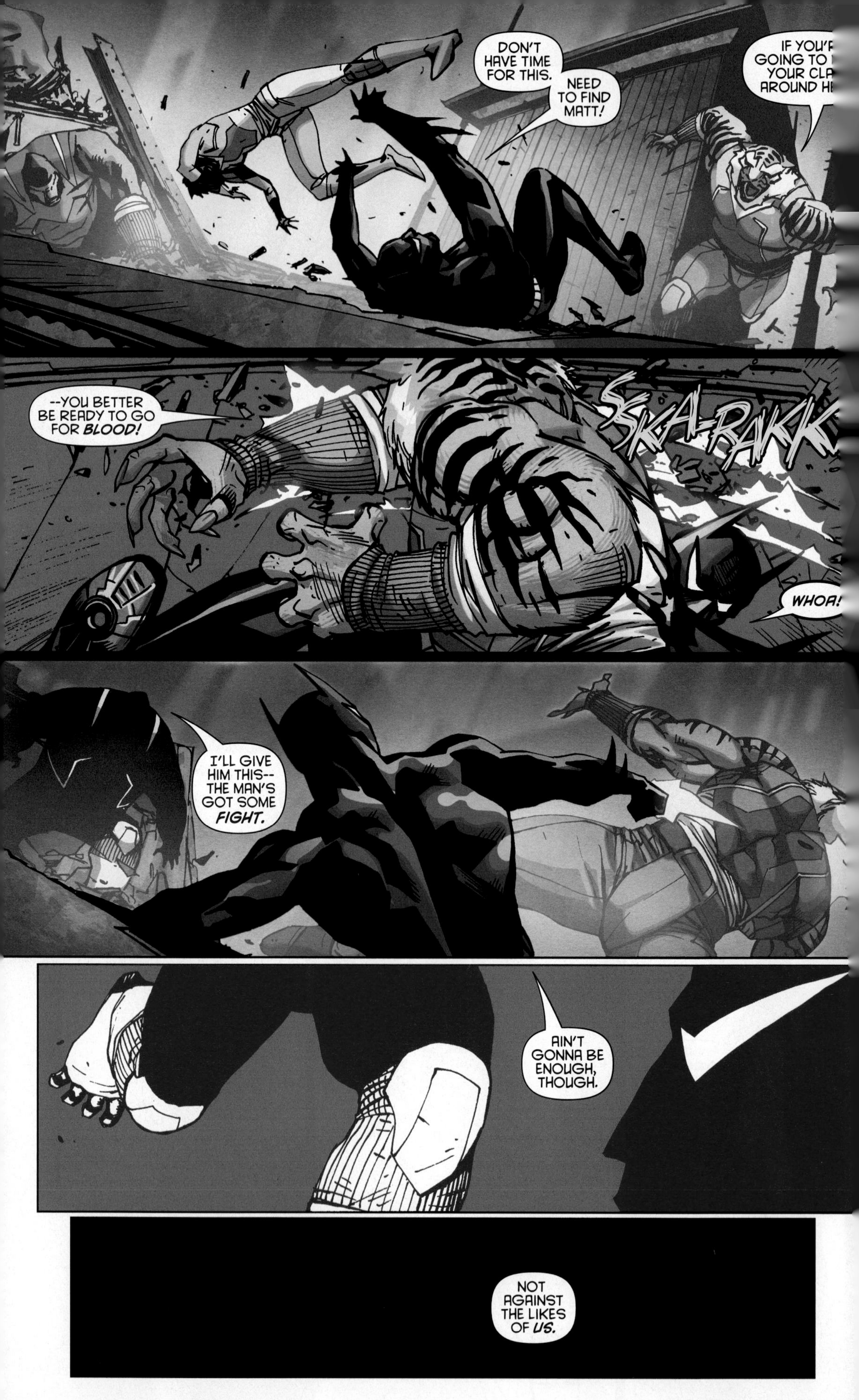
DON'T HAVE TIME FOR THIS.
NEED TO FIND MATT!
IF YOU'R GOING TO YOUR CLA AROUND HE
--YOU BETTER BE READY TO GO FOR BLOOD!
SKA-RAKK
WHOA!
I'LL GIVE HIM THIS-- THE MAN'S GOT SOME FIGHT.
AIN'T GONNA BE ENOUGH, THOUGH.
NOT AGAINST THE LIKES OF US.

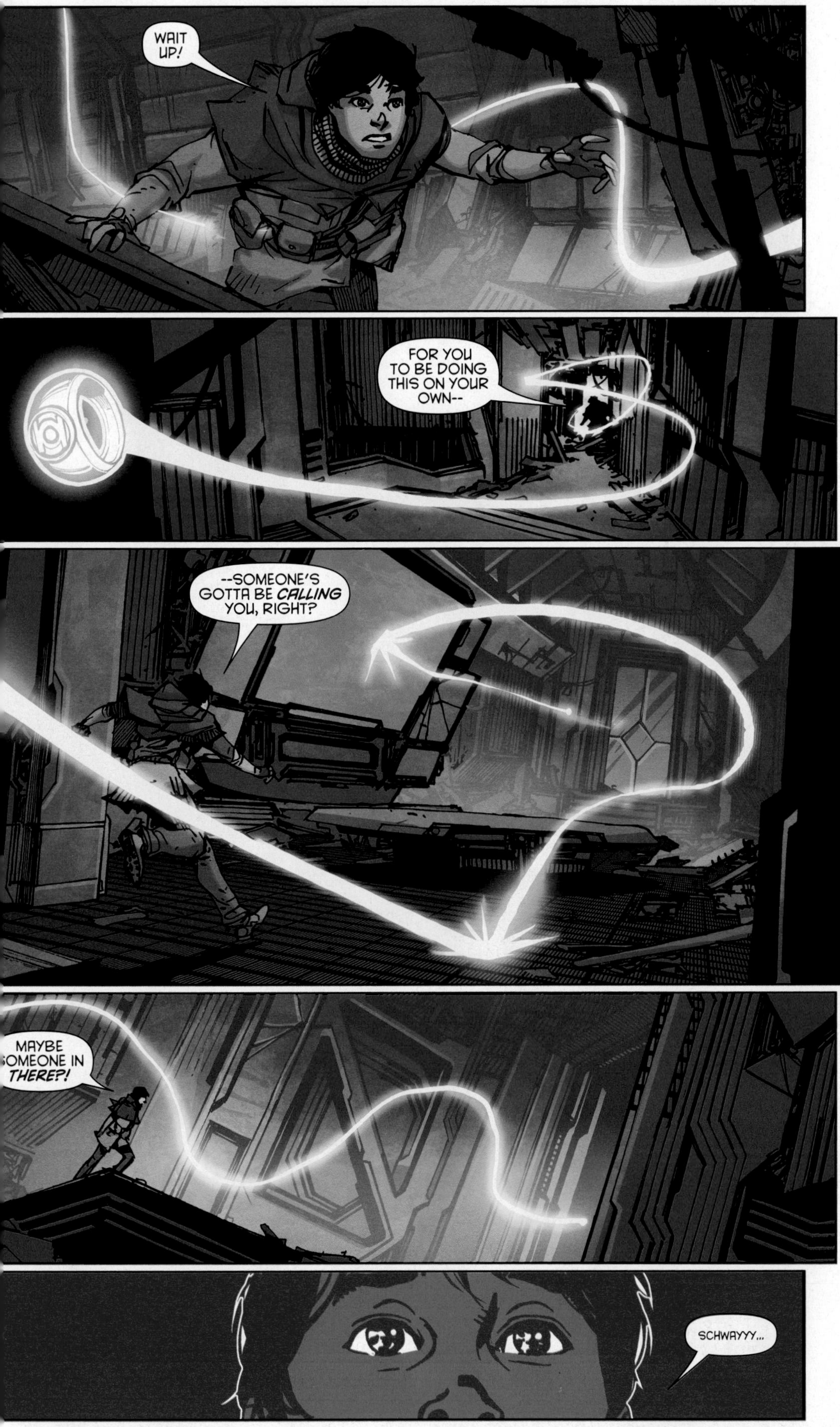
WAIT UP!
FOR YOU TO BE DOING THIS ON YOUR OWN--
--SOMEONE'S GOTTA BE *CALLING* YOU, RIGHT?
MAYBE SOMEONE IN *THERE?!*
SCHWAYYY...

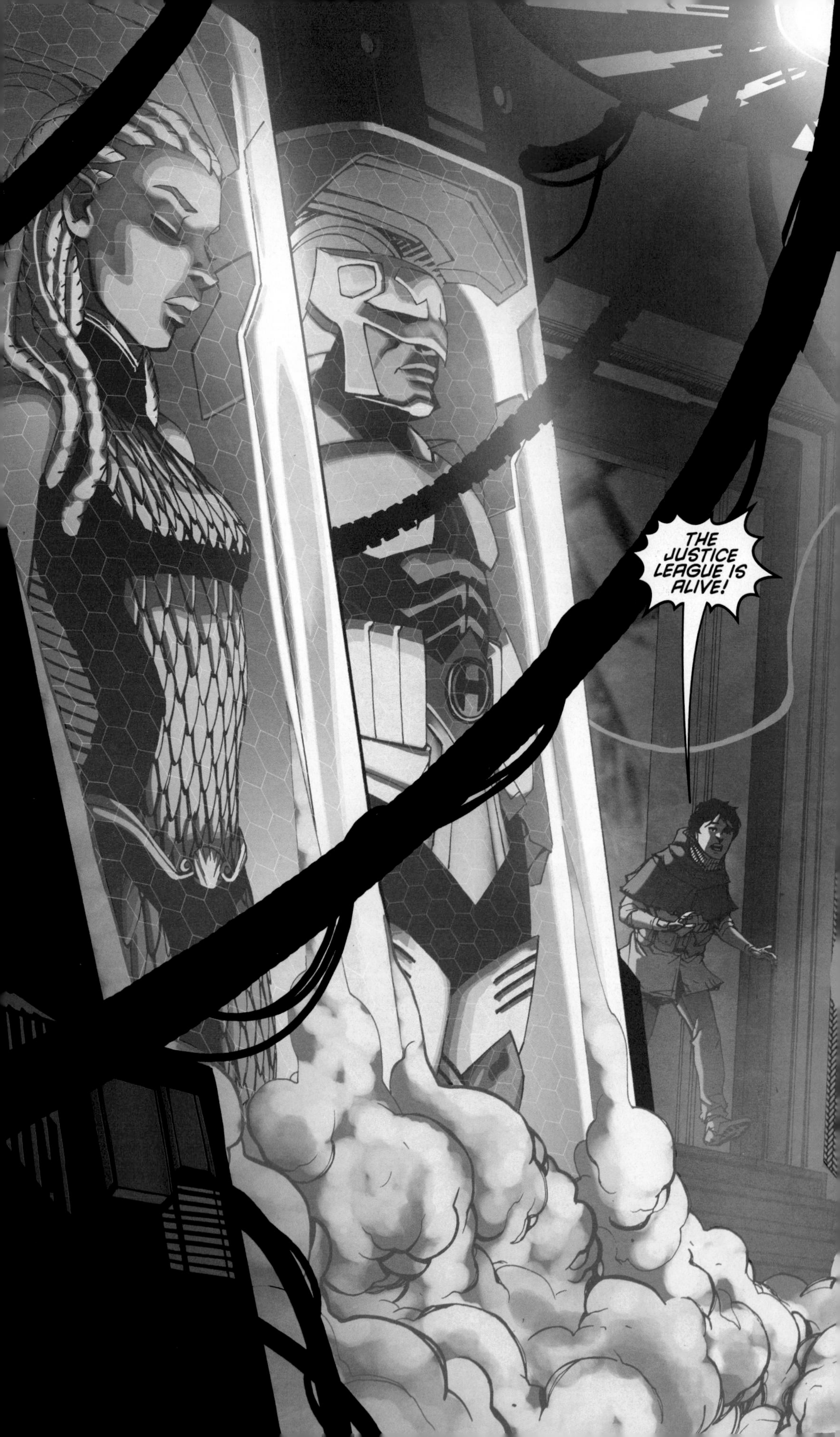
THE JUSTICE LEAGUE IS ALIVE!

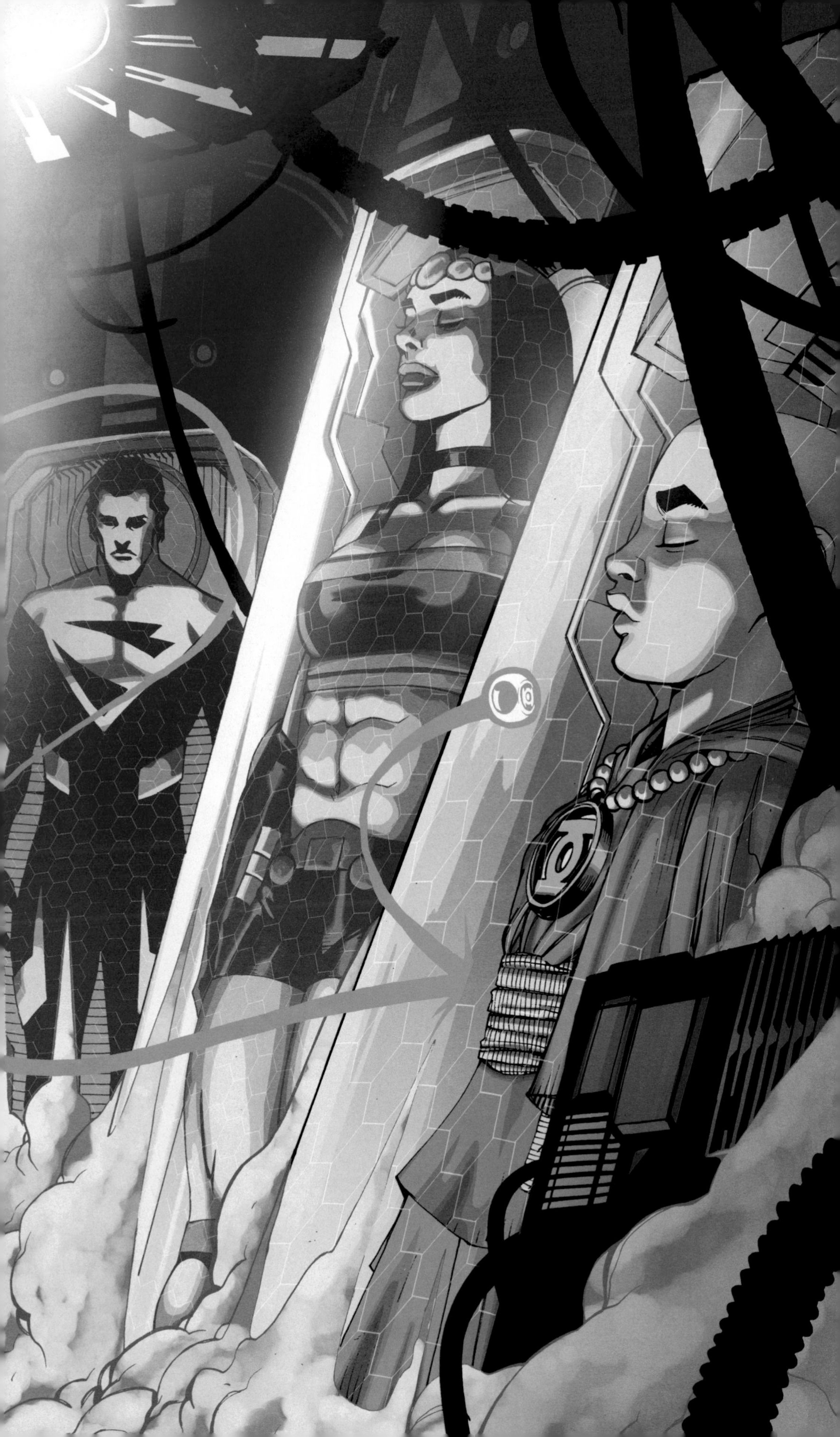

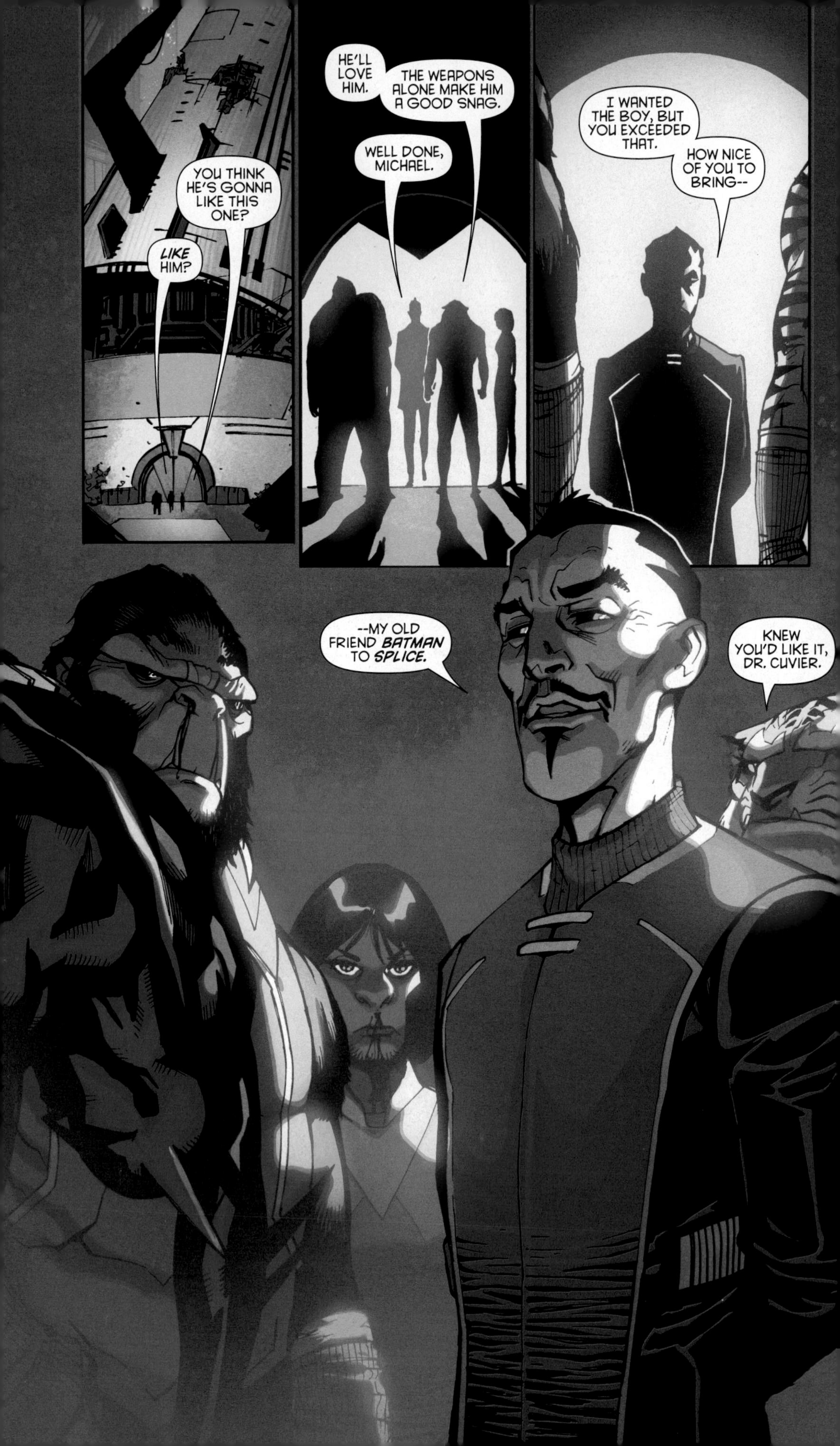
YOU THINK HE'S GONNA LIKE THIS ONE?
LIKE HIM?
HE'LL LOVE HIM.
THE WEAPONS ALONE MAKE HIM A GOOD SNAG.
WELL DONE, MICHAEL.
I WANTED THE BOY, BUT YOU EXCEEDED THAT.
HOW NICE OF YOU TO BRING--
--MY OLD FRIEND *BATMAN* TO *SPLICE.*
KNEW YOU'D LIKE IT, DR. CUVIER.

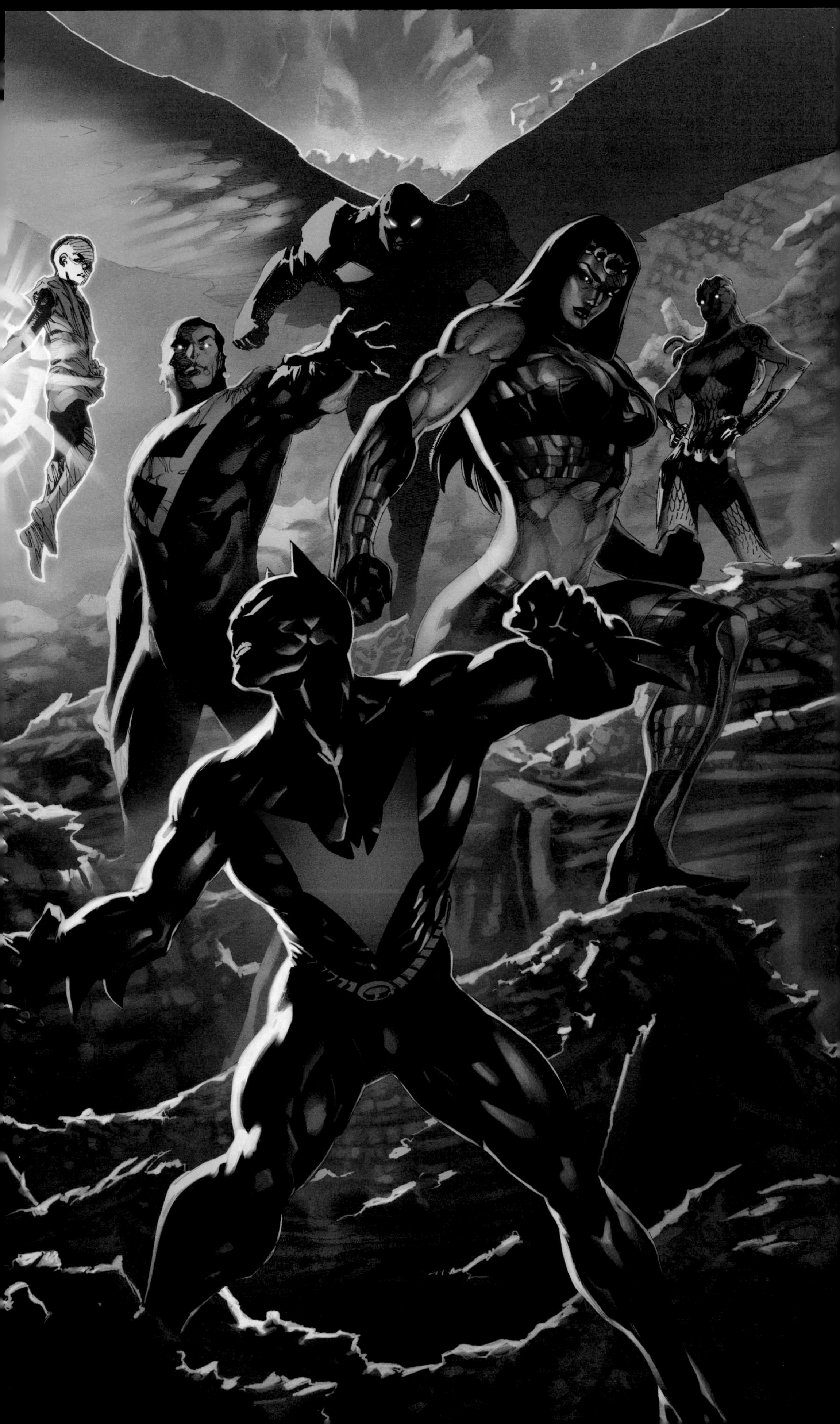

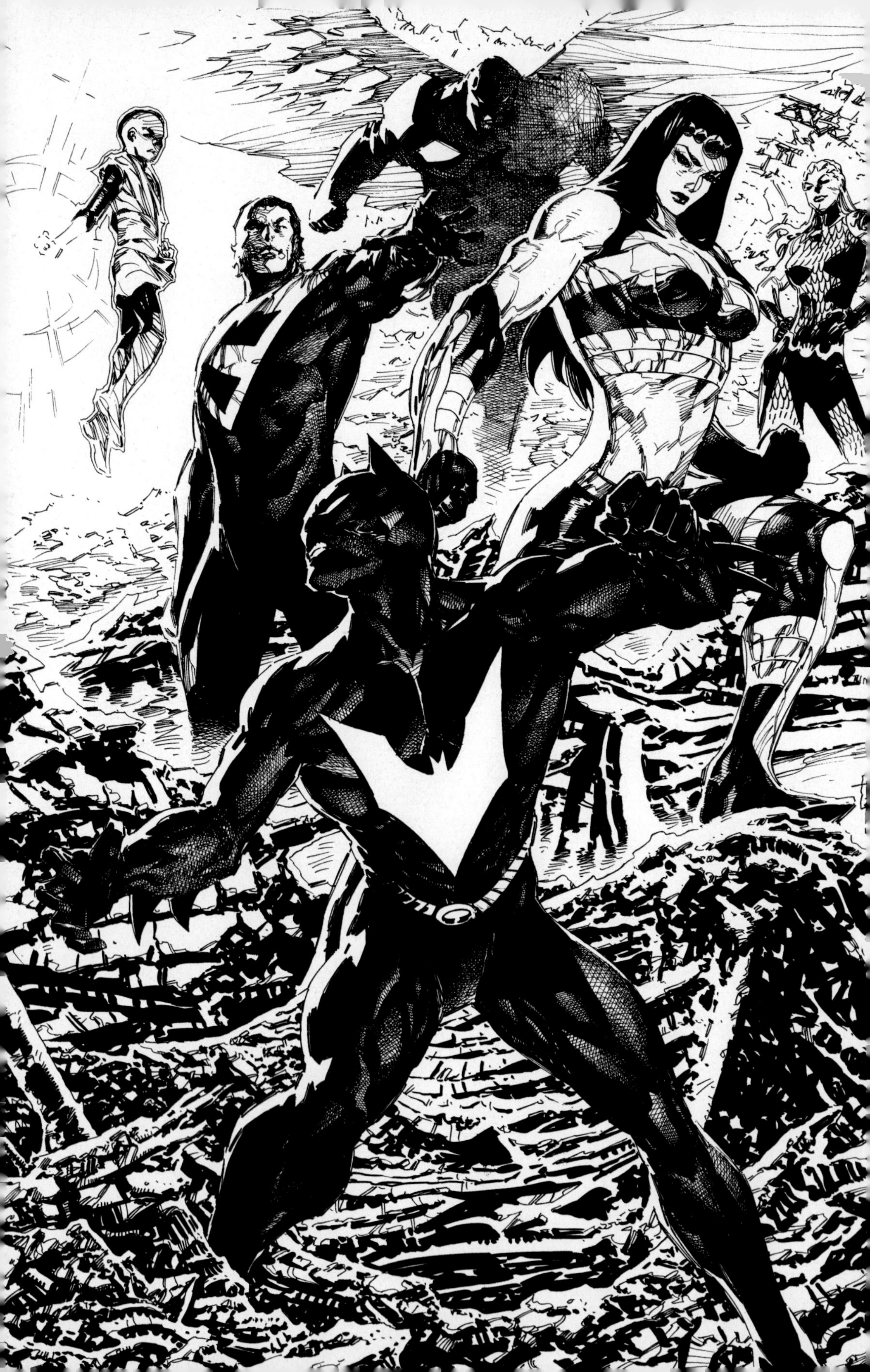

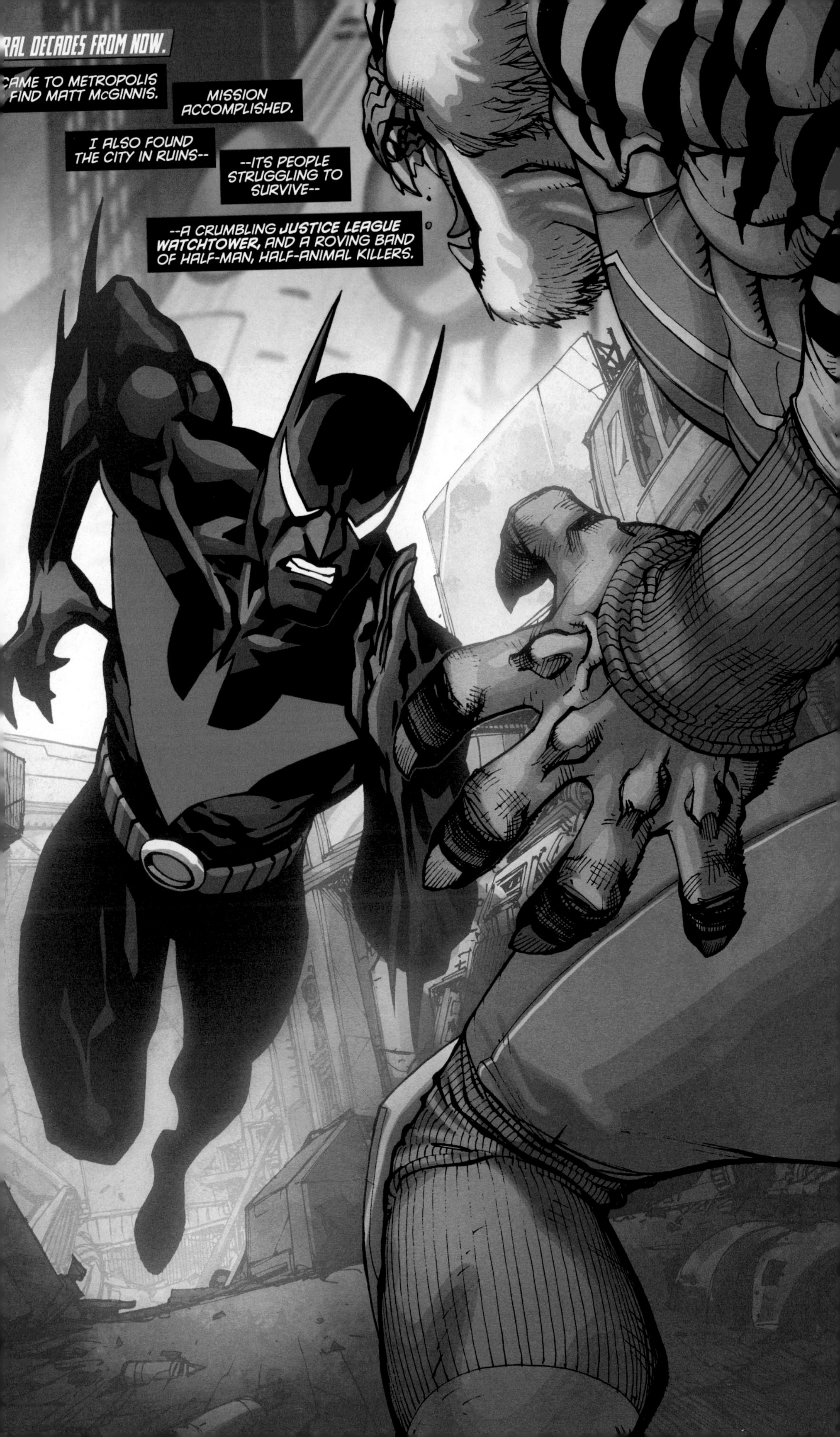
RAL DECADES FROM NOW.
CAME TO METROPOLIS FIND MATT McGINNIS.
MISSION ACCOMPLISHED.
I ALSO FOUND THE CITY IN RUINS--
--ITS PEOPLE STRUGGLING TO SURVIVE--
--A CRUMBLING JUSTICE LEAGUE WATCHTOWER, AND A ROVING BAND OF HALF-MAN, HALF-ANIMAL KILLERS.

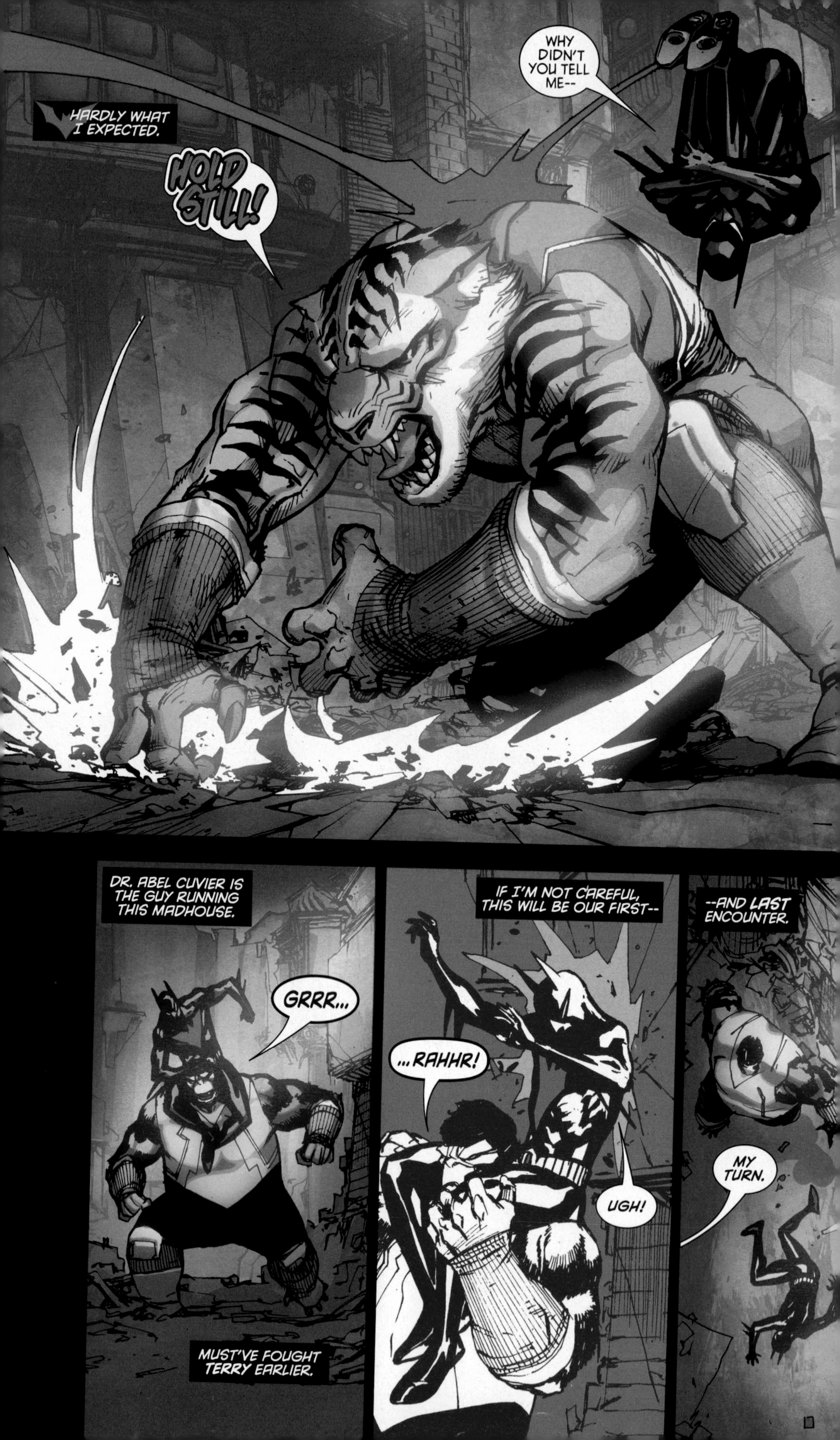
HARDLY WHAT I EXPECTED.
WHY DIDN'T YOU TELL ME--
HOLD STILL!
DR. ABEL CUVIER IS THE GUY RUNNING THIS MADHOUSE.
GRRR...
MUST'VE FOUGHT TERRY EARLIER.
IF I'M NOT CAREFUL, THIS WILL BE OUR FIRST--
...RAHHR!
UGH!
--AND LAST ENCOUNTER.
MY TURN.

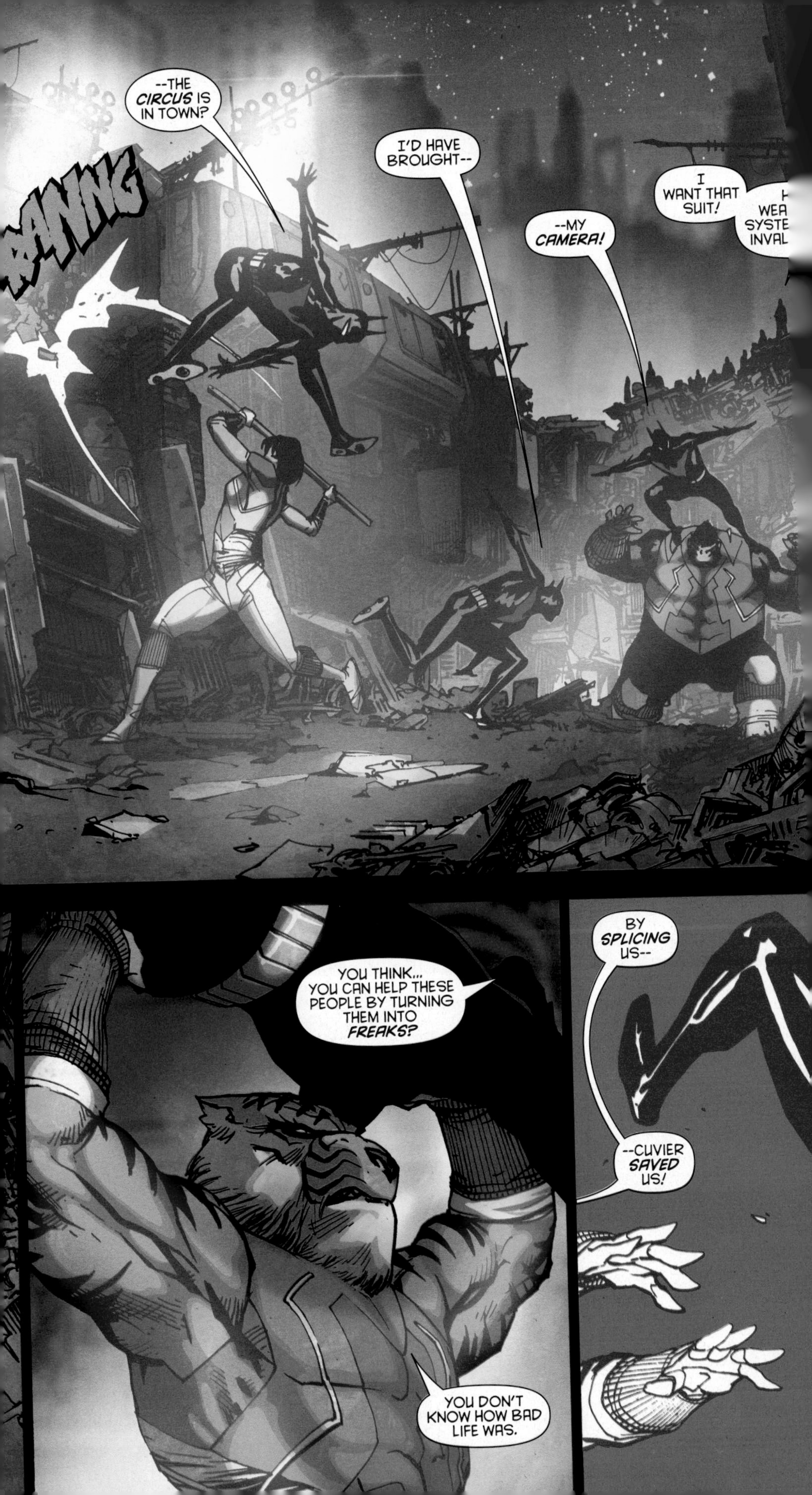
--THE CIRCUS IS IN TOWN?
I'D HAVE BROUGHT--
--MY CAMERA!
I WANT THAT SUIT!
YOU THINK... YOU CAN HELP THESE PEOPLE BY TURNING THEM INTO FREAKS?
YOU DON'T KNOW HOW BAD LIFE WAS.
BY SPLICING US--
--CUVIER SAVED US!

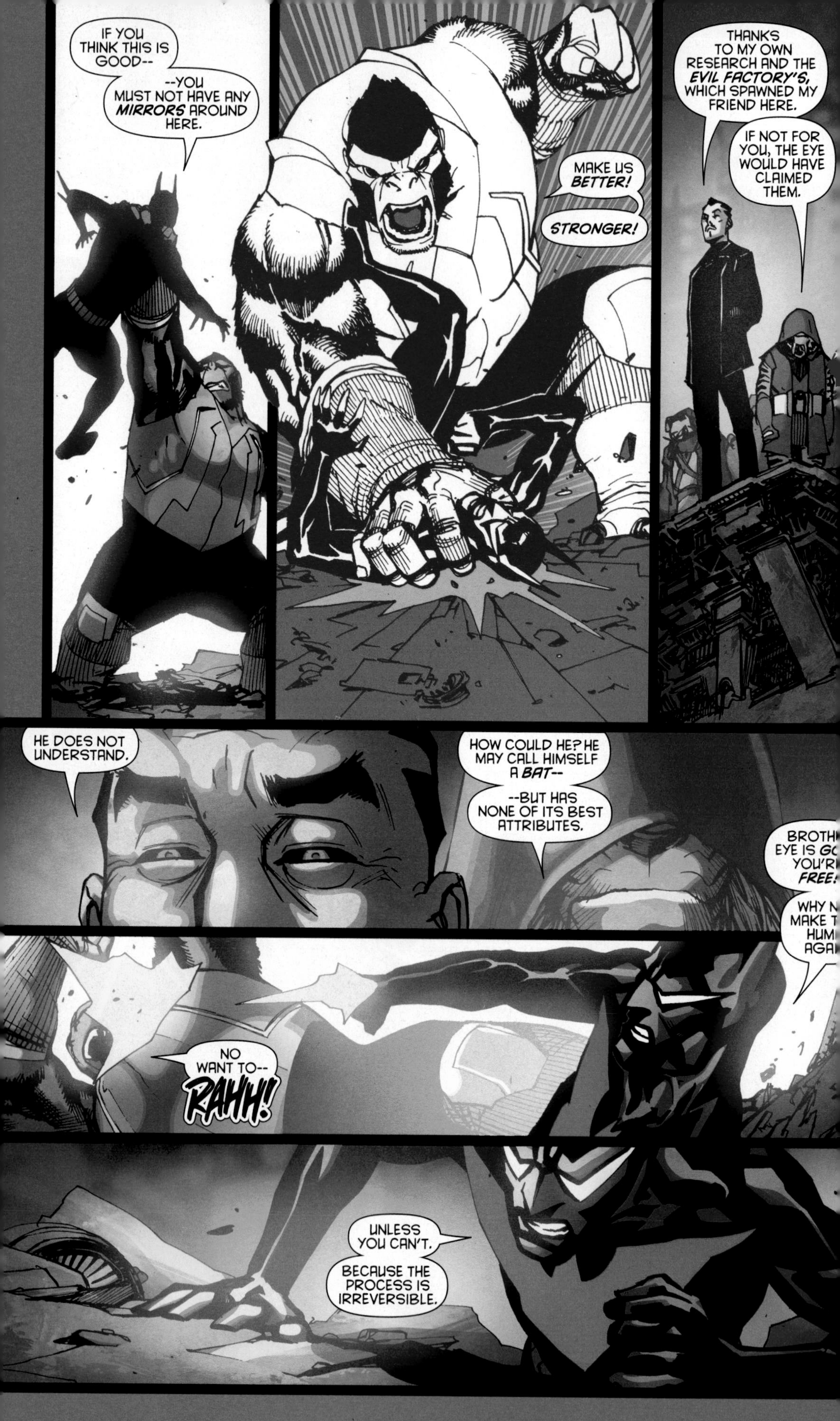
IF YOU THINK THIS IS GOOD--
--YOU MUST NOT HAVE ANY MIRRORS AROUND HERE.
MAKE US BETTER!
STRONGER!
THANKS TO MY OWN RESEARCH AND THE EVIL FACTORY'S, WHICH SPAWNED MY FRIEND HERE.
IF NOT FOR YOU, THE EYE WOULD HAVE CLAIMED THEM.
HE DOES NOT UNDERSTAND.
HOW COULD HE? HE MAY CALL HIMSELF A BAT--
--BUT HAS NONE OF ITS BEST ATTRIBUTES.
NO WANT TO--
RAHH!
UNLESS YOU CAN'T.
BECAUSE THE PROCESS IS IRREVERSIBLE.

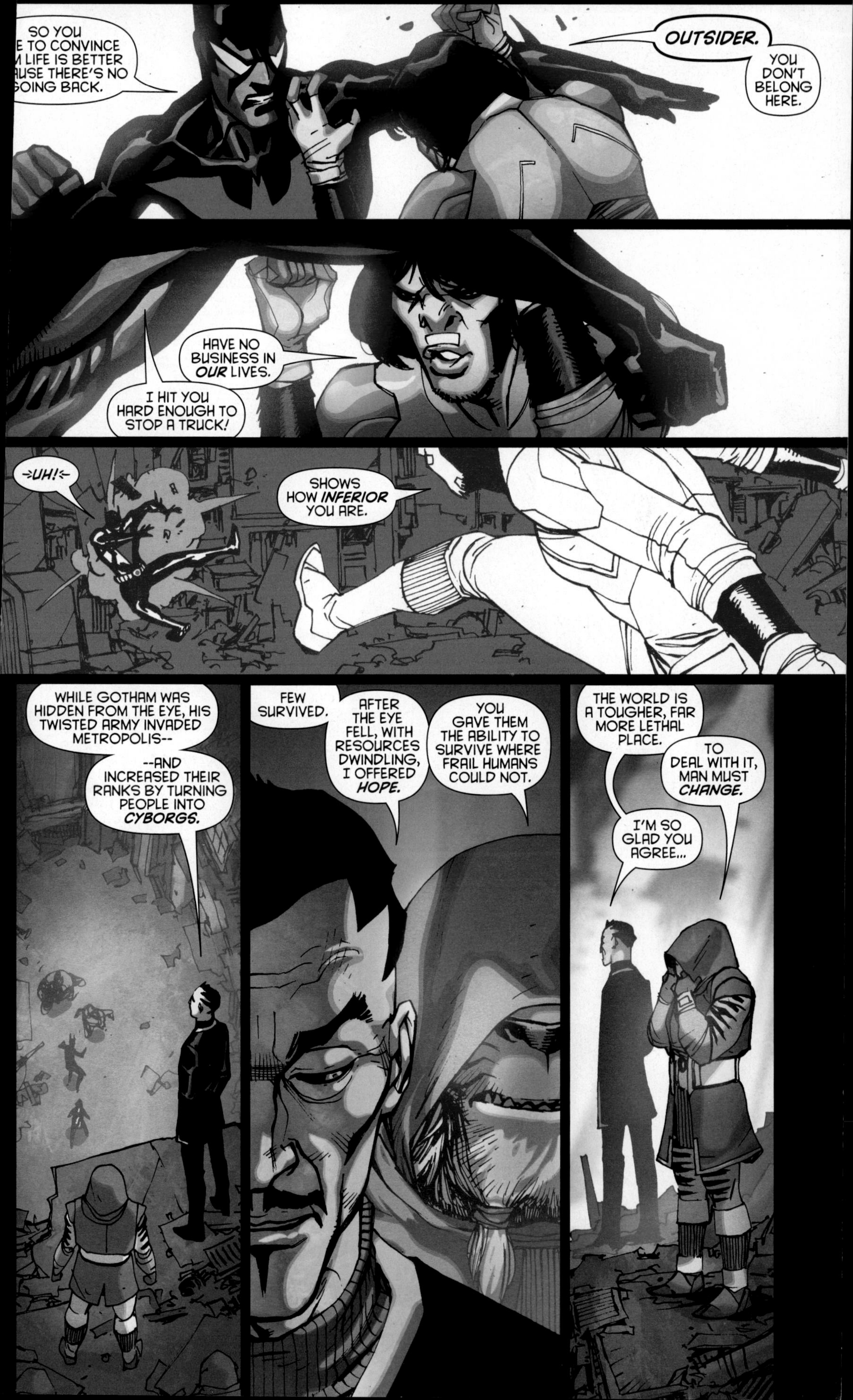
SO YOU
E TO CONVINCE
M LIFE IS BETTER
AUSE THERE'S NO
GOING BACK.
OUTSIDER.
YOU DON'T BELONG HERE.
HAVE NO BUSINESS IN OUR LIVES.
I HIT YOU HARD ENOUGH TO STOP A TRUCK!
UH!
SHOWS HOW INFERIOR YOU ARE.
WHILE GOTHAM WAS HIDDEN FROM THE EYE, HIS TWISTED ARMY INVADED METROPOLIS--
--AND INCREASED THEIR RANKS BY TURNING PEOPLE INTO CYBORGS.
FEW SURVIVED.
AFTER THE EYE FELL, WITH RESOURCES DWINDLING, I OFFERED HOPE.
YOU GAVE THEM THE ABILITY TO SURVIVE WHERE FRAIL HUMANS COULD NOT.
THE WORLD IS A TOUGHER, FAR MORE LETHAL PLACE.
TO DEAL WITH IT, MAN MUST CHANGE.
I'M SO GLAD YOU AGREE...

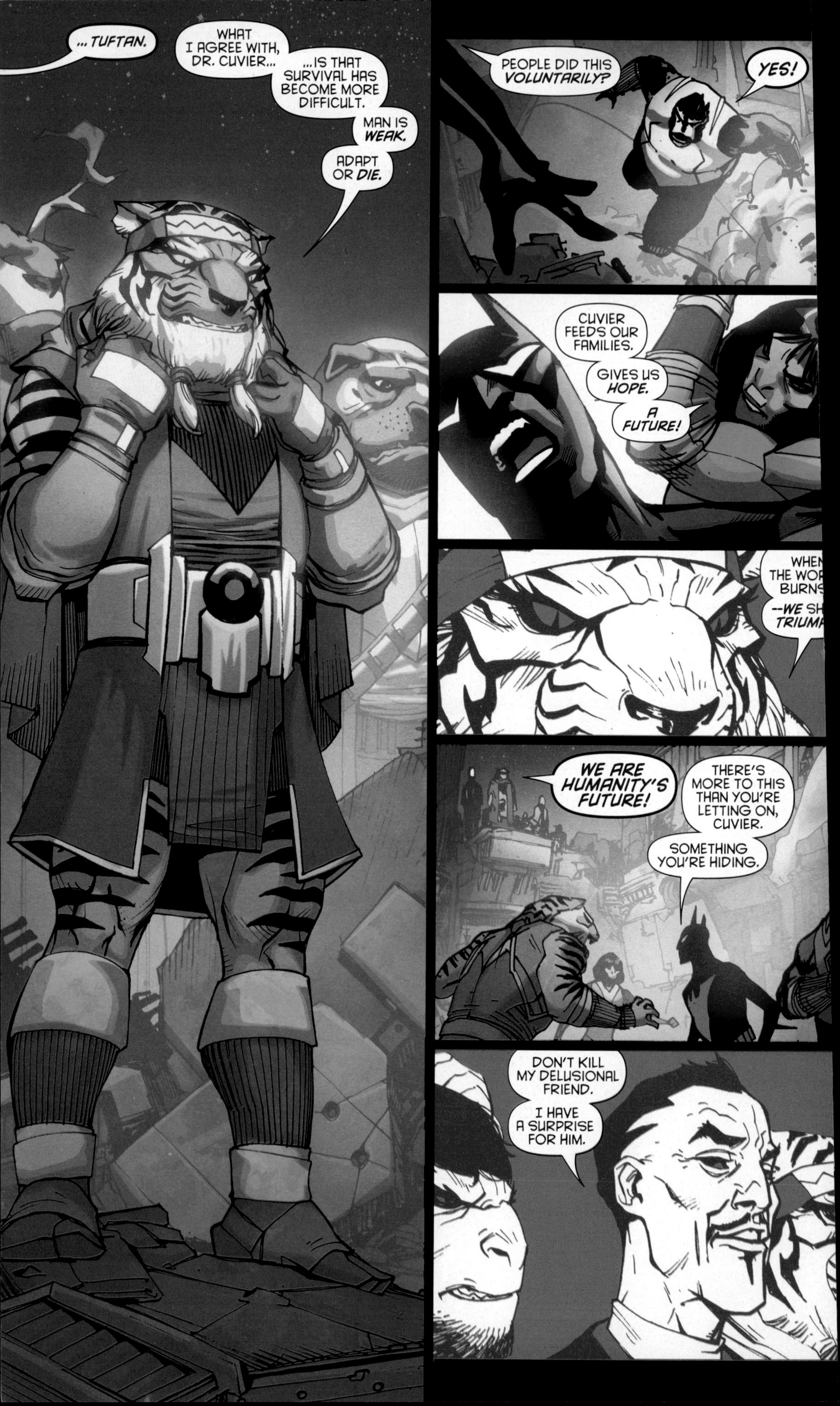
...TUFTAN.
WHAT I AGREE WITH, DR. CUVIER...
...IS THAT SURVIVAL HAS BECOME MORE DIFFICULT.
MAN IS WEAK.
ADAPT OR DIE.
PEOPLE DID THIS VOLUNTARILY?
YES!
CUVIER FEEDS OUR FAMILIES.
GIVES US HOPE.
A FUTURE!
WE ARE HUMANITY'S FUTURE!
THERE'S MORE TO THIS THAN YOU'RE LETTING ON, CUVIER.
SOMETHING YOU'RE HIDING.
DON'T KILL MY DELUSIONAL FRIEND.
I HAVE A SURPRISE FOR HIM.

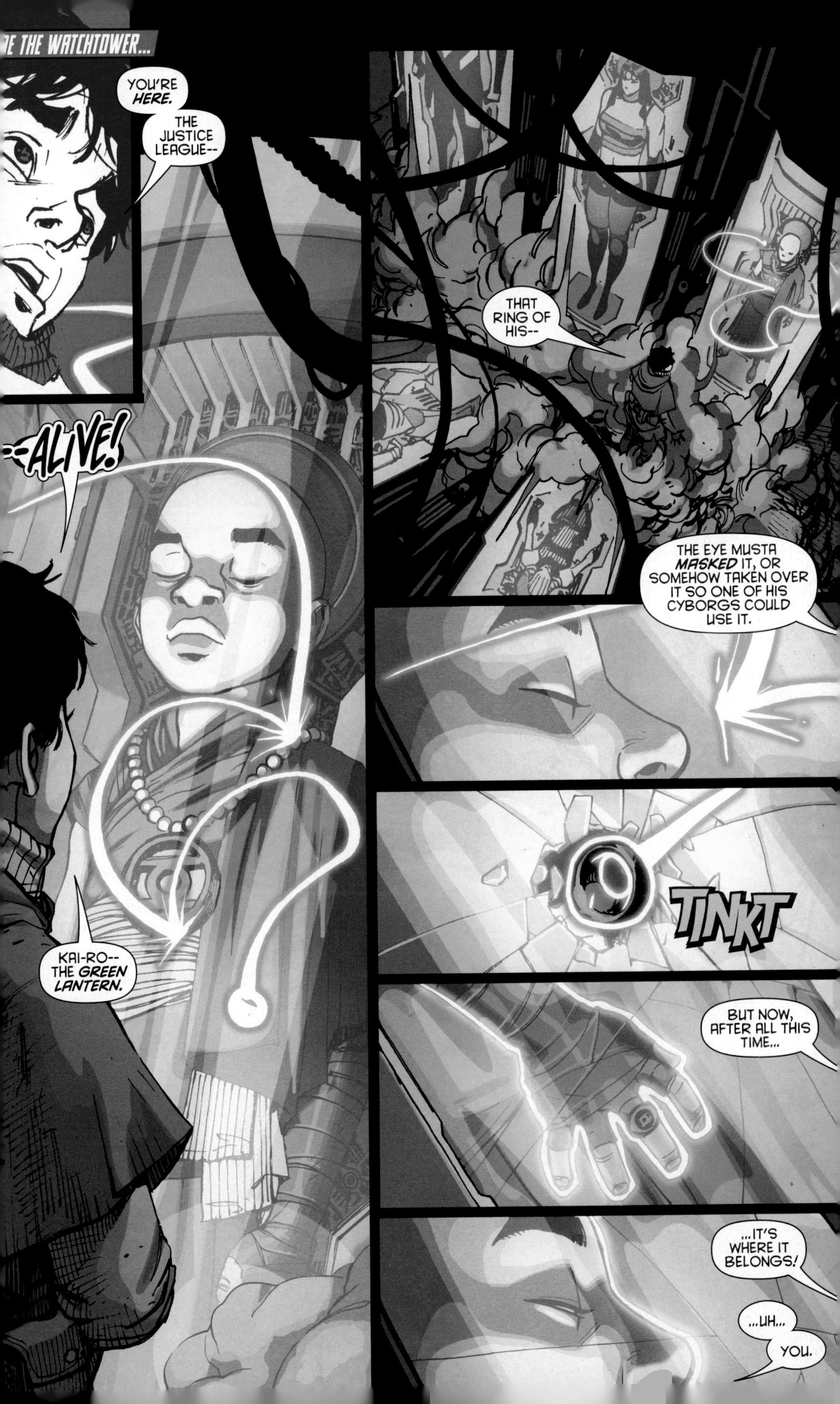
E THE WATCHTOWER...
YOU'RE HERE.
THE JUSTICE LEAGUE--
THAT RING OF HIS--
--ALIVE!
THE EYE MUSTA MASKED IT, OR SOMEHOW TAKEN OVER IT SO ONE OF HIS CYBORGS COULD USE IT.
TINKT
KAI-RO-- THE GREEN LANTERN.
BUT NOW, AFTER ALL THIS TIME...
...IT'S WHERE IT BELONGS!
...UH...
YOU.

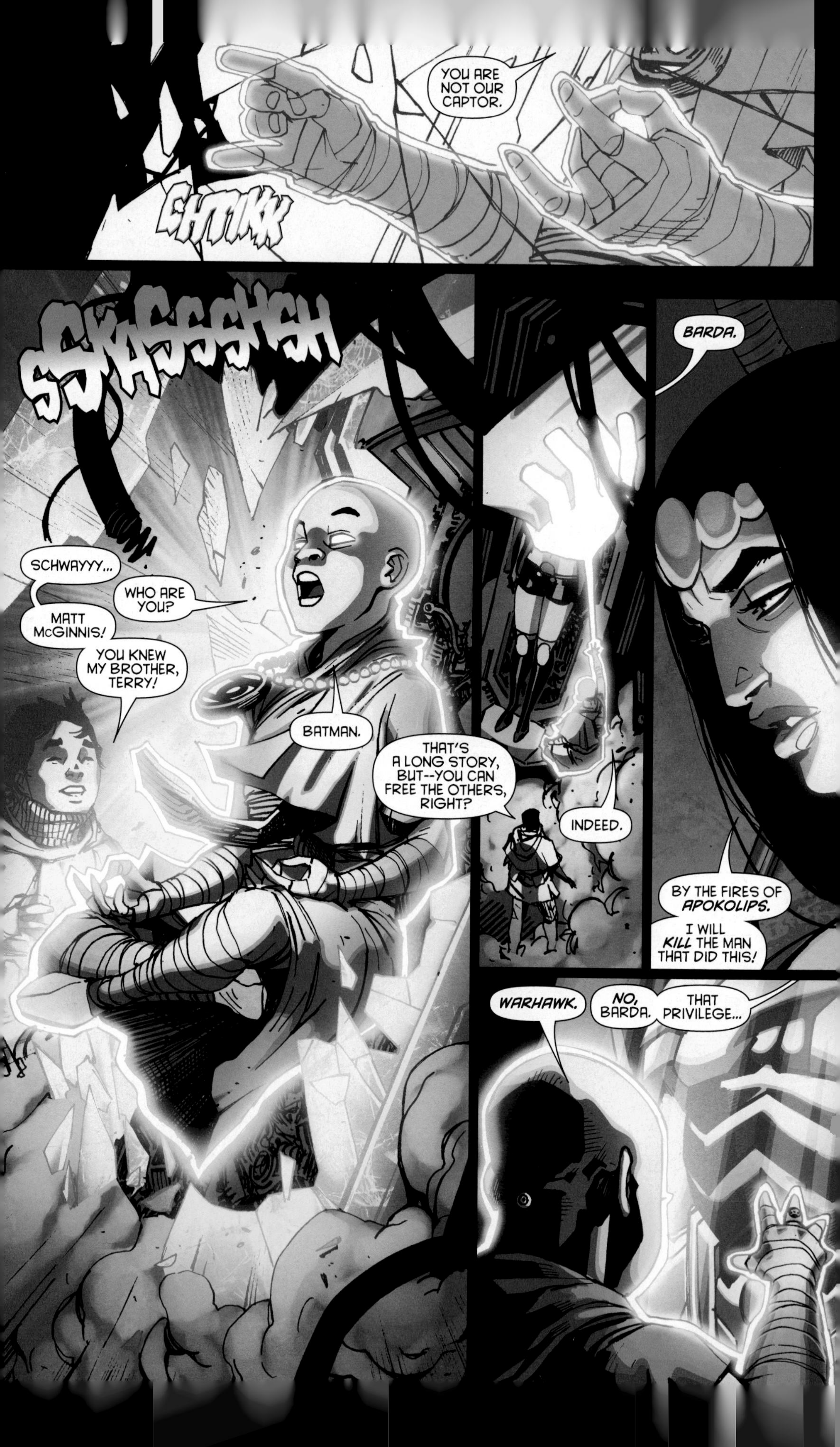
YOU ARE NOT OUR CAPTOR.
CHTIKK
SSKASSSHSH
SCHWAYYY...
WHO ARE YOU?
MATT McGINNIS!
YOU KNEW MY BROTHER, TERRY!
BATMAN.
THAT'S A LONG STORY, BUT--YOU CAN FREE THE OTHERS, RIGHT?
INDEED.
BARDA.
BY THE FIRES OF APOKOLIPS.
I WILL KILL THE MAN THAT DID THIS!
WARHAWK.
NO, BARDA.
THAT PRIVILEGE...

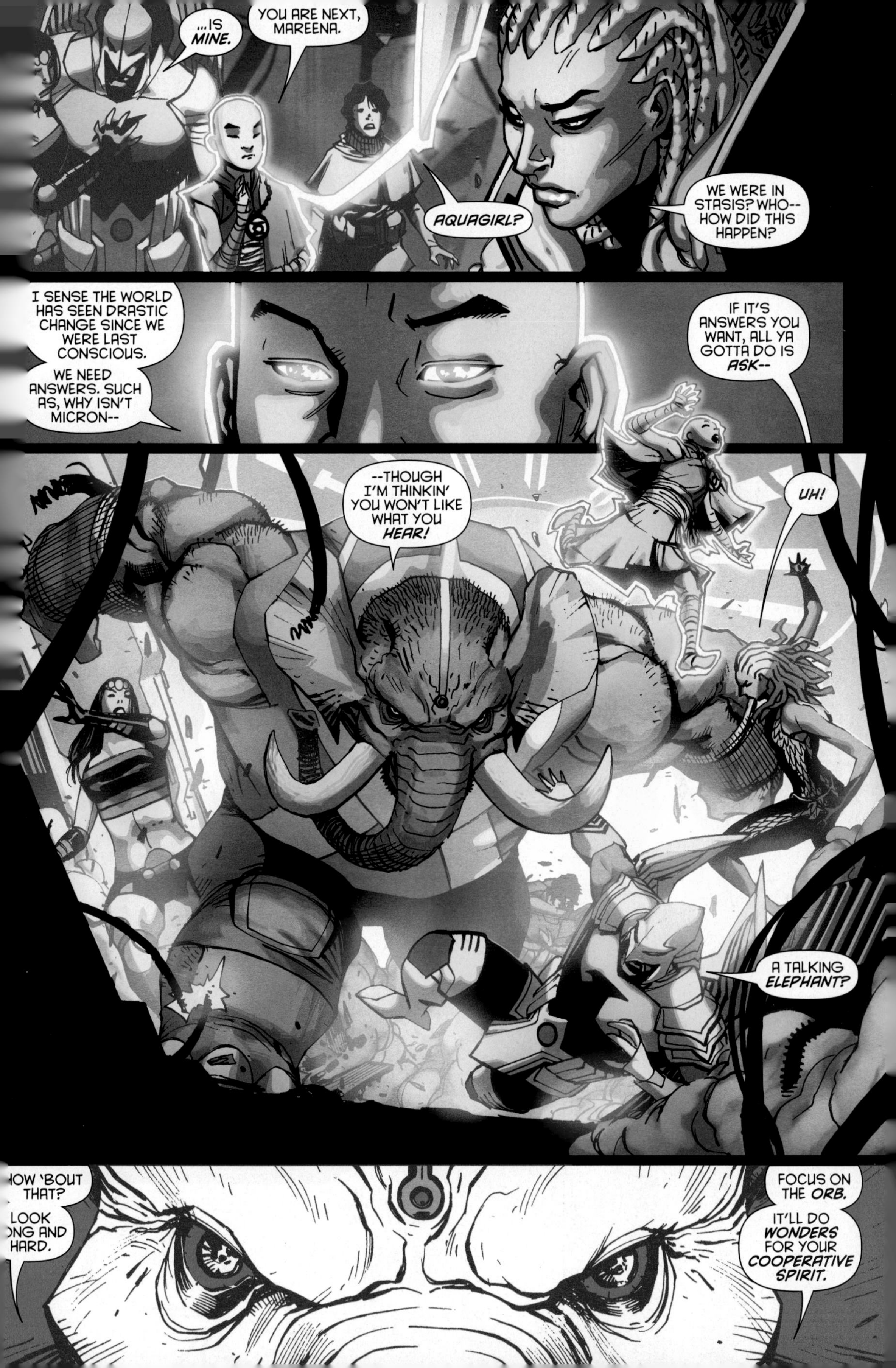

...IS *MINE.*
YOU ARE NEXT, MAREENA.
AQUAGIRL?
WE WERE IN STASIS? WHO-- HOW DID THIS HAPPEN?
I SENSE THE WORLD HAS SEEN DRASTIC CHANGE SINCE WE WERE LAST CONSCIOUS.
WE NEED ANSWERS. SUCH AS, WHY ISN'T MICRON--
IF IT'S ANSWERS YOU WANT, ALL YA GOTTA DO IS *ASK--*
--THOUGH I'M THINKIN' YOU WON'T LIKE WHAT YOU *HEAR!*
UH!
A TALKING *ELEPHANT?*
HOW 'BOUT THAT?
LOOK ONG AND HARD.
FOCUS ON THE *ORB.*
IT'LL DO *WONDERS* FOR YOUR *COOPERATIVE SPIRIT.*

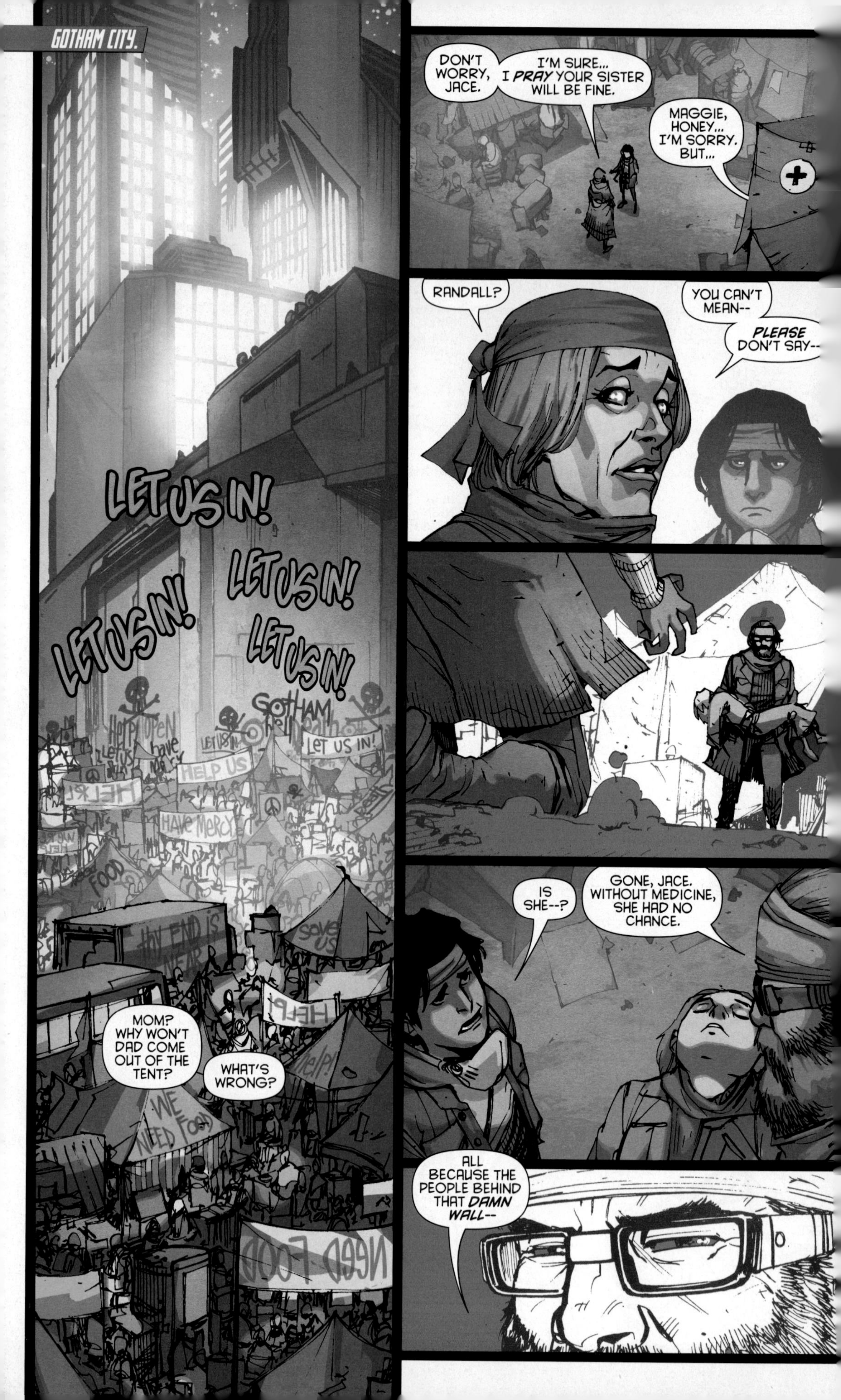
GOTHAM CITY.
LET US IN!
LET US IN!
LET US IN!
LET US IN!
GOTHAM
HELP
OPEN
LET US IN!
HELP US
HAVE MERCY
NEED FOOD
THE END IS NEAR
SAVE US
HELP!
MOM? WHY WON'T DAD COME OUT OF THE TENT?
WHAT'S WRONG?
WE NEED FOOD
NEED FOOD
DON'T WORRY, JACE.
I'M SURE... I PRAY YOUR SISTER WILL BE FINE.
MAGGIE, HONEY... I'M SORRY. BUT...
RANDALL?
YOU CAN'T MEAN--
PLEASE DON'T SAY--
IS SHE--?
GONE, JACE. WITHOUT MEDICINE, SHE HAD NO CHANCE.
ALL BECAUSE THE PEOPLE BEHIND THAT DAMN WALL--

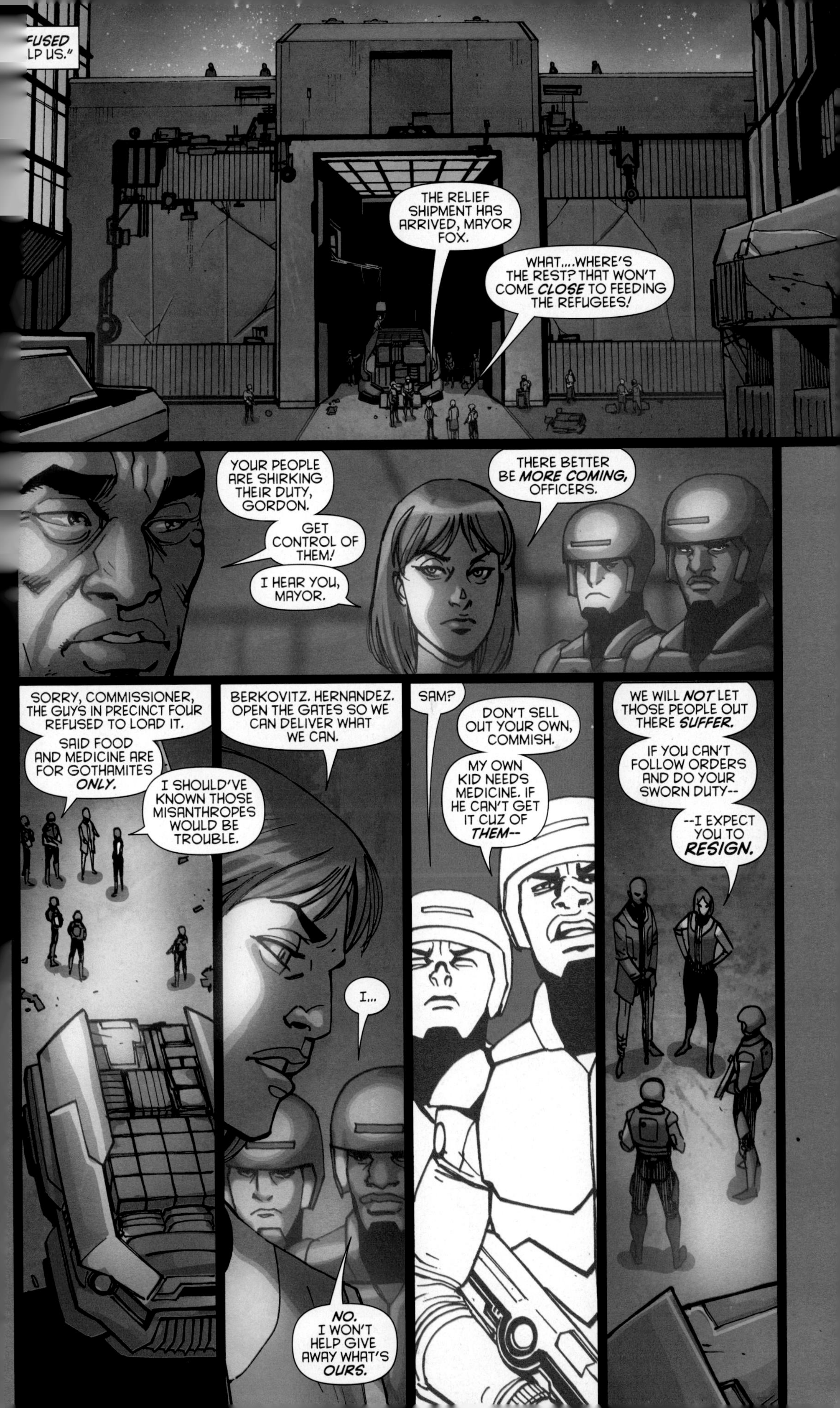
FUSED
LP US."
THE RELIEF SHIPMENT HAS ARRIVED, MAYOR FOX.
WHAT....WHERE'S THE REST? THAT WON'T COME *CLOSE* TO FEEDING THE REFUGEES!
YOUR PEOPLE ARE SHIRKING THEIR DUTY, GORDON.
GET CONTROL OF THEM!
I HEAR YOU, MAYOR.
THERE BETTER BE *MORE COMING,* OFFICERS.
SORRY, COMMISSIONER, THE GUYS IN PRECINCT FOUR REFUSED TO LOAD IT.
SAID FOOD AND MEDICINE ARE FOR GOTHAMITES *ONLY.*
I SHOULD'VE KNOWN THOSE MISANTHROPES WOULD BE TROUBLE.
BERKOVITZ. HERNANDEZ. OPEN THE GATES SO WE CAN DELIVER WHAT WE CAN.
I...
NO. I WON'T HELP GIVE AWAY WHAT'S *OURS.*
SAM?
DON'T SELL OUT YOUR OWN, COMMISH.
MY OWN KID NEEDS MEDICINE. IF HE CAN'T GET IT CUZ OF *THEM--*
WE WILL *NOT* LET THOSE PEOPLE OUT THERE *SUFFER.*
IF YOU CAN'T FOLLOW ORDERS AND DO YOUR SWORN DUTY--
--I EXPECT YOU TO *RESIGN.*

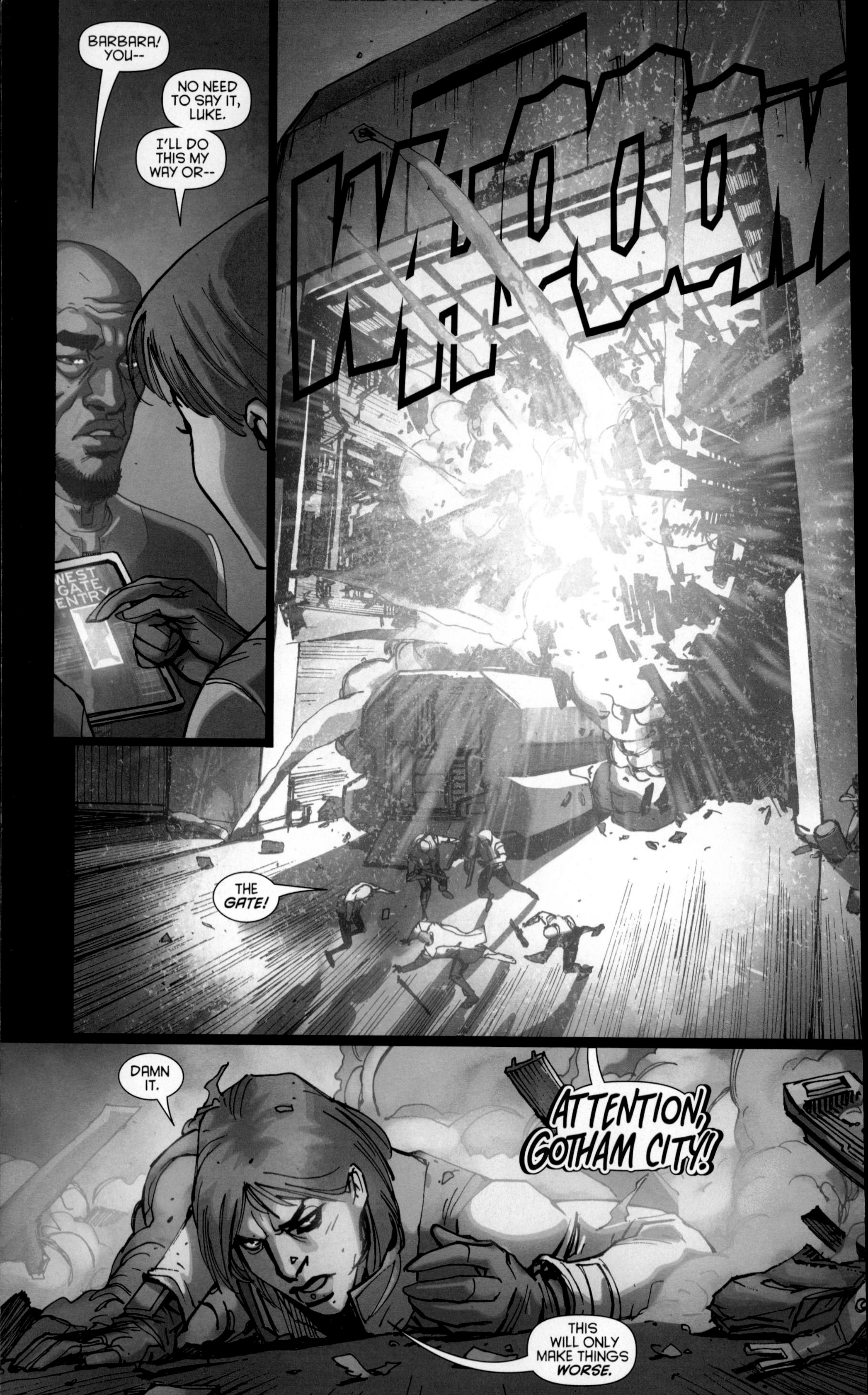
BARBARA! YOU--
NO NEED TO SAY IT, LUKE.
I'LL DO THIS MY WAY OR--
WEST GATE ENTRY
THE GATE!
DAMN IT.
ATTENTION, GOTHAM CITY!
THIS WILL ONLY MAKE THINGS WORSE.

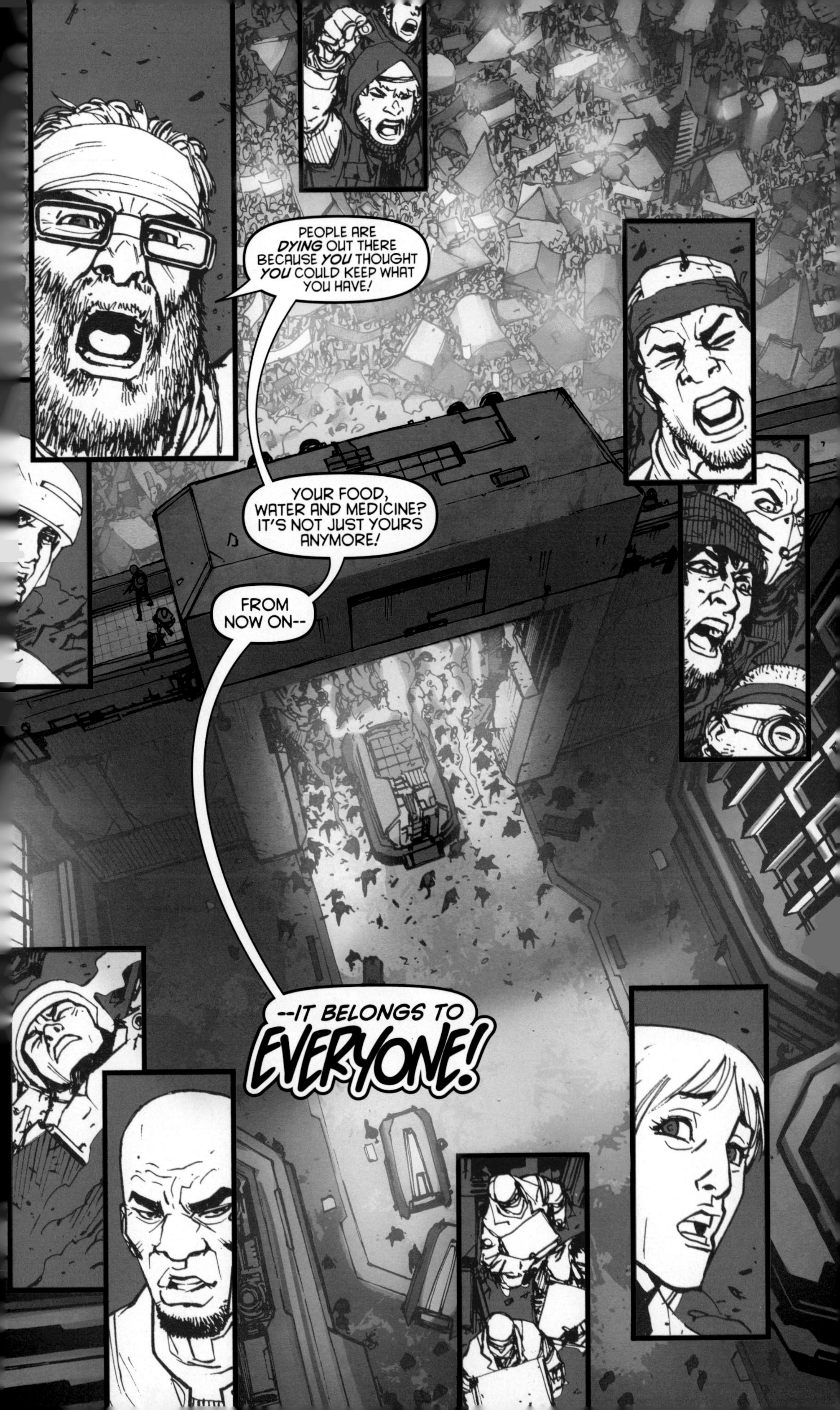
PEOPLE ARE DYING OUT THERE BECAUSE YOU THOUGHT YOU COULD KEEP WHAT YOU HAVE!
YOUR FOOD, WATER AND MEDICINE? IT'S NOT JUST YOURS ANYMORE!
FROM NOW ON--
--IT BELONGS TO EVERYONE!

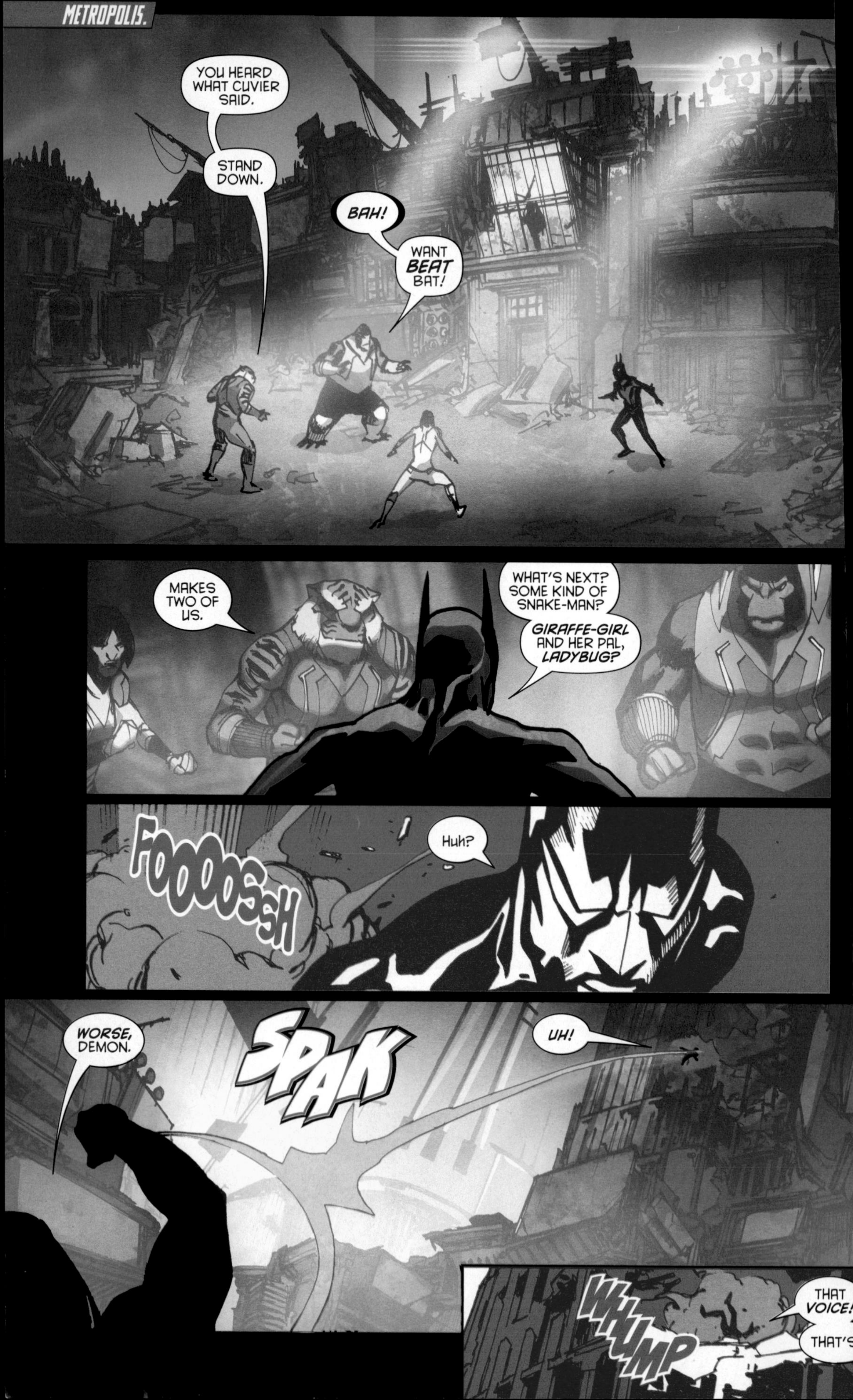
METROPOLIS.
YOU HEARD WHAT CUVIER SAID.
STAND DOWN.
BAH!
WANT BEAT BAT!
MAKES TWO OF US.
WHAT'S NEXT? SOME KIND OF SNAKE-MAN?
GIRAFFE-GIRL AND HER PAL, LADYBUG?
FOOOOSSH
Huh?
WORSE, DEMON.
SPAK
UH!
WHUMP
THAT VOICE!
THAT'S

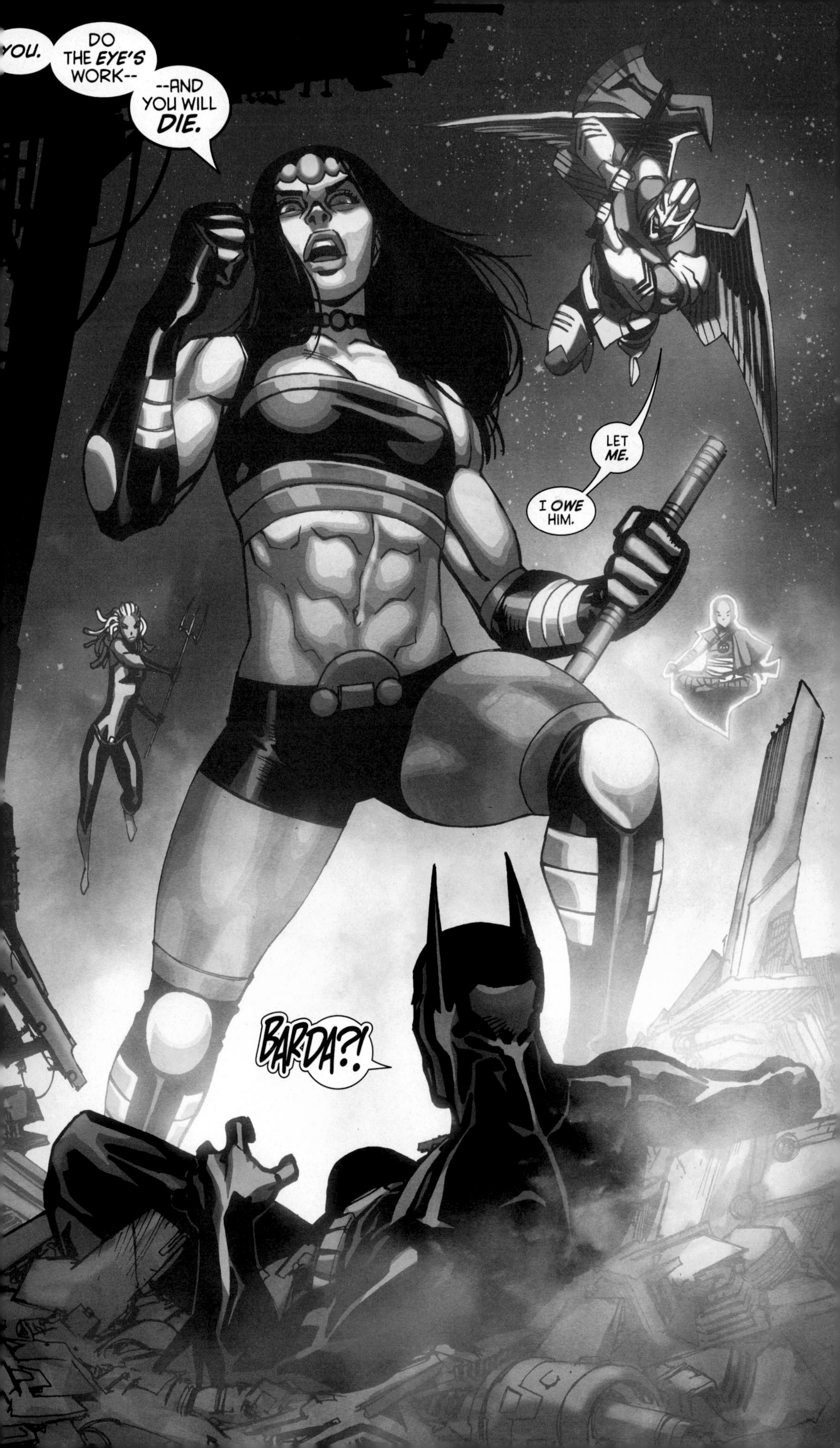
YOU.
DO THE EYE'S WORK--
--AND YOU WILL DIE.
LET ME.
I OWE HIM.
BARDA?!

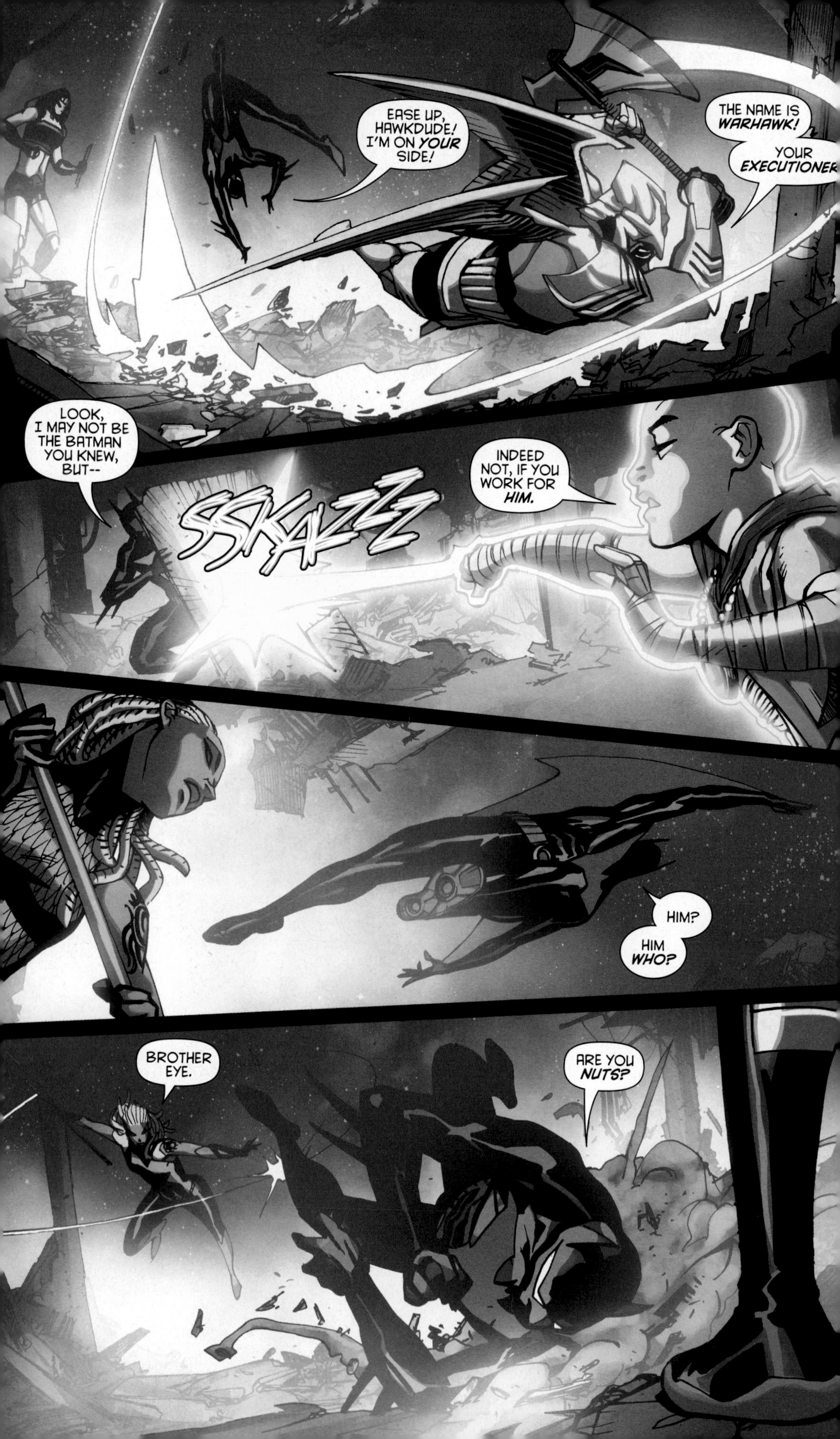
EASE UP, HAWKDUDE! I'M ON YOUR SIDE!
THE NAME IS WARHAWK!
YOUR EXECUTIONER
LOOK, I MAY NOT BE THE BATMAN YOU KNEW, BUT--
INDEED NOT, IF YOU WORK FOR HIM.
SSKAZZZZ
HIM?
HIM WHO?
BROTHER EYE.
ARE YOU NUTS?

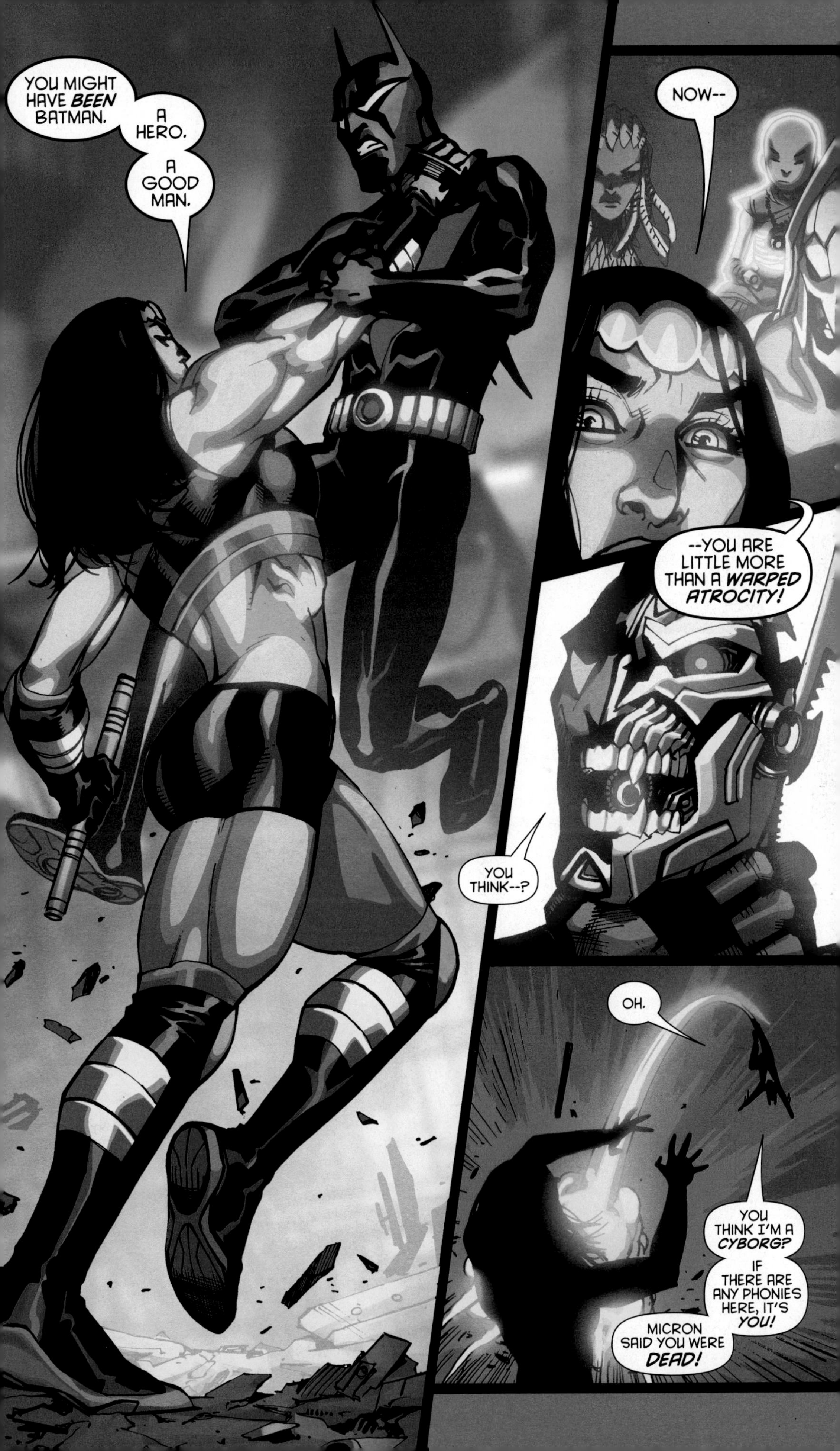
YOU MIGHT HAVE BEEN BATMAN.
A HERO.
A GOOD MAN.
NOW--
--YOU ARE LITTLE MORE THAN A WARPED ATROCITY!
YOU THINK--?
OH.
YOU THINK I'M A CYBORG?
IF THERE ARE ANY PHONIES HERE, IT'S YOU!
MICRON SAID YOU WERE DEAD!

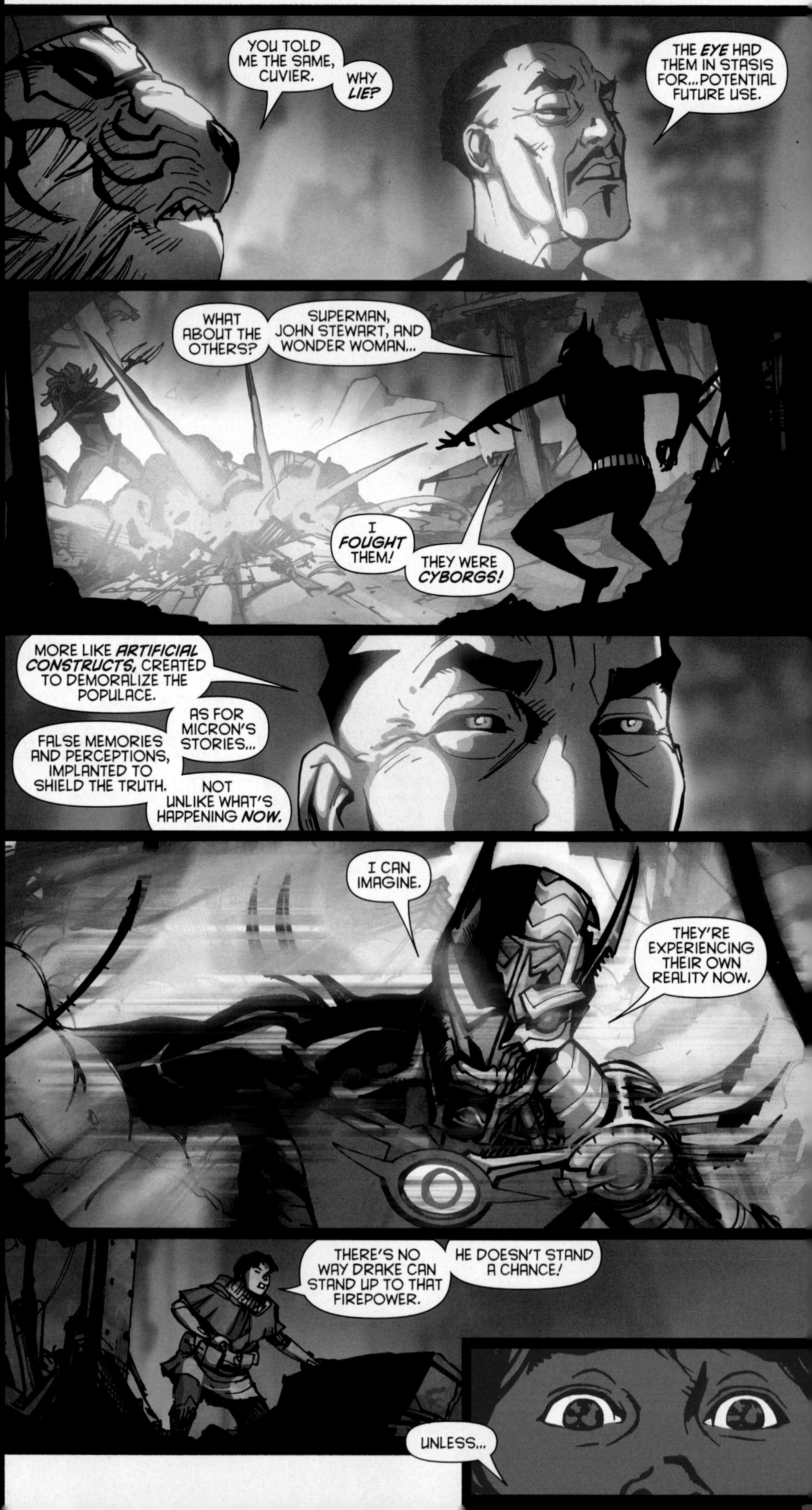

YOU TOLD ME THE SAME, CUVIER.
WHY LIE?
THE EYE HAD THEM IN STASIS FOR...POTENTIAL FUTURE USE.
WHAT ABOUT THE OTHERS?
SUPERMAN, JOHN STEWART, AND WONDER WOMAN...
I FOUGHT THEM!
THEY WERE CYBORGS!
MORE LIKE ARTIFICIAL CONSTRUCTS, CREATED TO DEMORALIZE THE POPULACE.
AS FOR MICRON'S STORIES...
FALSE MEMORIES AND PERCEPTIONS, IMPLANTED TO SHIELD THE TRUTH.
NOT UNLIKE WHAT'S HAPPENING NOW.
I CAN IMAGINE.
THEY'RE EXPERIENCING THEIR OWN REALITY NOW.
THERE'S NO WAY DRAKE CAN STAND UP TO THAT FIREPOWER.
HE DOESN'T STAND A CHANCE!
UNLESS...

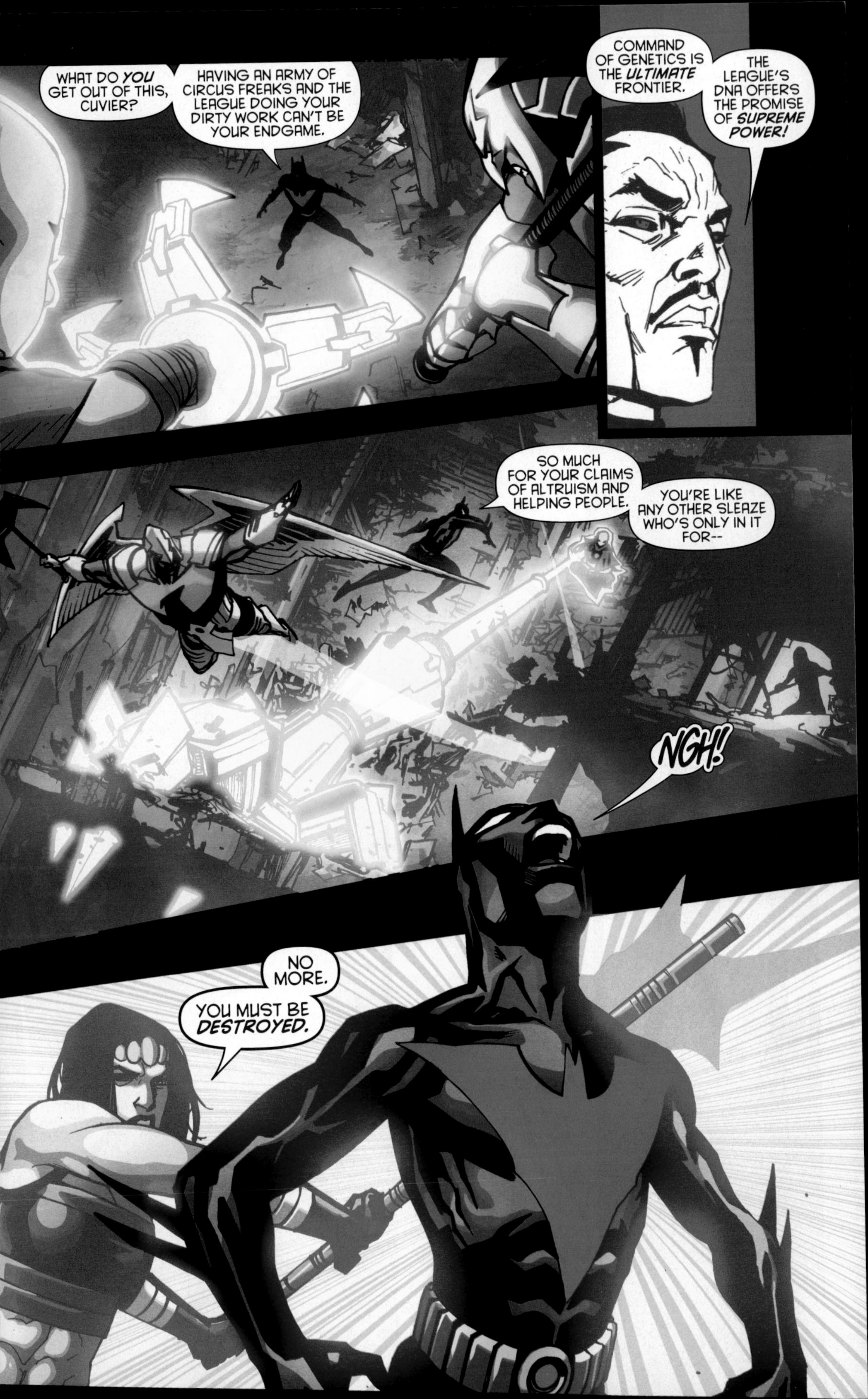

WHAT DO YOU GET OUT OF THIS, CUVIER?
HAVING AN ARMY OF CIRCUS FREAKS AND THE LEAGUE DOING YOUR DIRTY WORK CAN'T BE YOUR ENDGAME.
COMMAND OF GENETICS IS THE ULTIMATE FRONTIER.
THE LEAGUE'S DNA OFFERS THE PROMISE OF SUPREME POWER!
SO MUCH FOR YOUR CLAIMS OF ALTRUISM AND HELPING PEOPLE.
YOU'RE LIKE ANY OTHER SLEAZE WHO'S ONLY IN IT FOR--
NGH!
NO MORE.
YOU MUST BE DESTROYED.

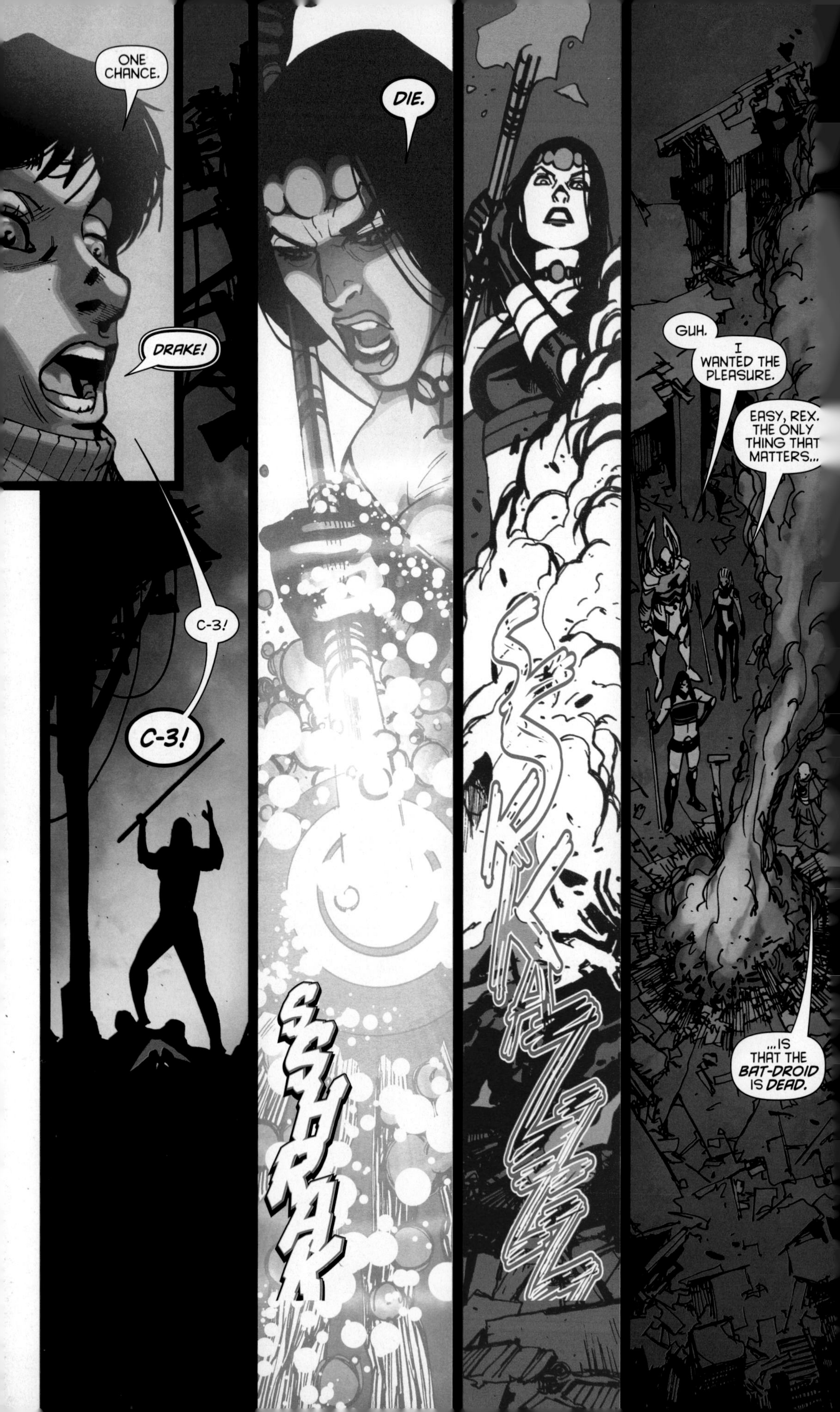
ONE CHANCE.
DRAKE!
C-3!
C-3!
DIE.
SSHRAK
SKKKAZZZZZ
GUH.
I WANTED THE PLEASURE.
EASY, REX. THE ONLY THING THAT MATTERS...
...IS THAT THE BAT-DROID IS DEAD.

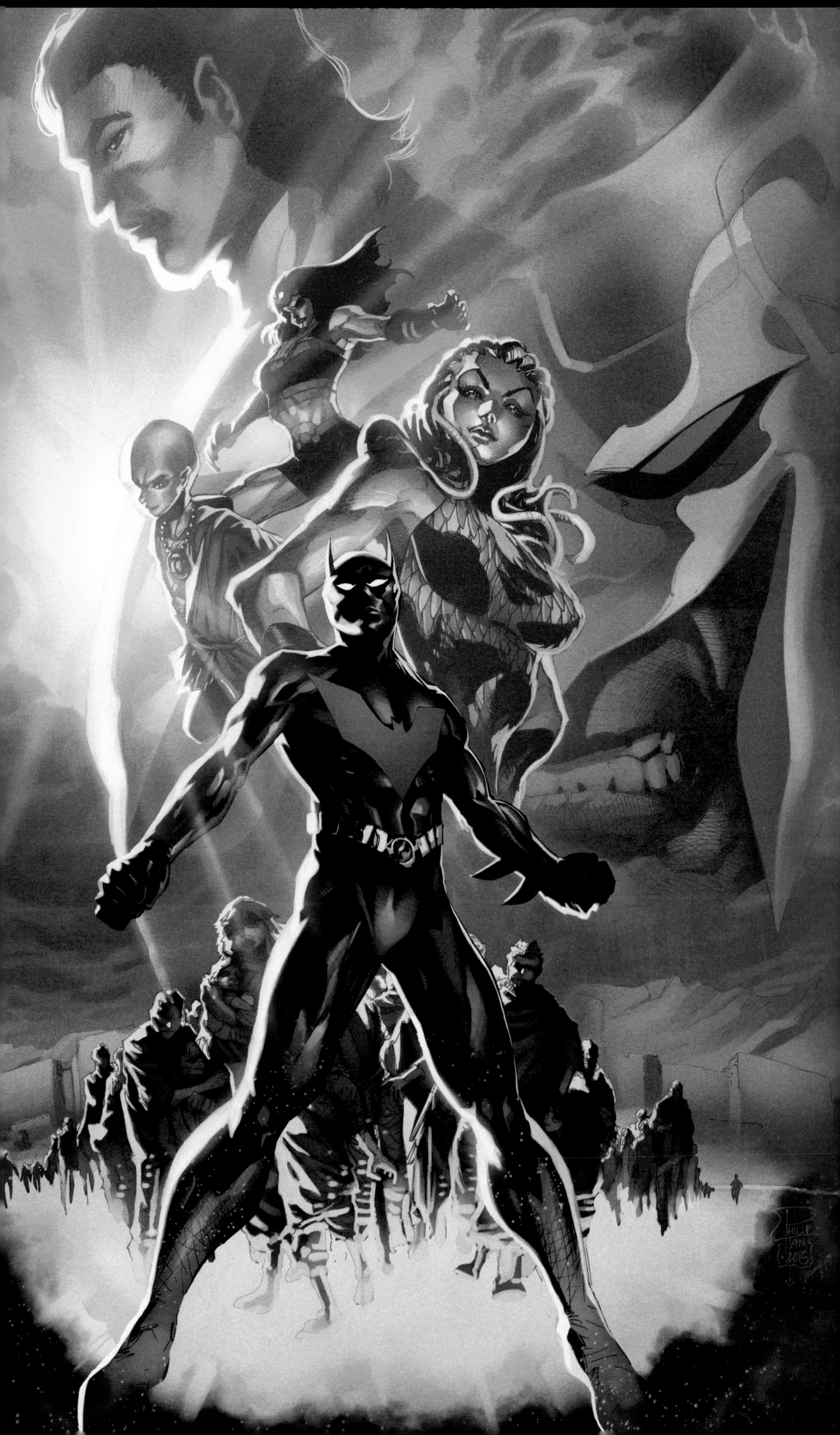
PHILIP TAN 2015

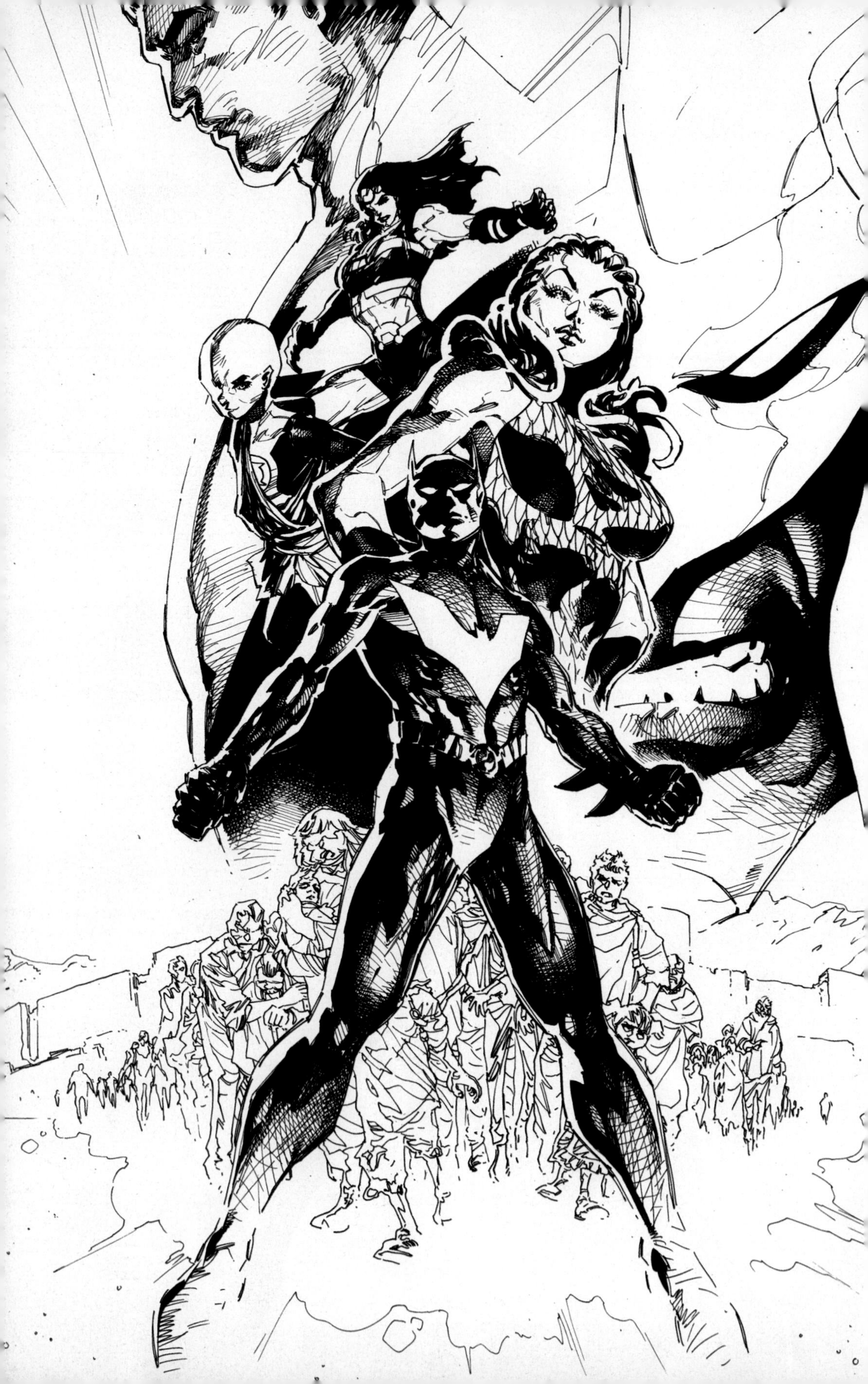

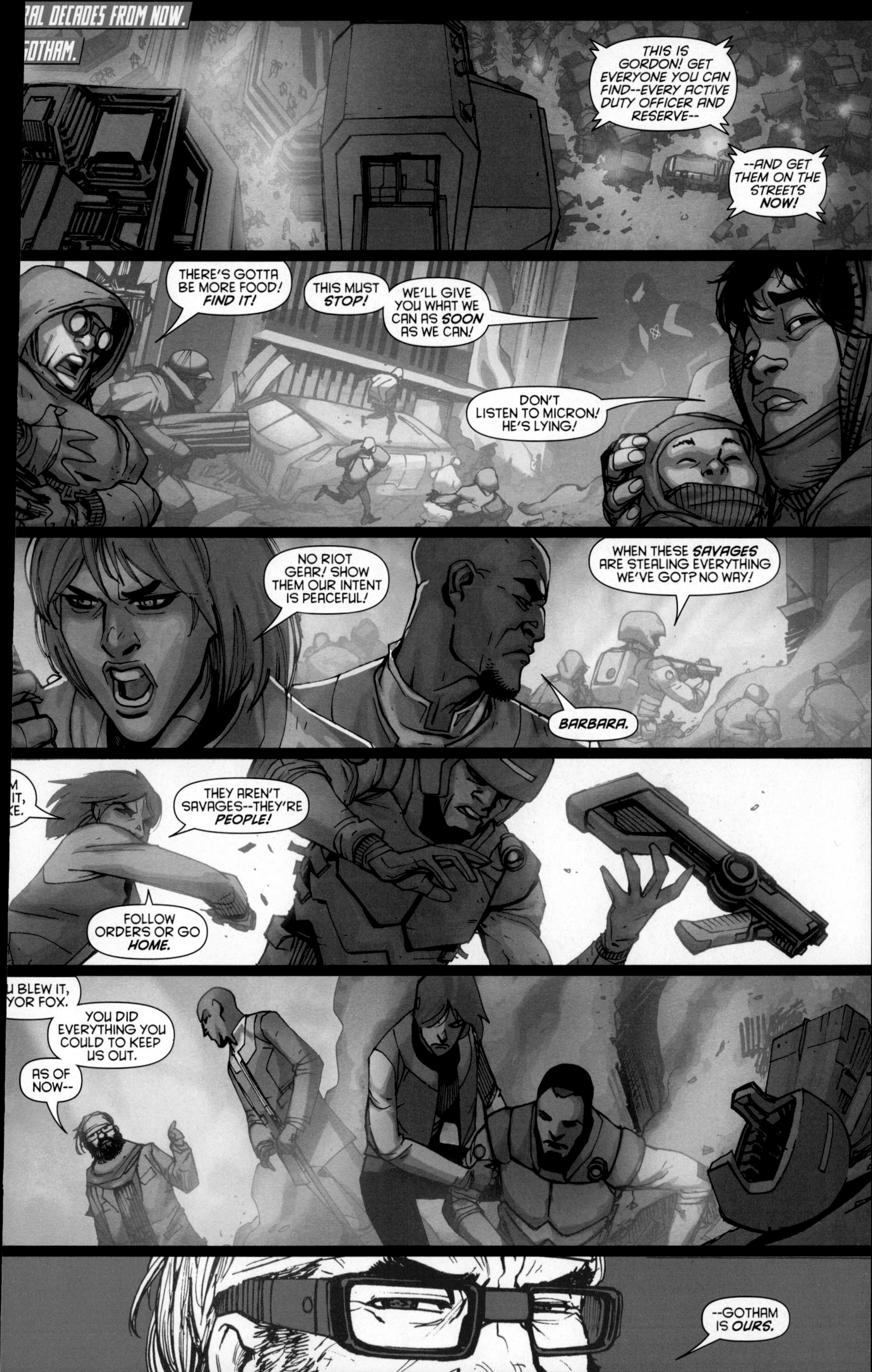

RAL DECADES FROM NOW.
GOTHAM.
THIS IS GORDON! GET EVERYONE YOU CAN FIND--EVERY ACTIVE DUTY OFFICER AND RESERVE--
--AND GET THEM ON THE STREETS NOW!
THERE'S GOTTA BE MORE FOOD! FIND IT!
THIS MUST STOP!
WE'LL GIVE YOU WHAT WE CAN AS SOON AS WE CAN!
DON'T LISTEN TO MICRON! HE'S LYING!
NO RIOT GEAR! SHOW THEM OUR INTENT IS PEACEFUL!
WHEN THESE SAVAGES ARE STEALING EVERYTHING WE'VE GOT? NO WAY!
BARBARA.
THEY AREN'T SAVAGES--THEY'RE PEOPLE!
FOLLOW ORDERS OR GO HOME.
U BLEW IT, YOR FOX.
YOU DID EVERYTHING YOU COULD TO KEEP US OUT.
AS OF NOW--
--GOTHAM IS OURS.

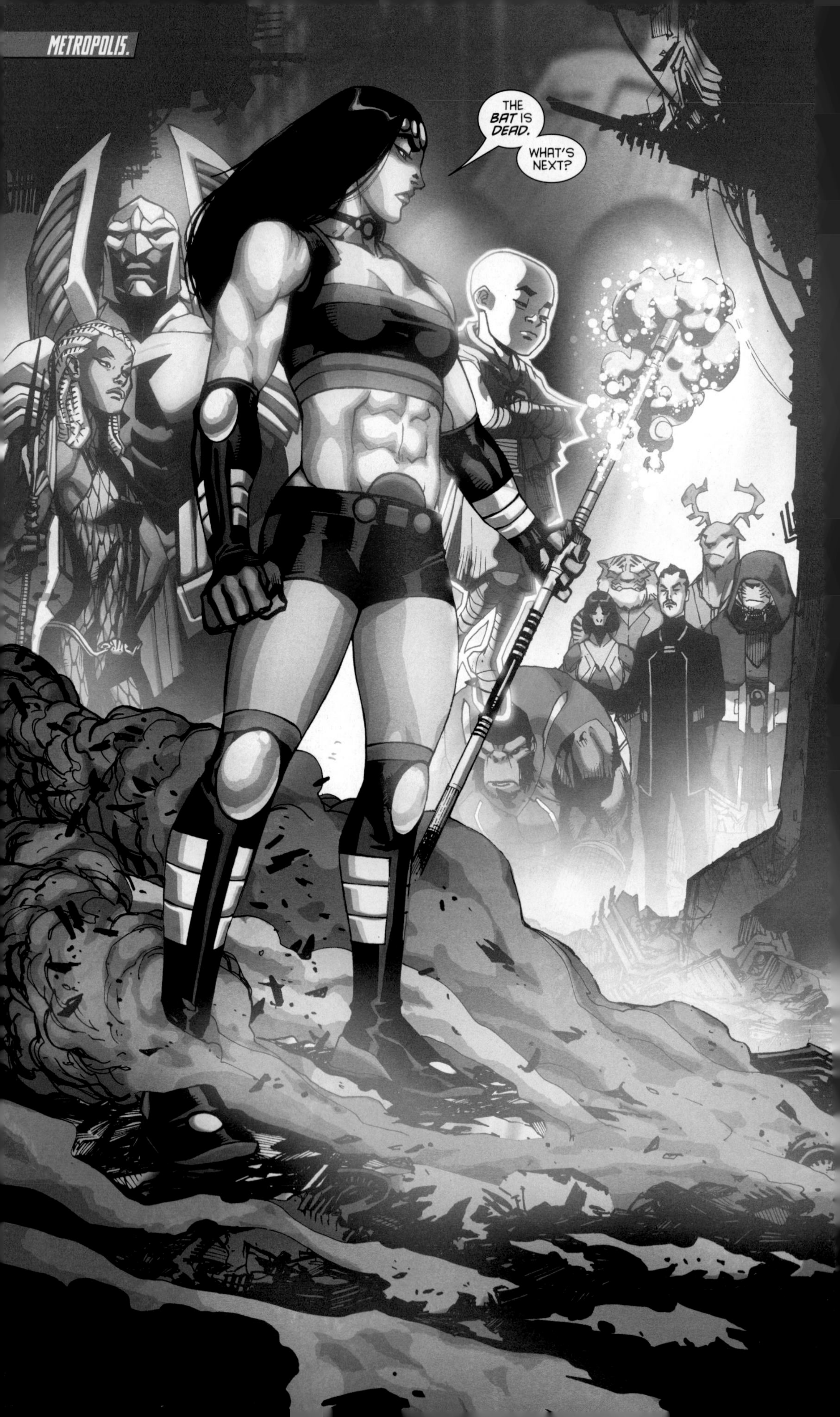
METROPOLIS.
THE BAT IS DEAD.
WHAT'S NEXT?

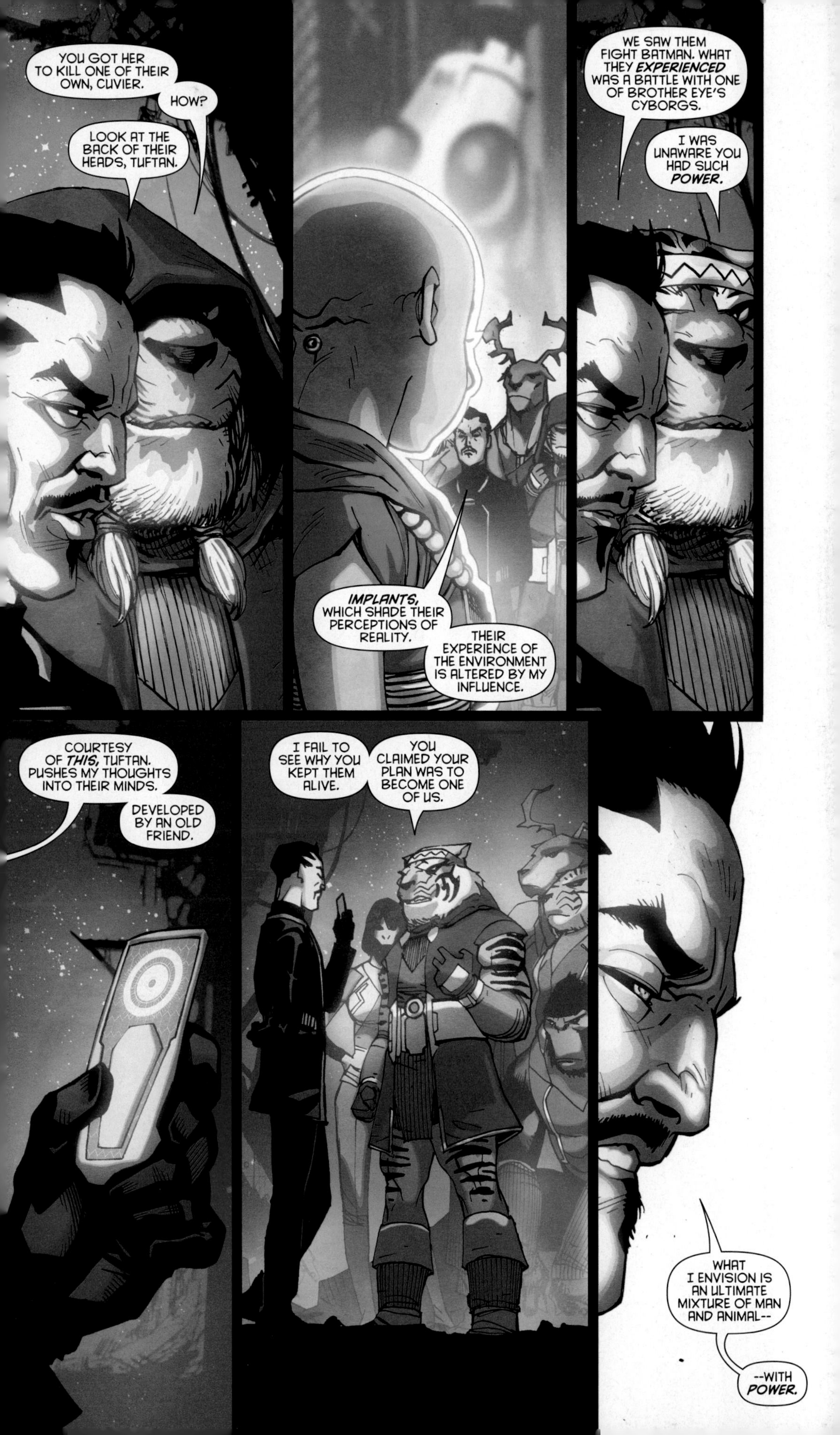
YOU GOT HER TO KILL ONE OF THEIR OWN, CUVIER.
HOW?
LOOK AT THE BACK OF THEIR HEADS, TUFTAN.
IMPLANTS, WHICH SHADE THEIR PERCEPTIONS OF REALITY.
THEIR EXPERIENCE OF THE ENVIRONMENT IS ALTERED BY MY INFLUENCE.
WE SAW THEM FIGHT BATMAN. WHAT THEY EXPERIENCED WAS A BATTLE WITH ONE OF BROTHER EYE'S CYBORGS.
I WAS UNAWARE YOU HAD SUCH POWER.
COURTESY OF THIS, TUFTAN. PUSHES MY THOUGHTS INTO THEIR MINDS.
DEVELOPED BY AN OLD FRIEND.
I FAIL TO SEE WHY YOU KEPT THEM ALIVE.
YOU CLAIMED YOUR PLAN WAS TO BECOME ONE OF US.
WHAT I ENVISION IS AN ULTIMATE MIXTURE OF MAN AND ANIMAL--
--WITH POWER.

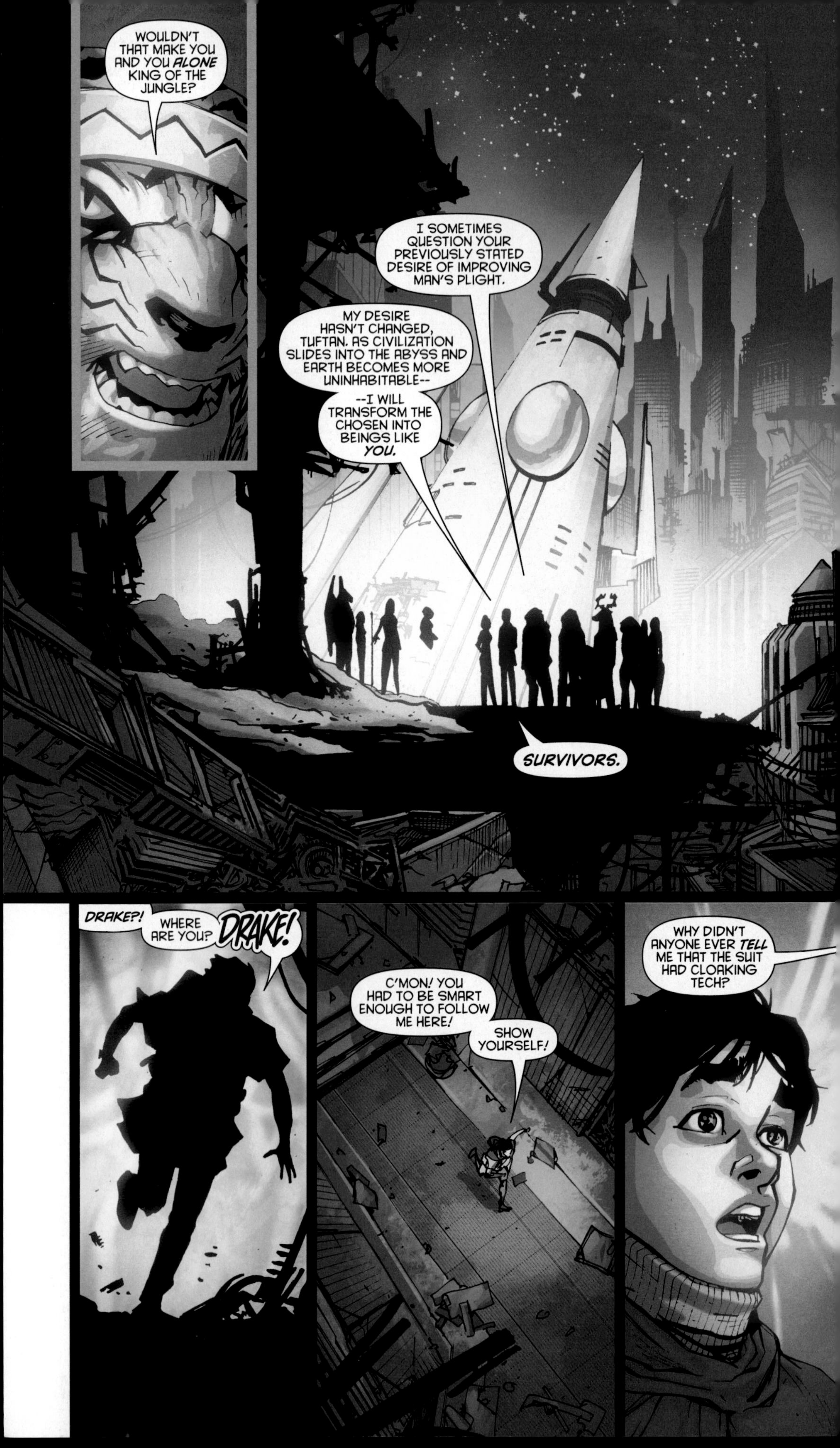
WOULDN'T THAT MAKE YOU AND YOU ALONE KING OF THE JUNGLE?
I SOMETIMES QUESTION YOUR PREVIOUSLY STATED DESIRE OF IMPROVING MAN'S PLIGHT.
MY DESIRE HASN'T CHANGED, TUFTAN. AS CIVILIZATION SLIDES INTO THE ABYSS AND EARTH BECOMES MORE UNINHABITABLE--
--I WILL TRANSFORM THE CHOSEN INTO BEINGS LIKE YOU.
SURVIVORS.
DRAKE?!
WHERE ARE YOU?
DRAKE!
C'MON! YOU HAD TO BE SMART ENOUGH TO FOLLOW ME HERE!
SHOW YOURSELF!
WHY DIDN'T ANYONE EVER TELL ME THAT THE SUIT HAD CLOAKING TECH?

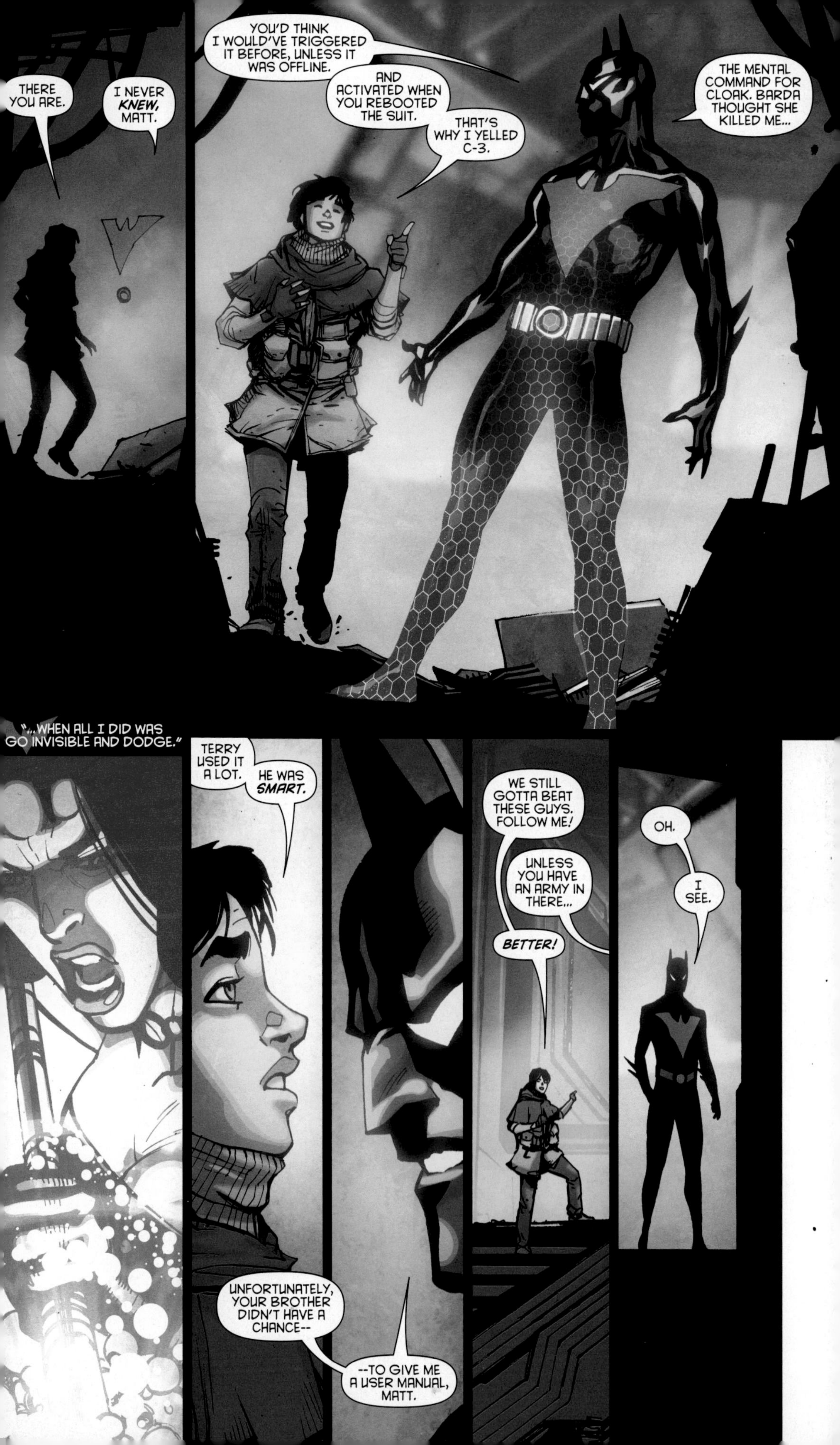
THERE YOU ARE.
I NEVER **KNEW,** MATT.
YOU'D THINK I WOULD'VE TRIGGERED IT BEFORE, UNLESS IT WAS OFFLINE.
AND ACTIVATED WHEN YOU REBOOTED THE SUIT.
THAT'S WHY I YELLED C-3.
THE MENTAL COMMAND FOR CLOAK. BARDA THOUGHT SHE KILLED ME...
"...WHEN ALL I DID WAS GO INVISIBLE AND DODGE."
TERRY USED IT A LOT.
HE WAS ***SMART.***
UNFORTUNATELY, YOUR BROTHER DIDN'T HAVE A CHANCE--
--TO GIVE ME A USER MANUAL, MATT.
WE STILL GOTTA BEAT THESE GUYS. FOLLOW ME!
UNLESS YOU HAVE AN ARMY IN THERE...
BETTER!
OH.
I SEE.

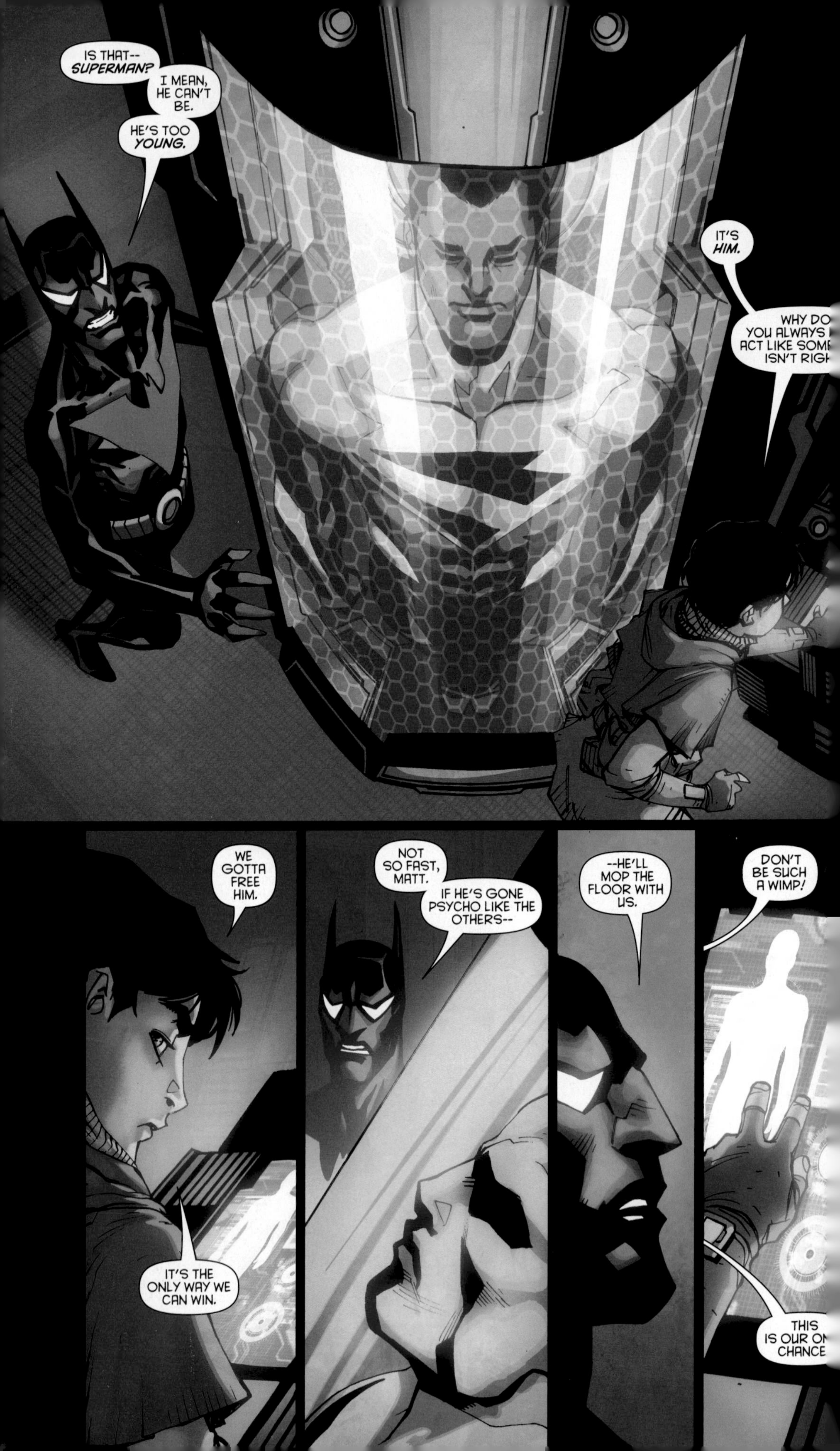
IS THAT-- SUPERMAN?
I MEAN, HE CAN'T BE.
HE'S TOO YOUNG.
IT'S HIM.
WHY DO YOU ALWAYS ACT LIKE SOME ISN'T RIGH
WE GOTTA FREE HIM.
IT'S THE ONLY WAY WE CAN WIN.
NOT SO FAST, MATT.
IF HE'S GONE PSYCHO LIKE THE OTHERS--
--HE'LL MOP THE FLOOR WITH US.
DON'T BE SUCH A WIMP!
THIS IS OUR ON CHANCE

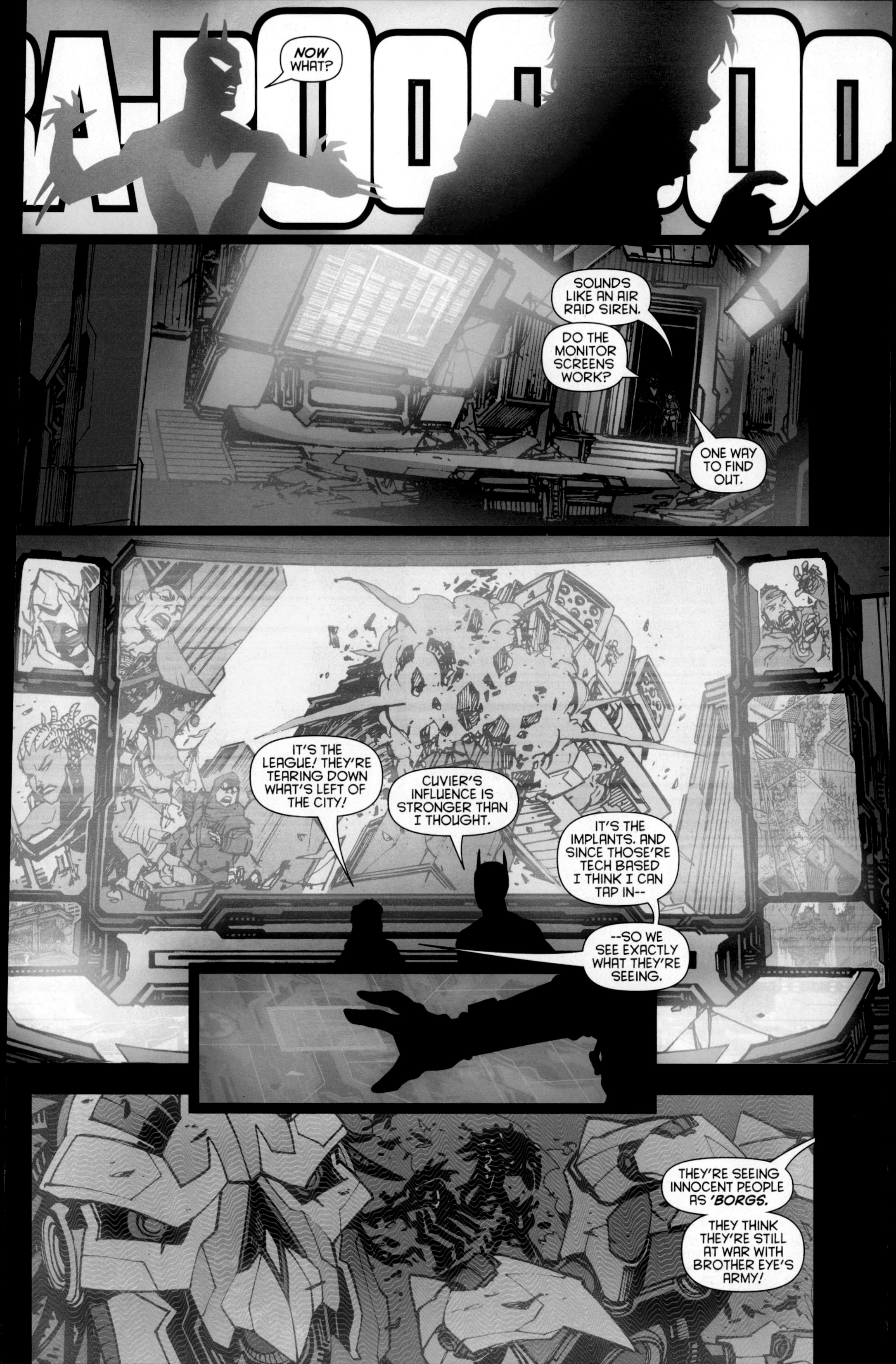
NOW WHAT?
SOUNDS LIKE AN AIR RAID SIREN.
DO THE MONITOR SCREENS WORK?
ONE WAY TO FIND OUT.
IT'S THE LEAGUE! THEY'RE TEARING DOWN WHAT'S LEFT OF THE CITY!
CUVIER'S INFLUENCE IS STRONGER THAN I THOUGHT.
IT'S THE IMPLANTS. AND SINCE THOSE'RE TECH BASED I THINK I CAN TAP IN--
--SO WE SEE EXACTLY WHAT THEY'RE SEEING.
THEY'RE SEEING INNOCENT PEOPLE AS 'BORGS.
THEY THINK THEY'RE STILL AT WAR WITH BROTHER EYE'S ARMY!

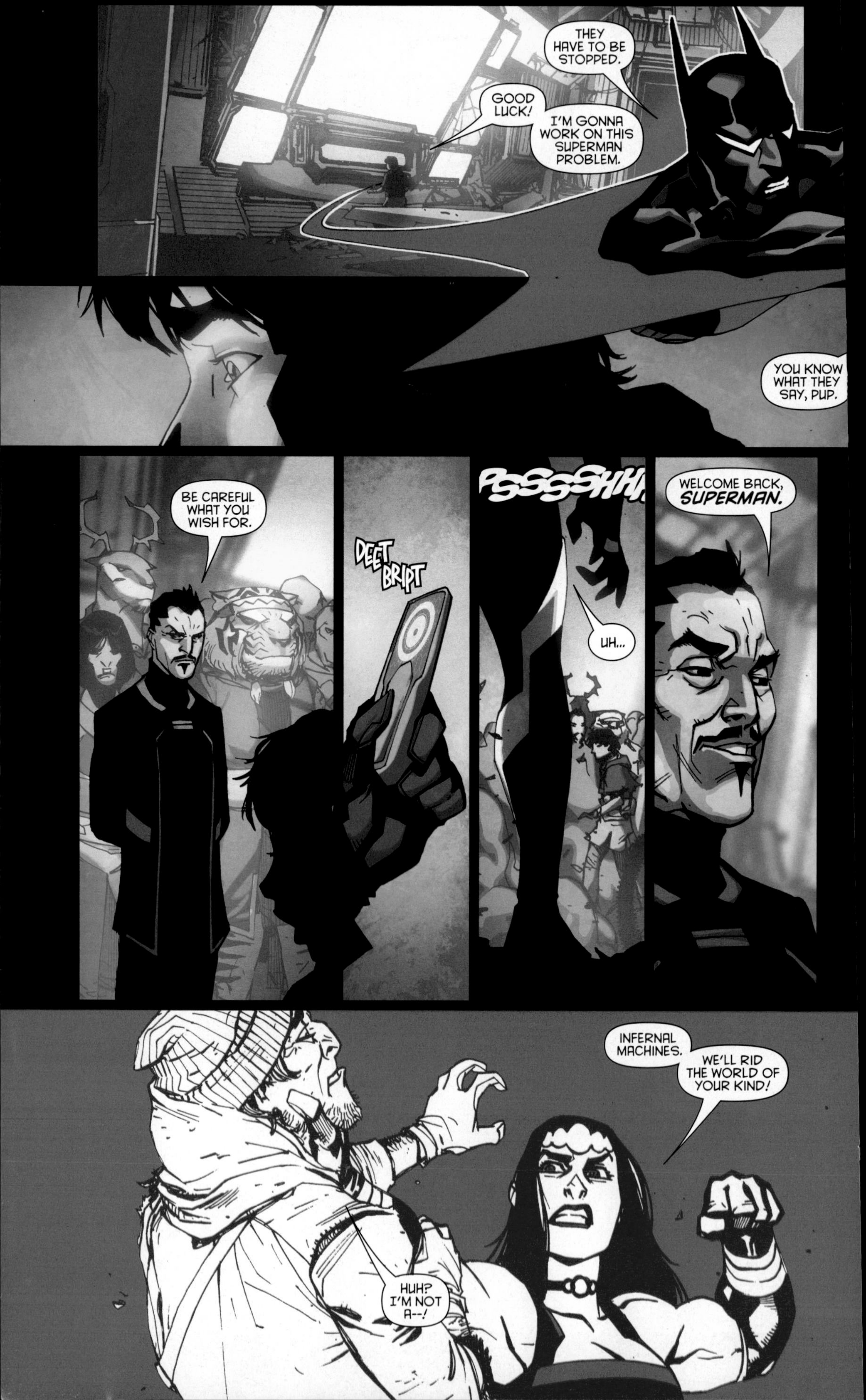
THEY HAVE TO BE STOPPED.
GOOD LUCK!
I'M GONNA WORK ON THIS SUPERMAN PROBLEM.
YOU KNOW WHAT THEY SAY, PUP.
BE CAREFUL WHAT YOU WISH FOR.
DEEET BRIPT
PSSSSHHH
UH...
WELCOME BACK, SUPERMAN.
INFERNAL MACHINES.
WE'LL RID THE WORLD OF YOUR KIND!
HUH? I'M NOT A--!

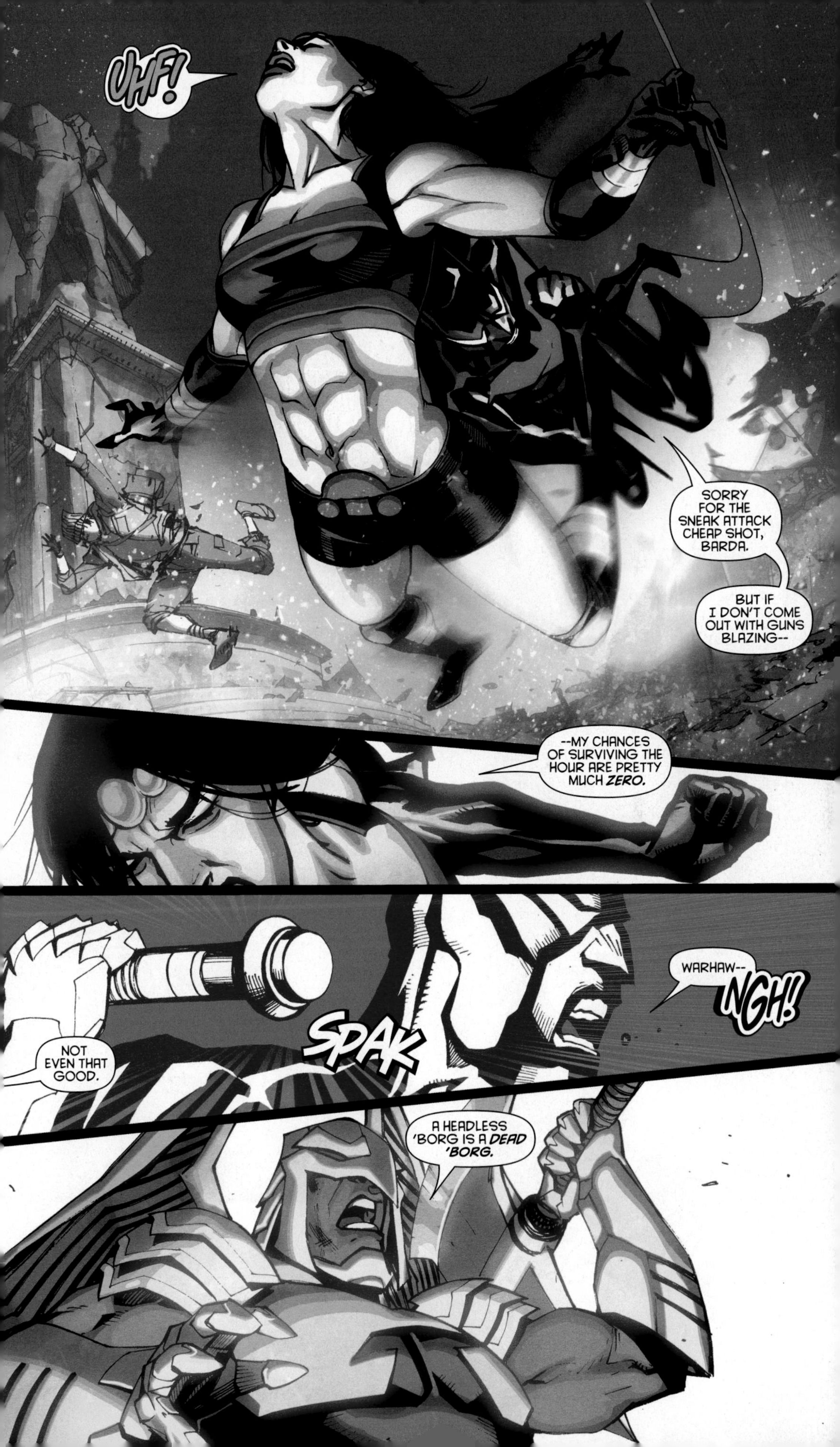
UHF!
SORRY FOR THE SNEAK ATTACK CHEAP SHOT, BARDA.
BUT IF I DON'T COME OUT WITH GUNS BLAZING--
--MY CHANCES OF SURVIVING THE HOUR ARE PRETTY MUCH ZERO.
WARHAW--
NGH!
SPAK
NOT EVEN THAT GOOD.
A HEADLESS 'BORG IS A DEAD 'BORG.

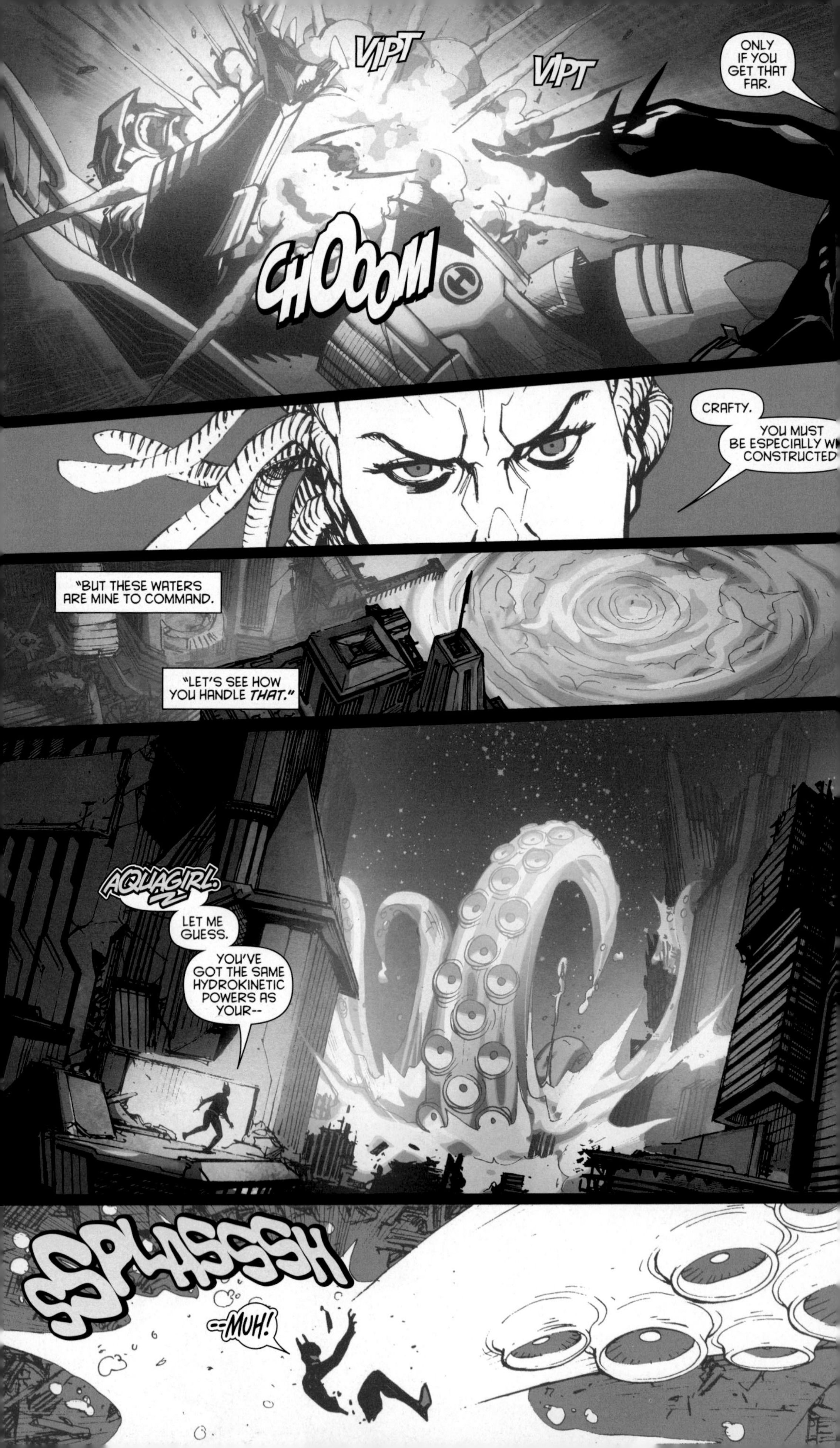
VIPT
VIPT
ONLY IF YOU GET THAT FAR.
CHOOOOM
CRAFTY.
YOU MUST BE ESPECIALLY W
CONSTRUCTED
"BUT THESE WATERS ARE MINE TO COMMAND.
"LET'S SEE HOW YOU HANDLE THAT."
AQUAGIRL.
LET ME GUESS.
YOU'VE GOT THE SAME HYDROKINETIC POWERS AS YOUR--
SPLASSSH
--MUH!

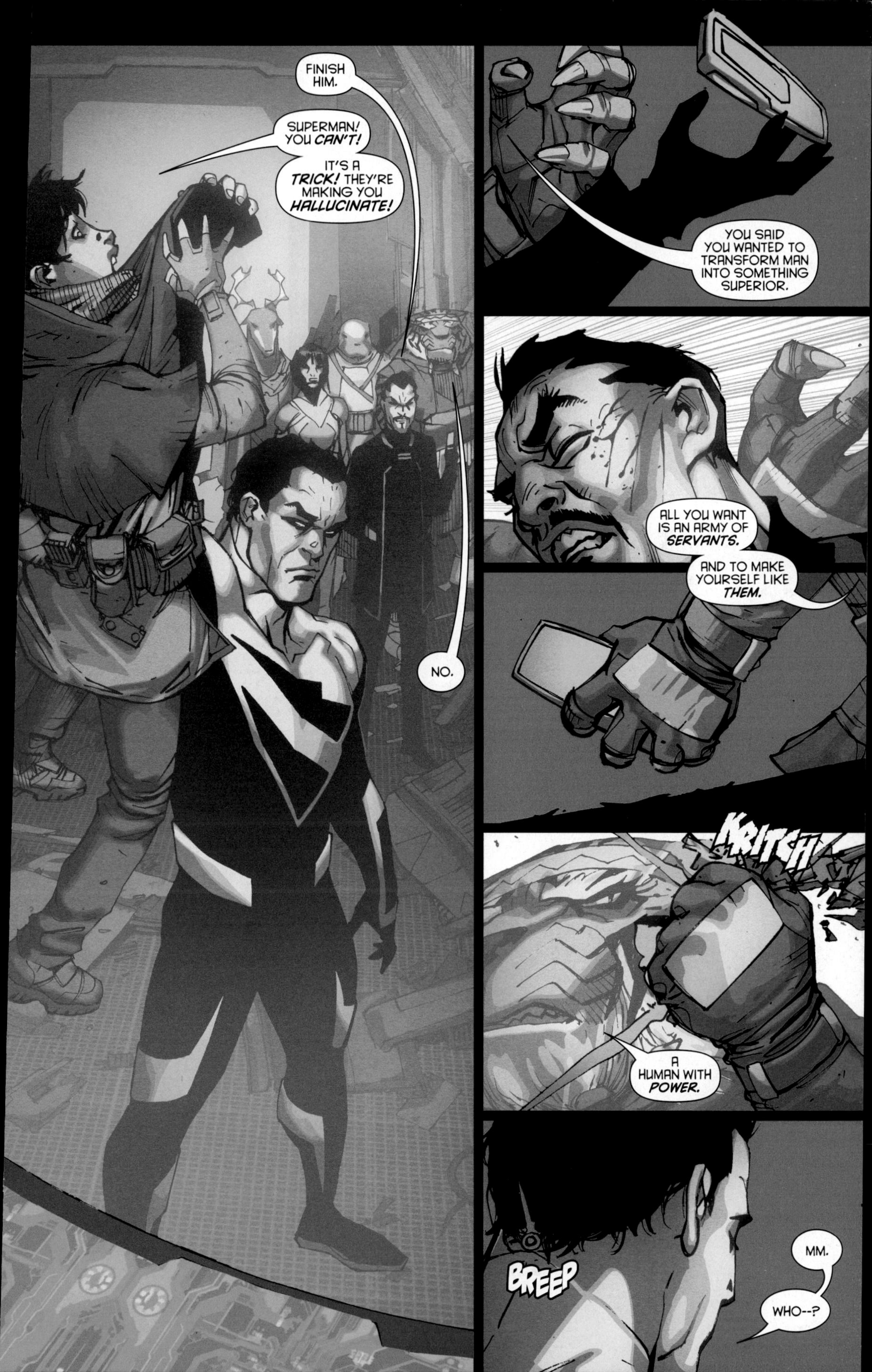
FINISH HIM.
SUPERMAN! YOU CAN'T!
IT'S A TRICK! THEY'RE MAKING YOU HALLUCINATE!
NO.
YOU SAID YOU WANTED TO TRANSFORM MAN INTO SOMETHING SUPERIOR.
ALL YOU WANT IS AN ARMY OF SERVANTS.
AND TO MAKE YOURSELF LIKE THEM.
KRITCH
A HUMAN WITH POWER.
BREEP
MM.
WHO--?

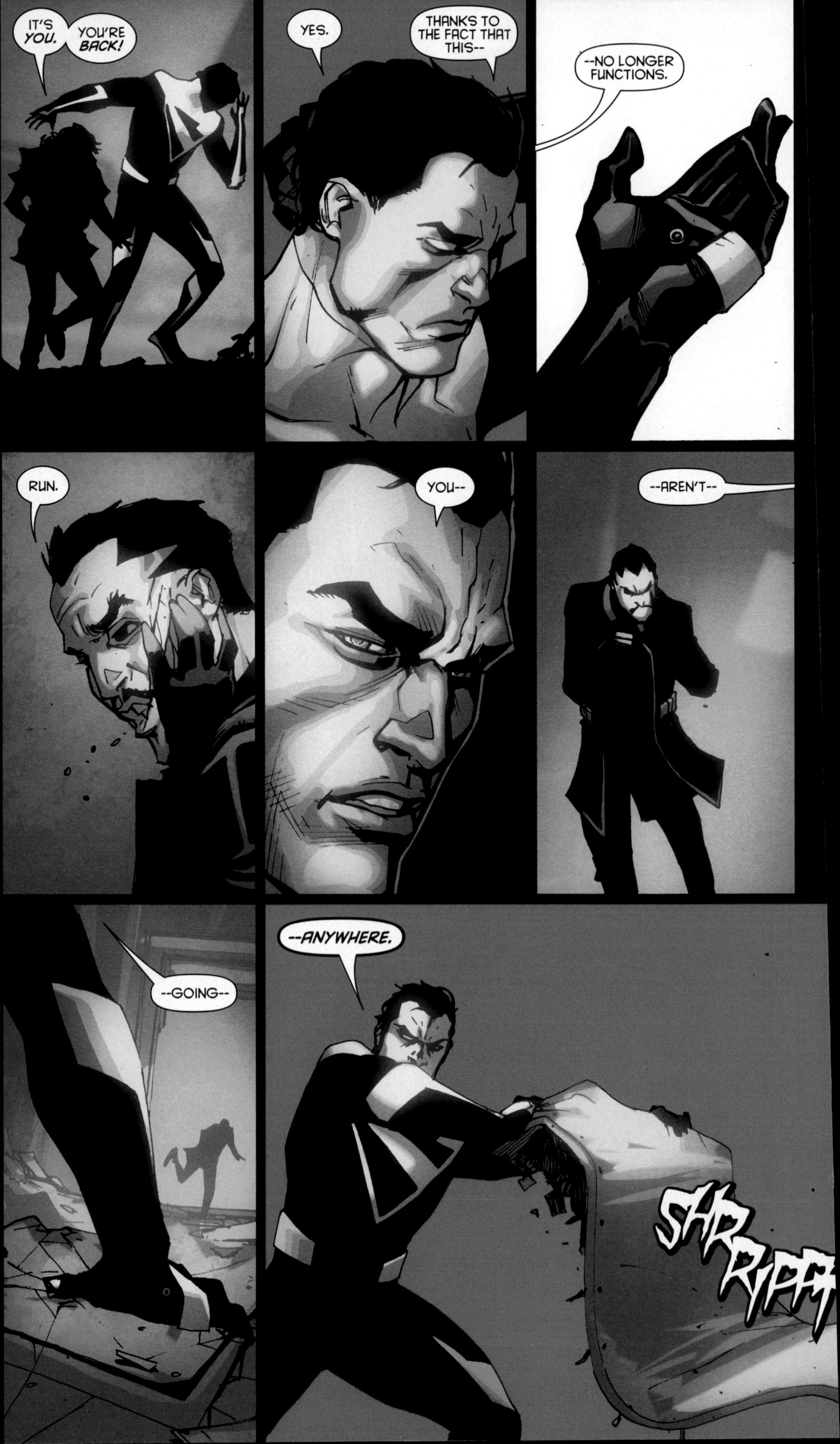
IT'S *YOU.*
YOU'RE *BACK!*
YES.
THANKS TO THE FACT THAT THIS--
--NO LONGER FUNCTIONS.
RUN.
YOU--
--AREN'T--
--GOING--
--ANYWHERE.
SHRRIPPP

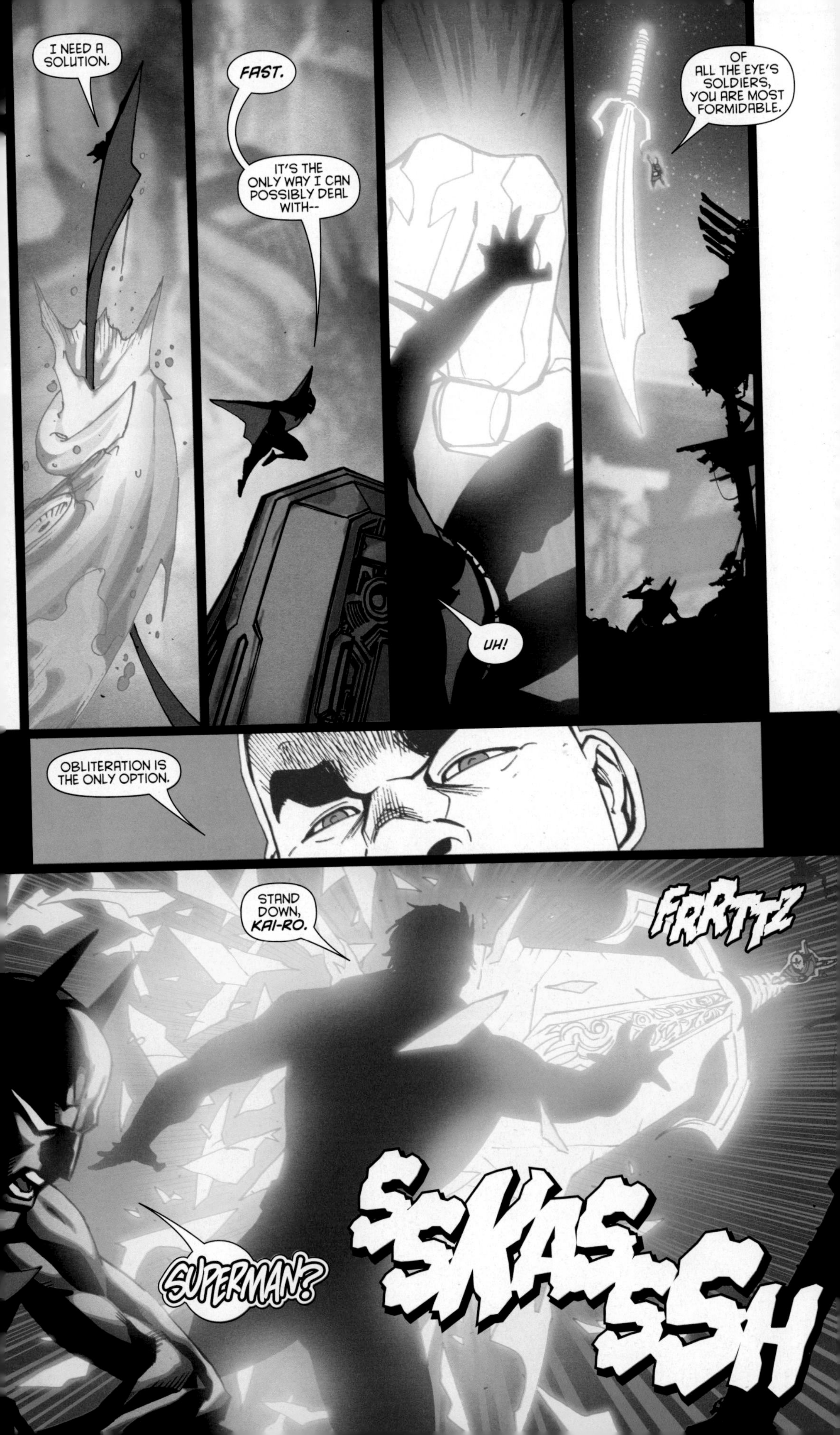
I NEED A SOLUTION.
FAST.
IT'S THE ONLY WAY I CAN POSSIBLY DEAL WITH--
UH!
OF ALL THE EYE'S SOLDIERS, YOU ARE MOST FORMIDABLE.
OBLITERATION IS THE ONLY OPTION.
STAND DOWN, KAI-RO.
FRTTZ
SUPERMAN?
SKASSSH

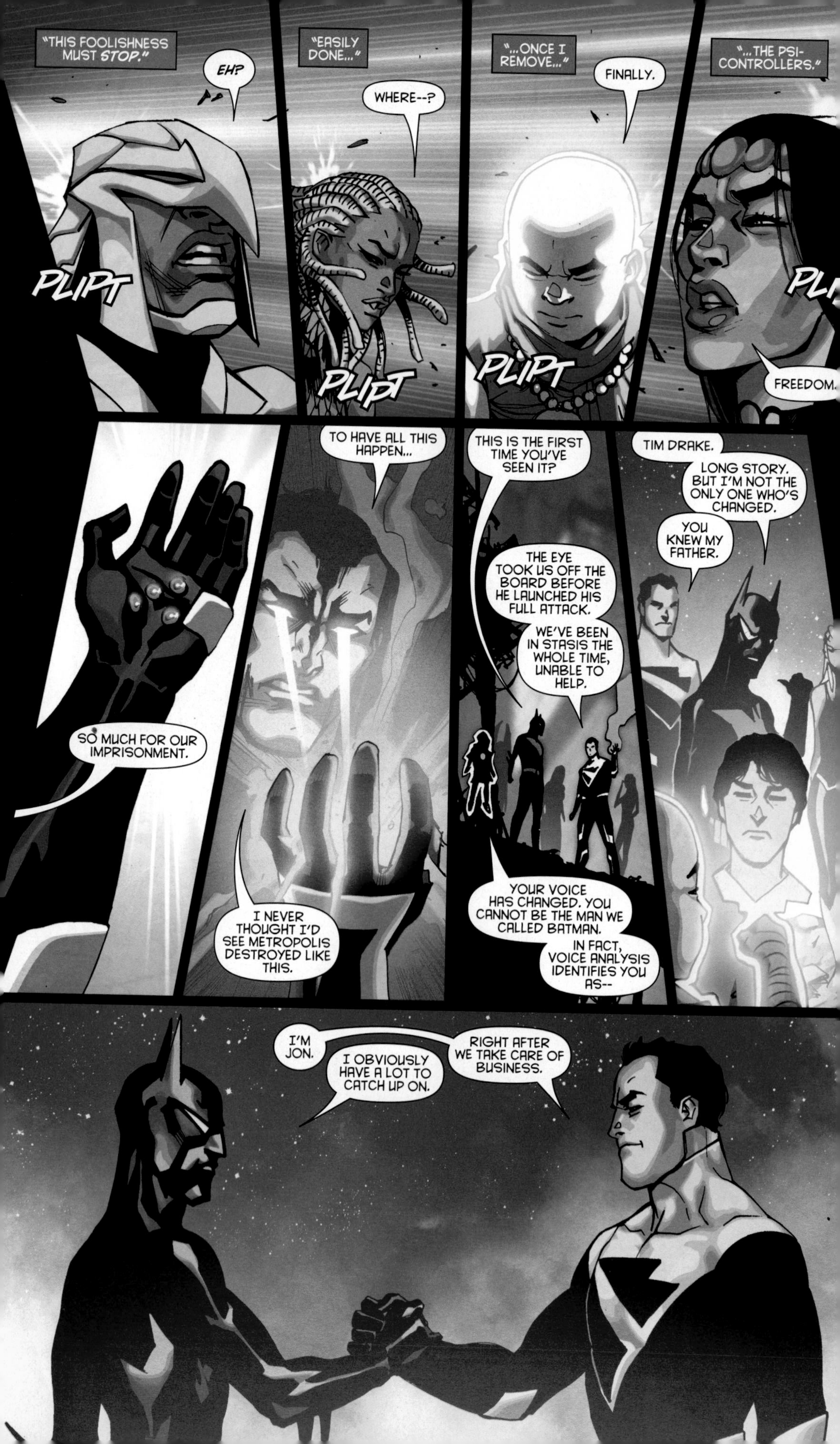
"THIS FOOLISHNESS MUST STOP."
EH?
PLIPT
"EASILY DONE..."
WHERE--?
PLIPT
"...ONCE I REMOVE..."
FINALLY.
PLIPT
"...THE PSI-CONTROLLERS."
FREEDOM.
SO MUCH FOR OUR IMPRISONMENT.
TO HAVE ALL THIS HAPPEN...
I NEVER THOUGHT I'D SEE METROPOLIS DESTROYED LIKE THIS.
THIS IS THE FIRST TIME YOU'VE SEEN IT?
THE EYE TOOK US OFF THE BOARD BEFORE HE LAUNCHED HIS FULL ATTACK.
WE'VE BEEN IN STASIS THE WHOLE TIME, UNABLE TO HELP.
YOUR VOICE HAS CHANGED. YOU CANNOT BE THE MAN WE CALLED BATMAN.
IN FACT, VOICE ANALYSIS IDENTIFIES YOU AS--
TIM DRAKE.
LONG STORY. BUT I'M NOT THE ONLY ONE WHO'S CHANGED.
YOU KNEW MY FATHER.
I'M JON.
RIGHT AFTER WE TAKE CARE OF BUSINESS.
I OBVIOUSLY HAVE A LOT TO CATCH UP ON.

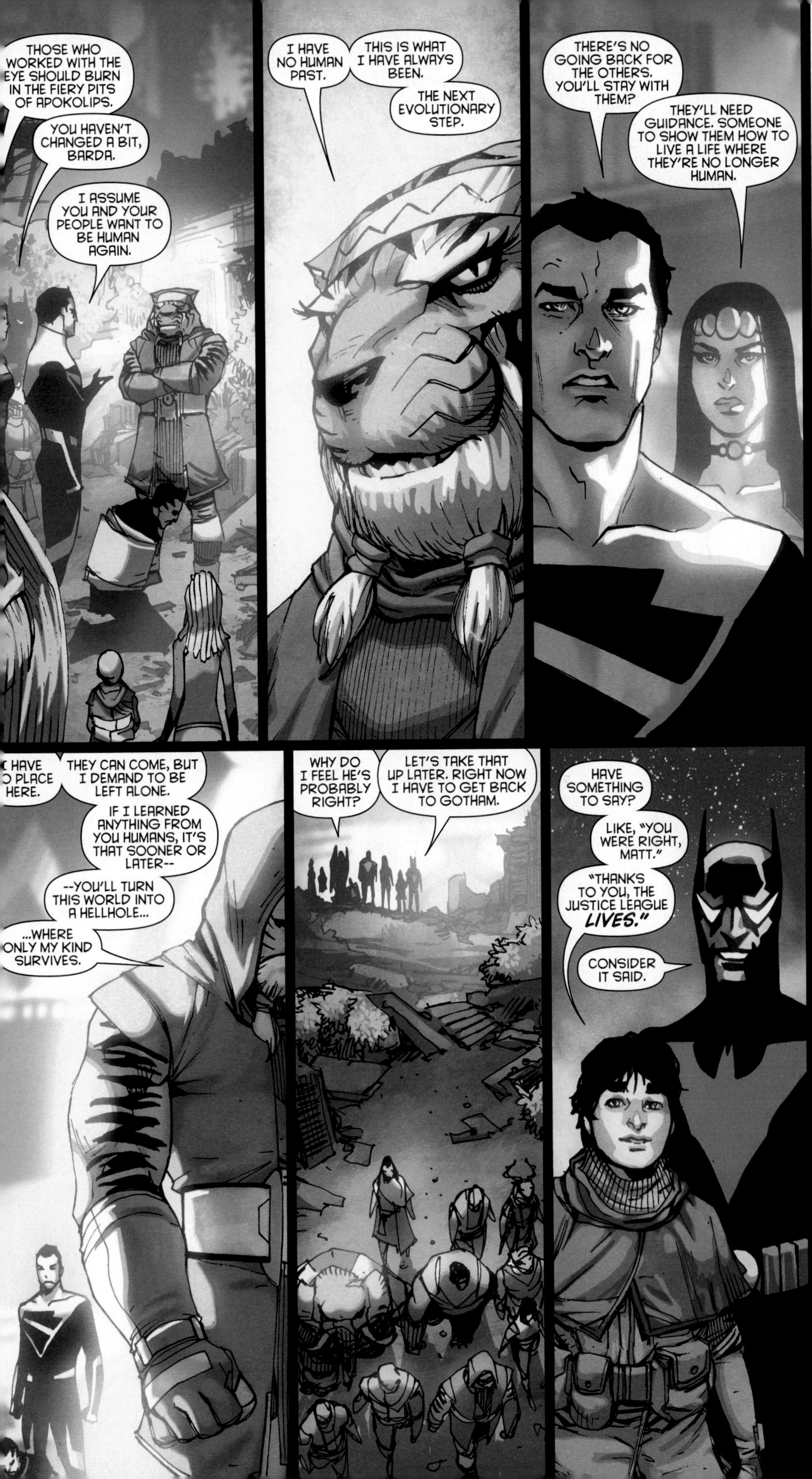

THOSE WHO WORKED WITH THE EYE SHOULD BURN IN THE FIERY PITS OF APOKOLIPS.
YOU HAVEN'T CHANGED A BIT, BARDA.
I ASSUME YOU AND YOUR PEOPLE WANT TO BE HUMAN AGAIN.
I HAVE NO HUMAN PAST.
THIS IS WHAT I HAVE ALWAYS BEEN.
THE NEXT EVOLUTIONARY STEP.
THERE'S NO GOING BACK FOR THE OTHERS. YOU'LL STAY WITH THEM?
THEY'LL NEED GUIDANCE. SOMEONE TO SHOW THEM HOW TO LIVE A LIFE WHERE THEY'RE NO LONGER HUMAN.
HAVE PLACE HERE.
THEY CAN COME, BUT I DEMAND TO BE LEFT ALONE.
IF I LEARNED ANYTHING FROM YOU HUMANS, IT'S THAT SOONER OR LATER--
--YOU'LL TURN THIS WORLD INTO A HELLHOLE...
...WHERE ONLY MY KIND SURVIVES.
WHY DO I FEEL HE'S PROBABLY RIGHT?
LET'S TAKE THAT UP LATER. RIGHT NOW I HAVE TO GET BACK TO GOTHAM.
HAVE SOMETHING TO SAY?
LIKE, "YOU WERE RIGHT, MATT."
"THANKS TO YOU, THE JUSTICE LEAGUE *LIVES.*"
CONSIDER IT SAID.

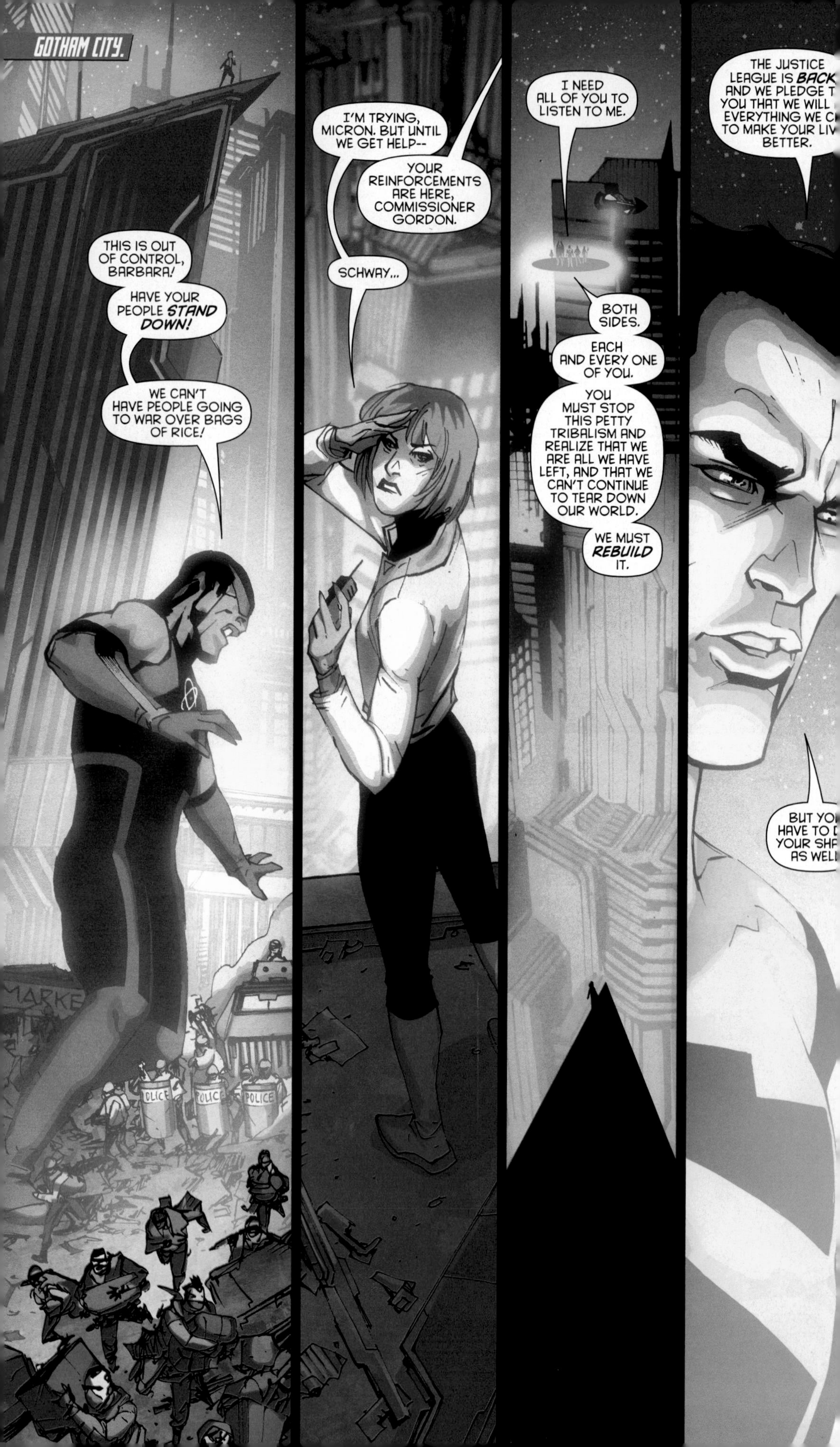

GOTHAM CITY.
THIS IS OUT OF CONTROL, BARBARA!
HAVE YOUR PEOPLE STAND DOWN!
WE CAN'T HAVE PEOPLE GOING TO WAR OVER BAGS OF RICE!
MARKE
POLICE
POLICE
POLICE
I'M TRYING, MICRON. BUT UNTIL WE GET HELP--
YOUR REINFORCEMENTS ARE HERE, COMMISSIONER GORDON.
SCHWAY...
I NEED ALL OF YOU TO LISTEN TO ME.
BOTH SIDES.
EACH AND EVERY ONE OF YOU.
YOU MUST STOP THIS PETTY TRIBALISM AND REALIZE THAT WE ARE ALL WE HAVE LEFT, AND THAT WE CAN'T CONTINUE TO TEAR DOWN OUR WORLD.
WE MUST REBUILD IT.
THE JUSTICE LEAGUE IS BACK AND WE PLEDGE T YOU THAT WE WILL EVERYTHING WE C TO MAKE YOUR LIV BETTER.
BUT YO HAVE TO D YOUR SHA AS WELL

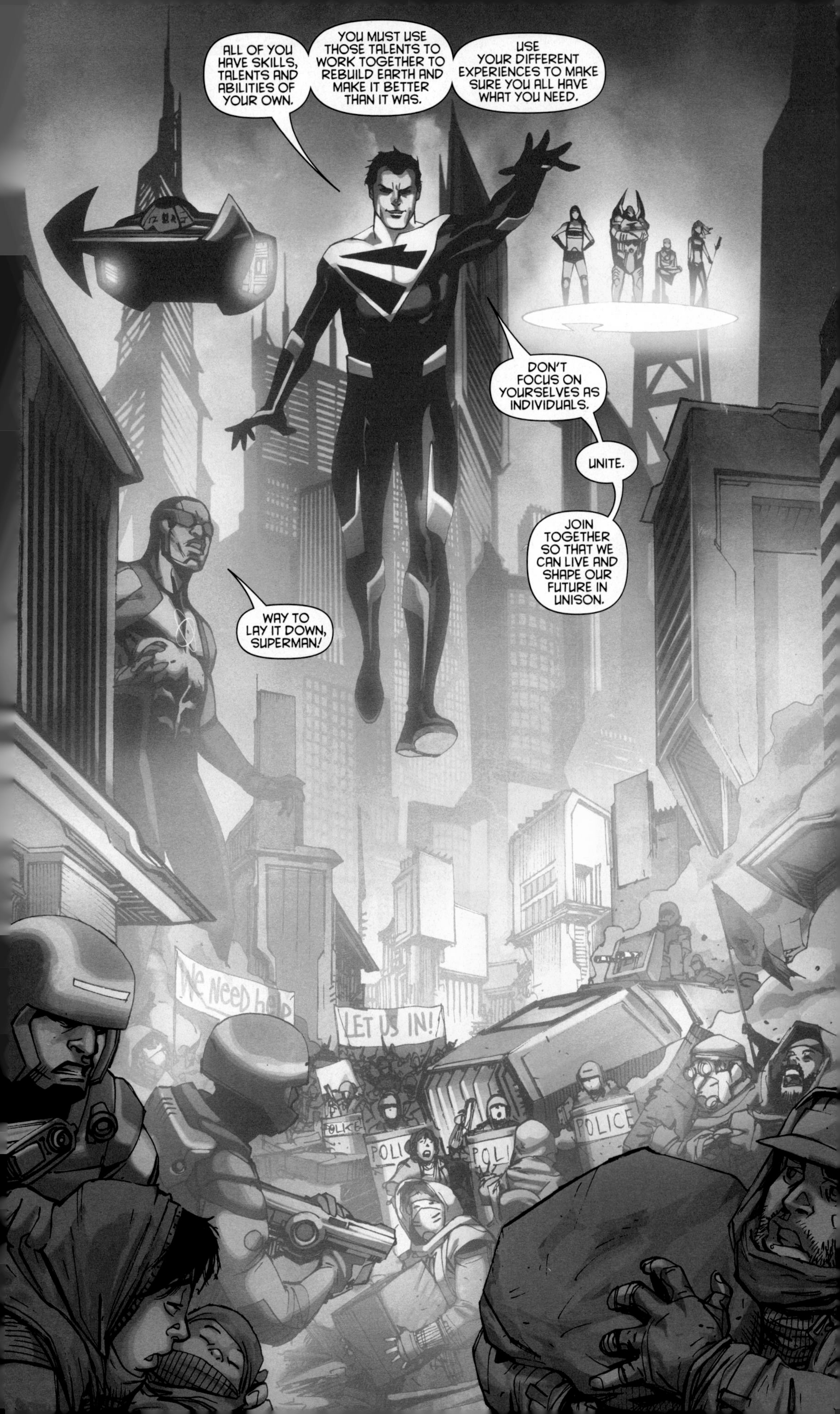
ALL OF YOU HAVE SKILLS, TALENTS AND ABILITIES OF YOUR OWN.
YOU MUST USE THOSE TALENTS TO WORK TOGETHER TO REBUILD EARTH AND MAKE IT BETTER THAN IT WAS.
USE YOUR DIFFERENT EXPERIENCES TO MAKE SURE YOU ALL HAVE WHAT YOU NEED.
DON'T FOCUS ON YOURSELVES AS INDIVIDUALS.
UNITE.
JOIN TOGETHER SO THAT WE CAN LIVE AND SHAPE OUR FUTURE IN UNISON.
WAY TO LAY IT DOWN, SUPERMAN!
We NEED help
LET US IN!
POLICE
POLICE

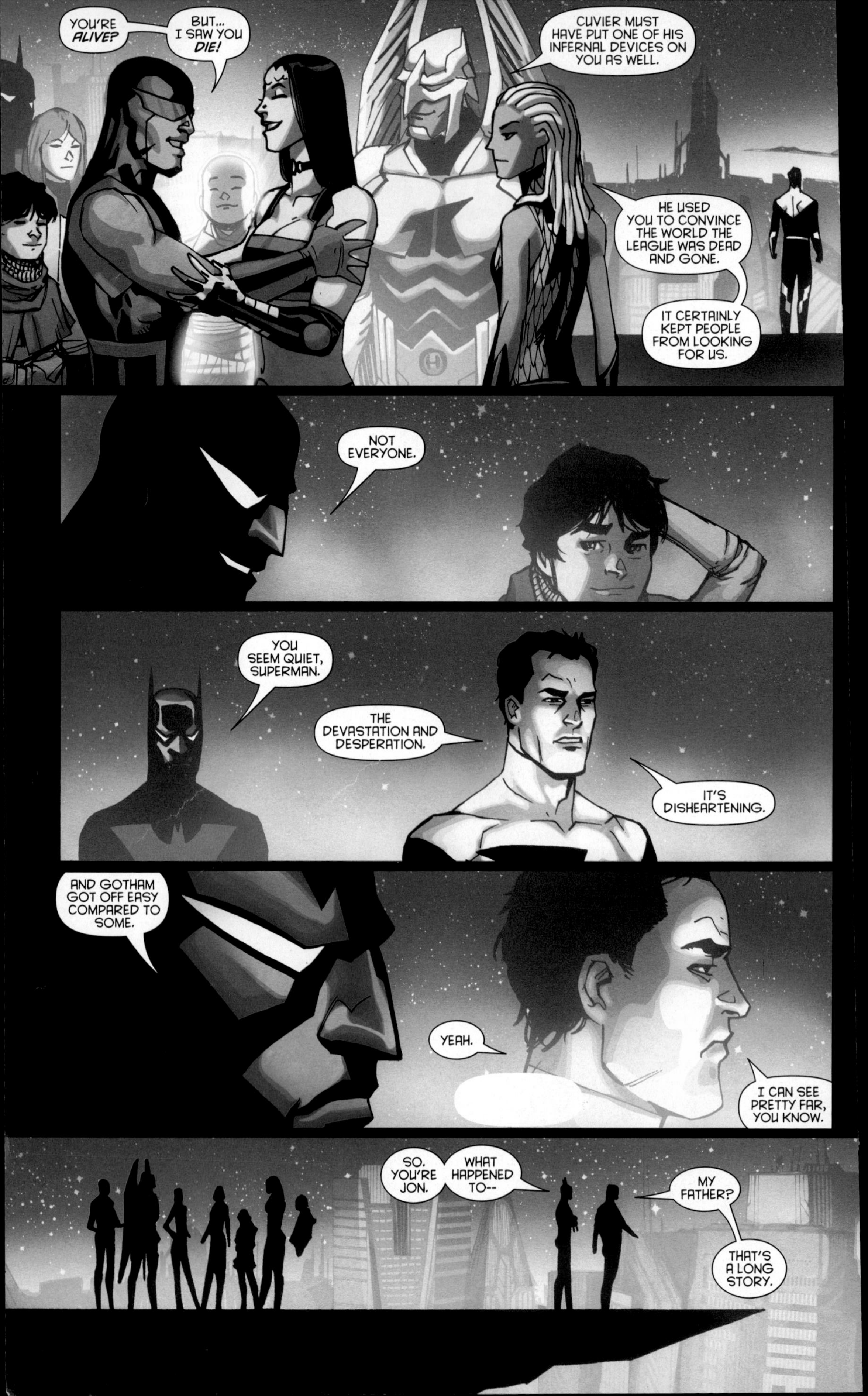
YOU'RE ALIVE?
BUT... I SAW YOU DIE!
CUVIER MUST HAVE PUT ONE OF HIS INFERNAL DEVICES ON YOU AS WELL.
HE USED YOU TO CONVINCE THE WORLD THE LEAGUE WAS DEAD AND GONE.
IT CERTAINLY KEPT PEOPLE FROM LOOKING FOR US.
NOT EVERYONE.
YOU SEEM QUIET, SUPERMAN.
THE DEVASTATION AND DESPERATION.
IT'S DISHEARTENING.
AND GOTHAM GOT OFF EASY COMPARED TO SOME.
YEAH.
I CAN SEE PRETTY FAR, YOU KNOW.
SO. YOU'RE JON.
WHAT HAPPENED TO--
MY FATHER?
THAT'S A LONG STORY.

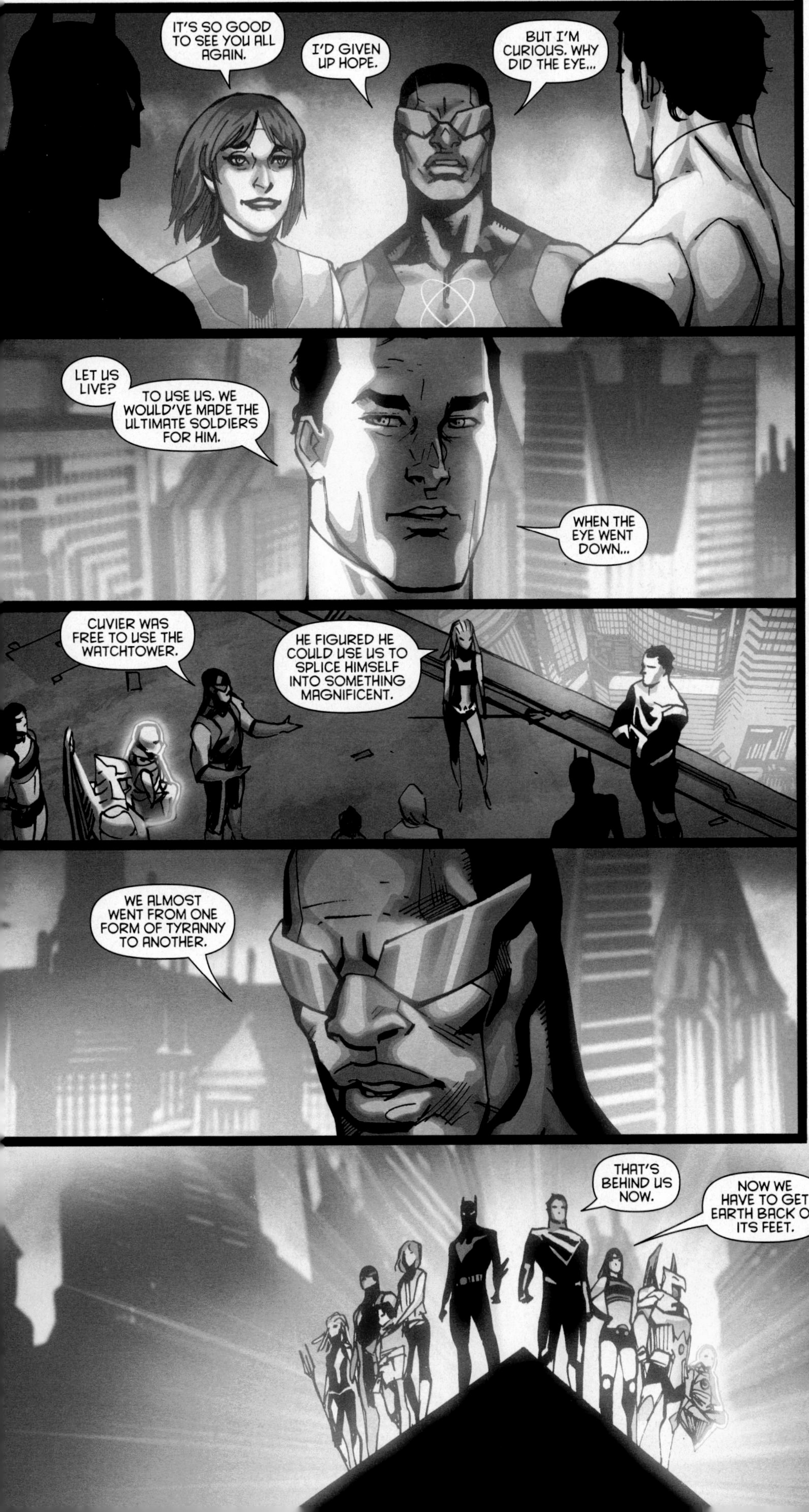
IT'S SO GOOD TO SEE YOU ALL AGAIN.
I'D GIVEN UP HOPE.
BUT I'M CURIOUS. WHY DID THE EYE...
LET US LIVE?
TO USE US. WE WOULD'VE MADE THE ULTIMATE SOLDIERS FOR HIM.
WHEN THE EYE WENT DOWN...
CUVIER WAS FREE TO USE THE WATCHTOWER.
HE FIGURED HE COULD USE US TO SPLICE HIMSELF INTO SOMETHING MAGNIFICENT.
WE ALMOST WENT FROM ONE FORM OF TYRANNY TO ANOTHER.
THAT'S BEHIND US NOW.
NOW WE HAVE TO GET EARTH BACK ON ITS FEET.

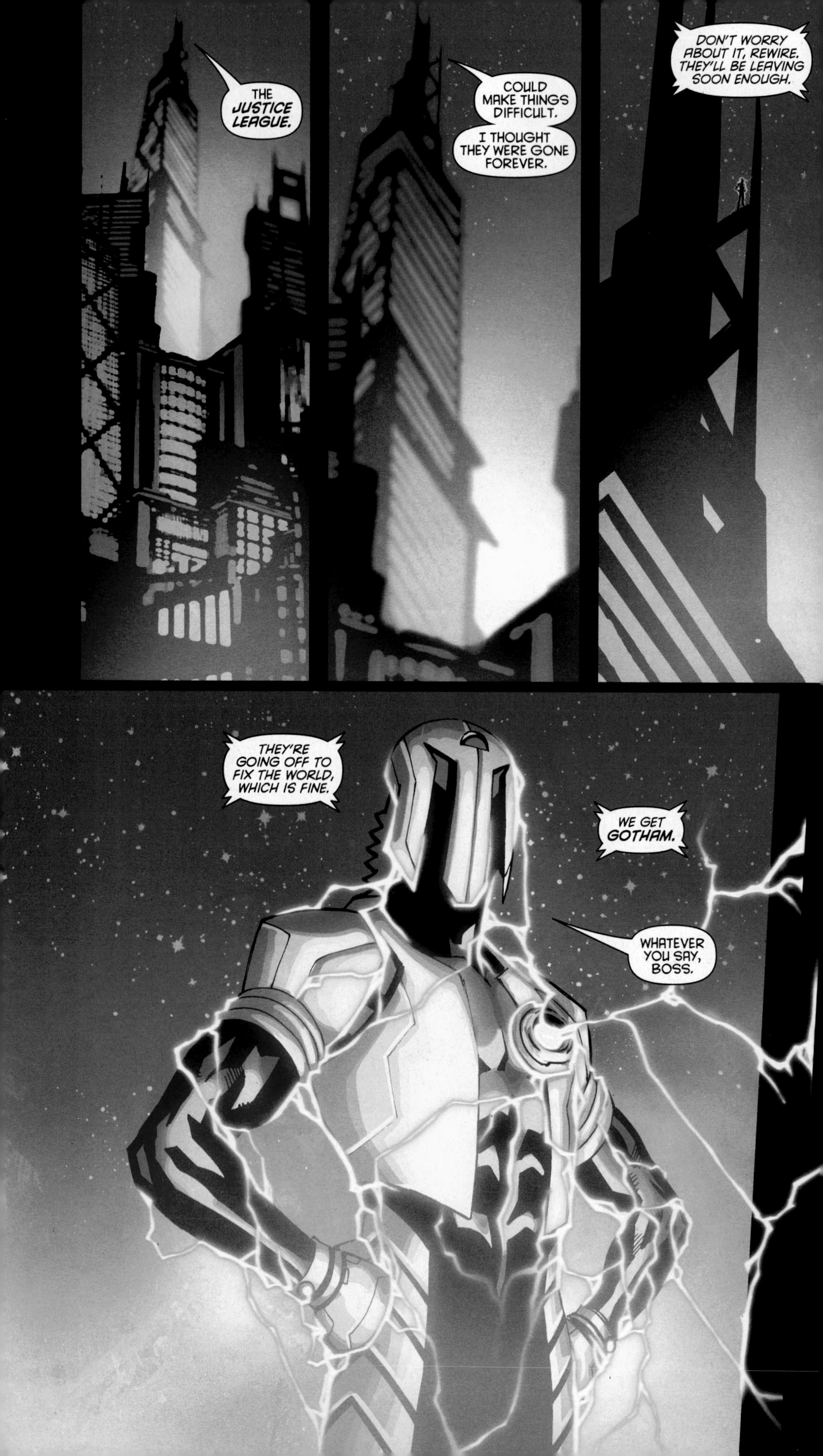
THE JUSTICE LEAGUE.
COULD MAKE THINGS DIFFICULT.
I THOUGHT THEY WERE GONE FOREVER.
DON'T WORRY ABOUT IT, REWIRE. THEY'LL BE LEAVING SOON ENOUGH.
THEY'RE GOING OFF TO FIX THE WORLD, WHICH IS FINE.
WE GET GOTHAM.
WHATEVER YOU SAY, BOSS.

VARIANT COVER & SKETCH GALLERY

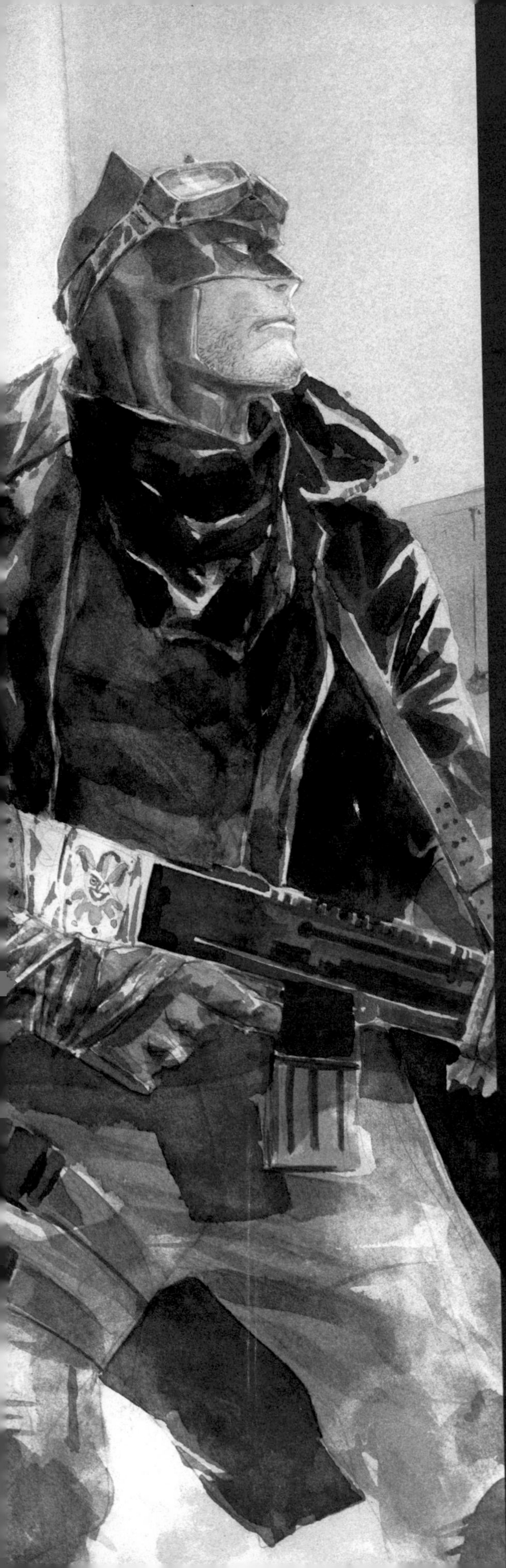

BATMAN BEYOND #10
BATMAN v SUPERMAN VARIANT
BY DUSTIN NGUYEN

CHARACTER SKETCHES
BY BERNARD CHANG

COVER SKETCHES
BY PHILIP TAN

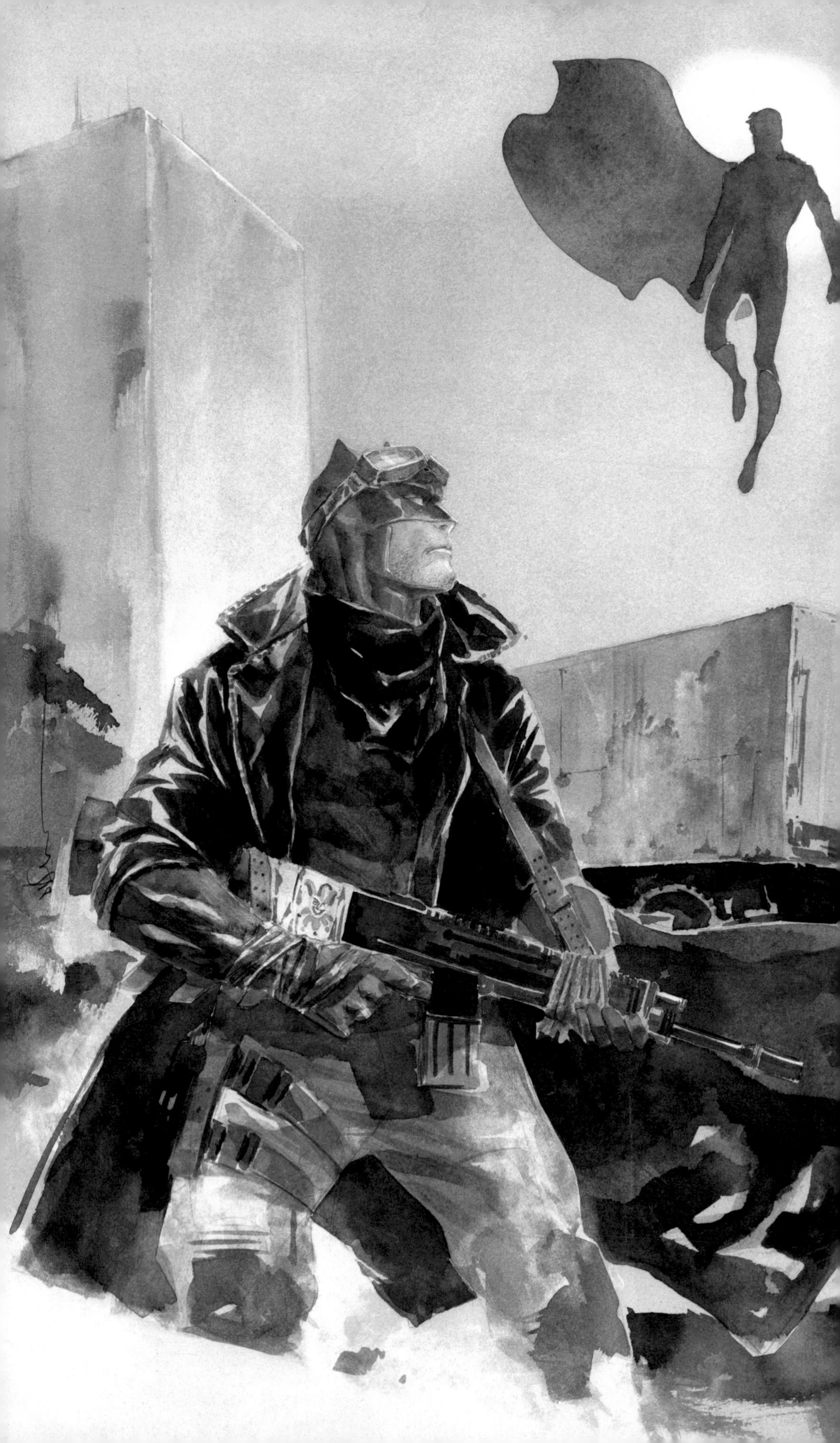

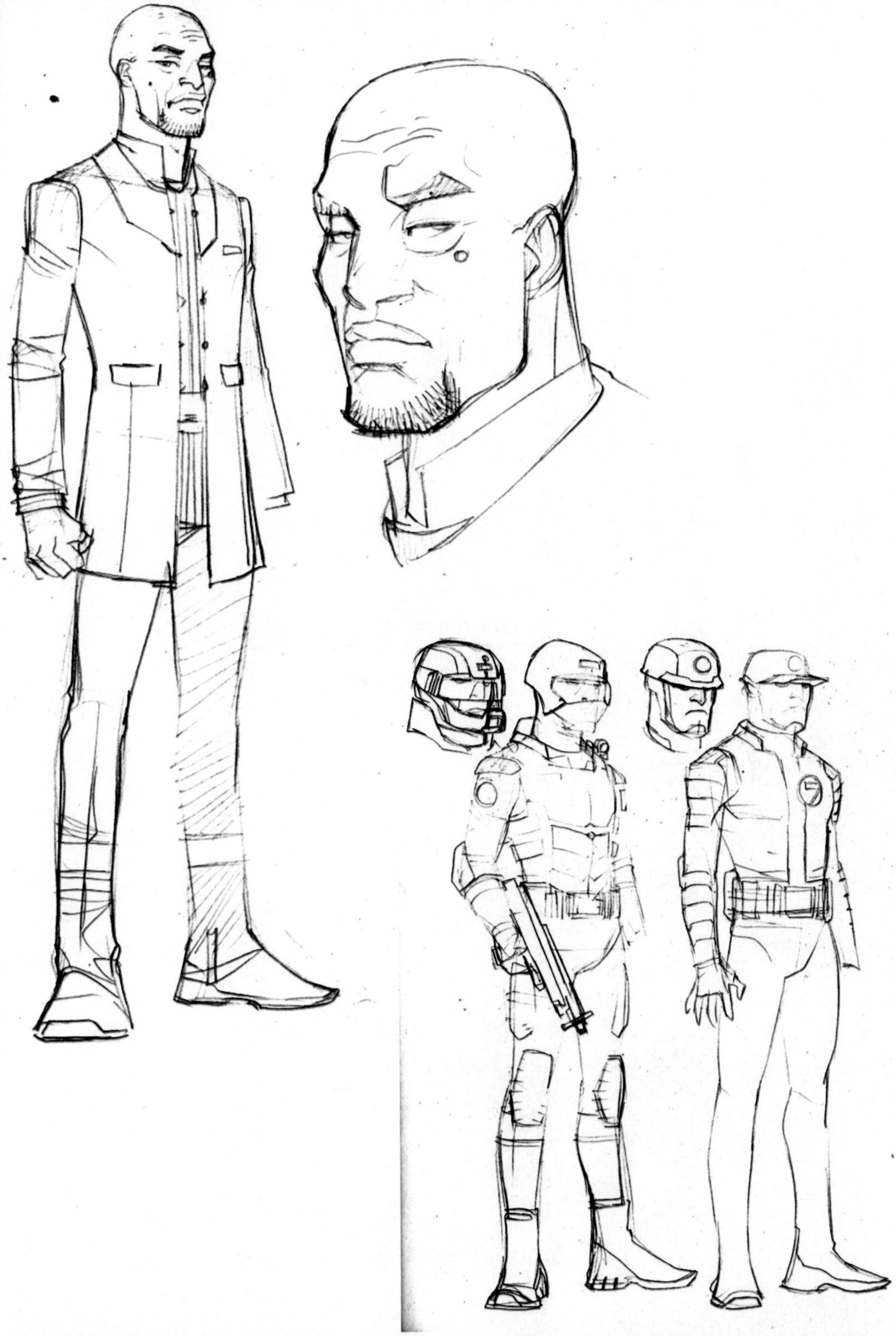

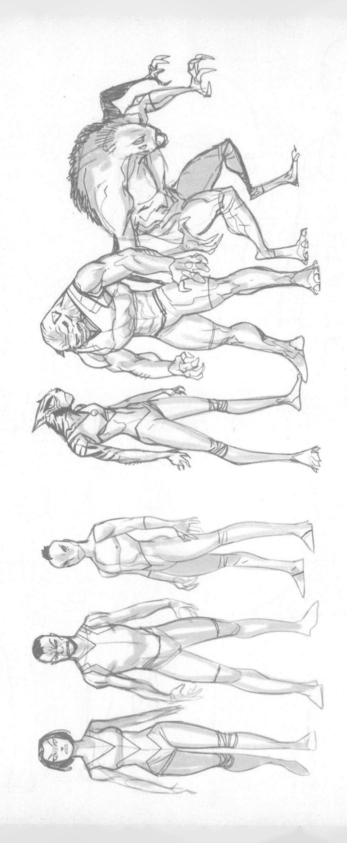

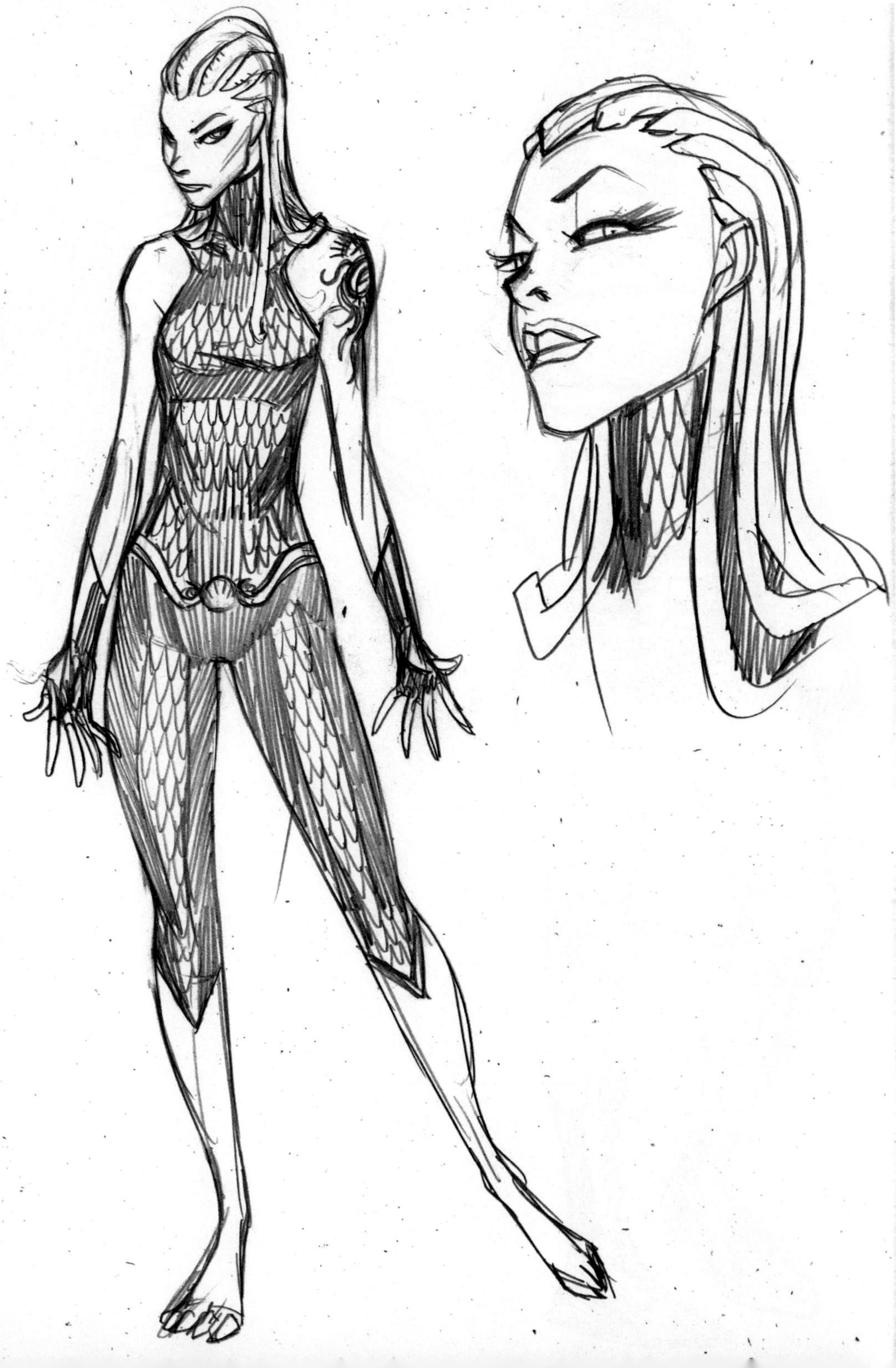

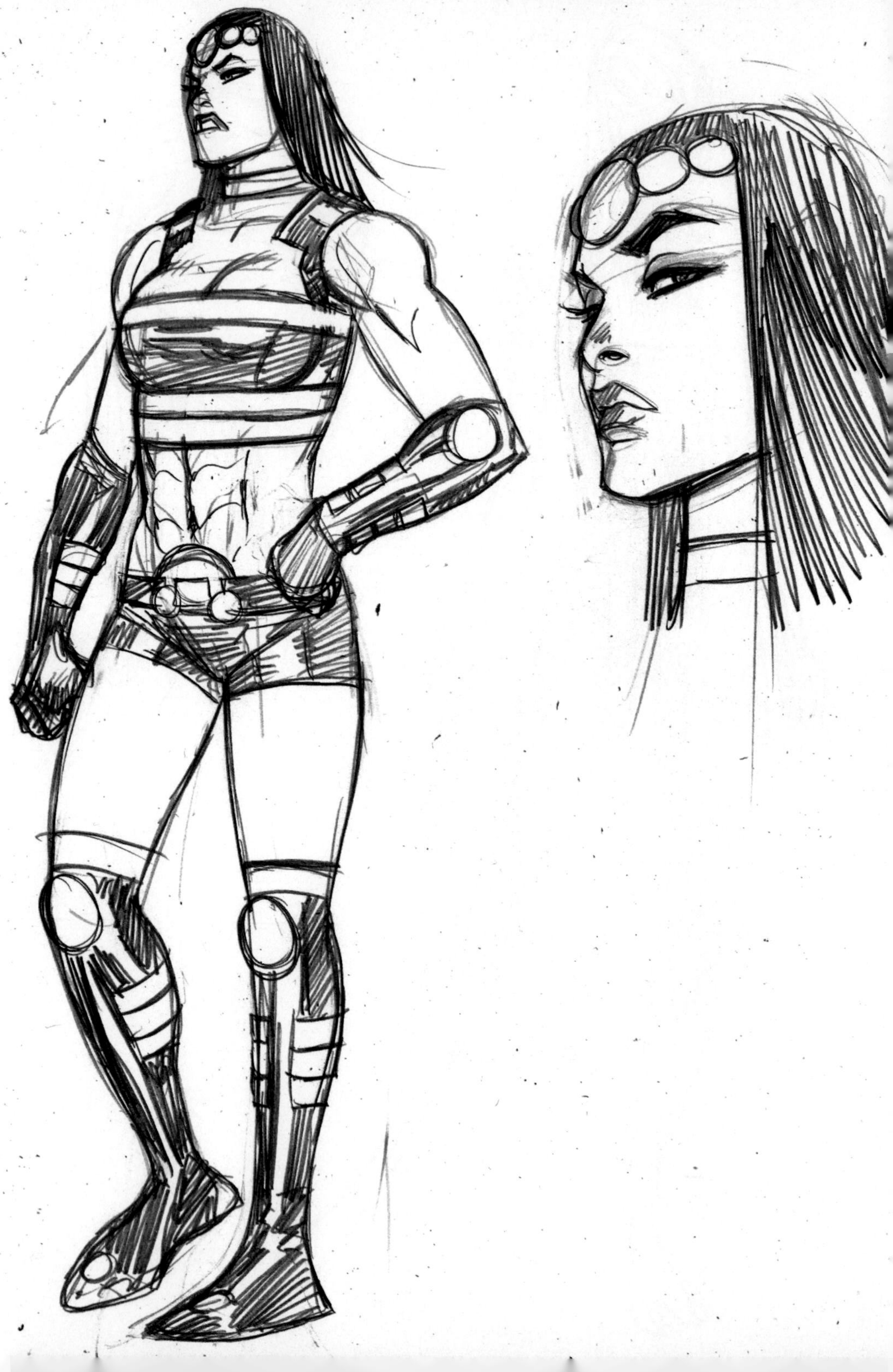

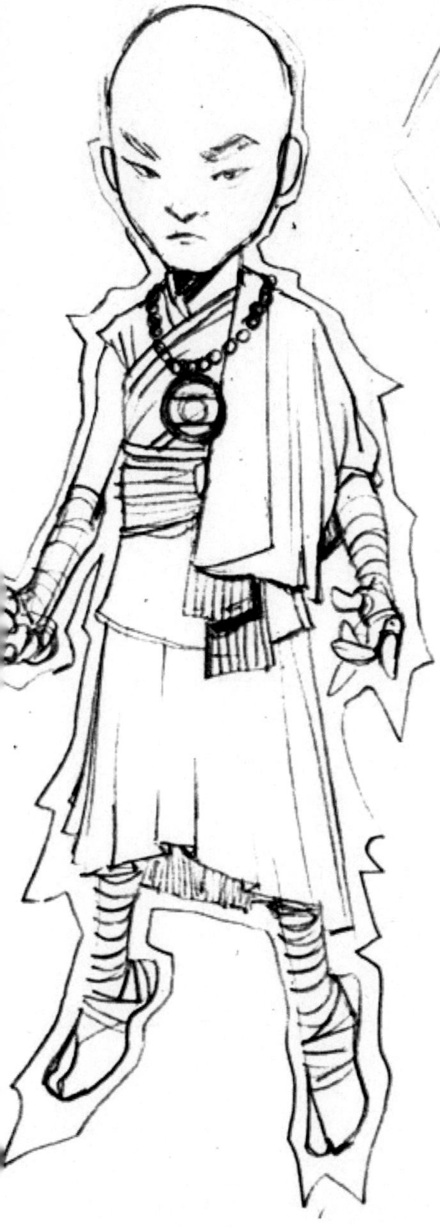
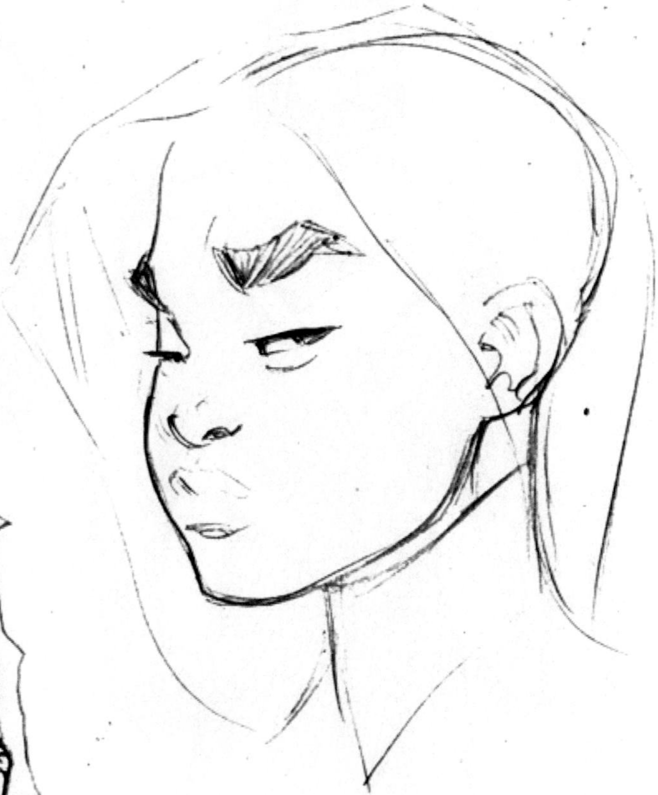

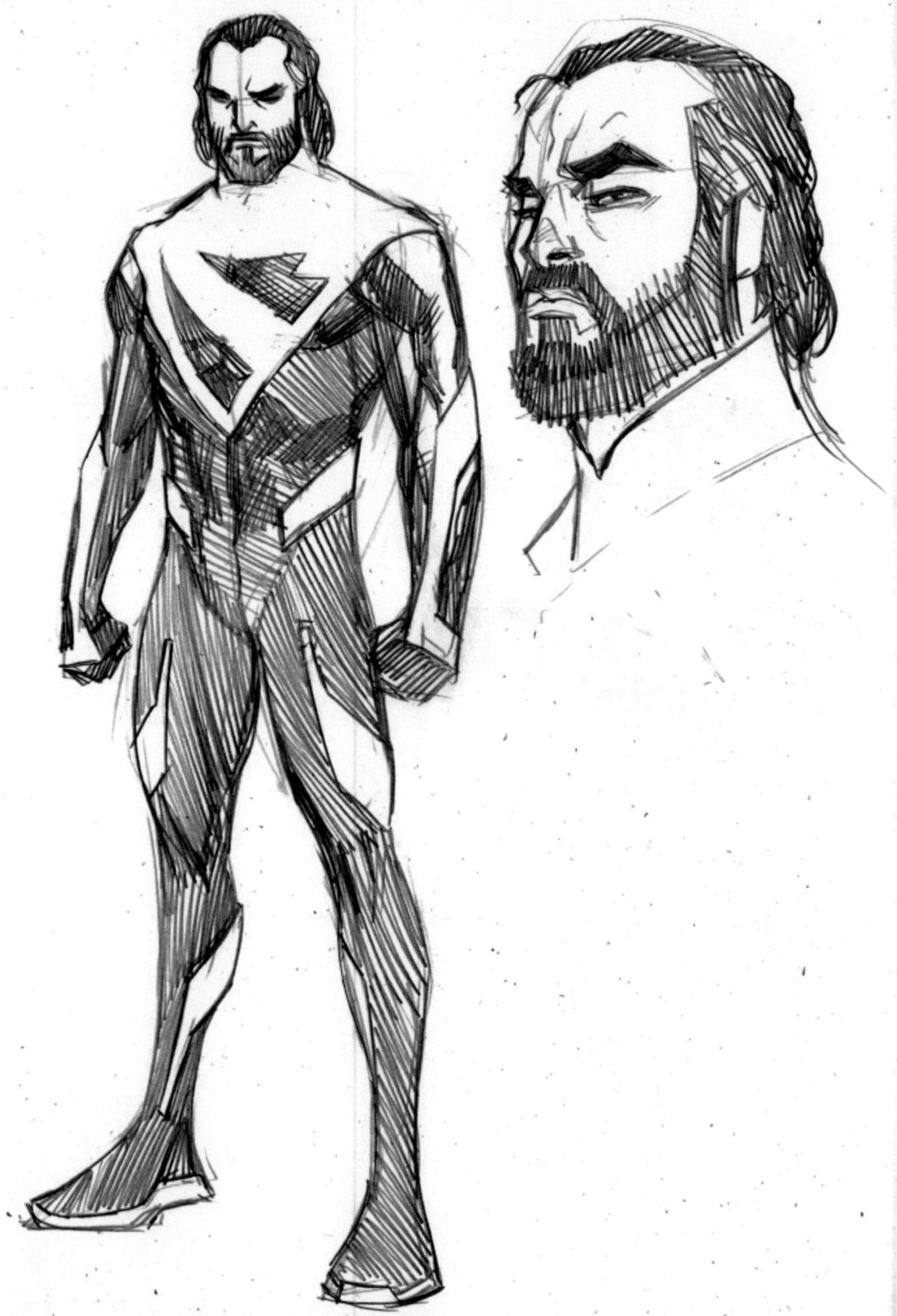

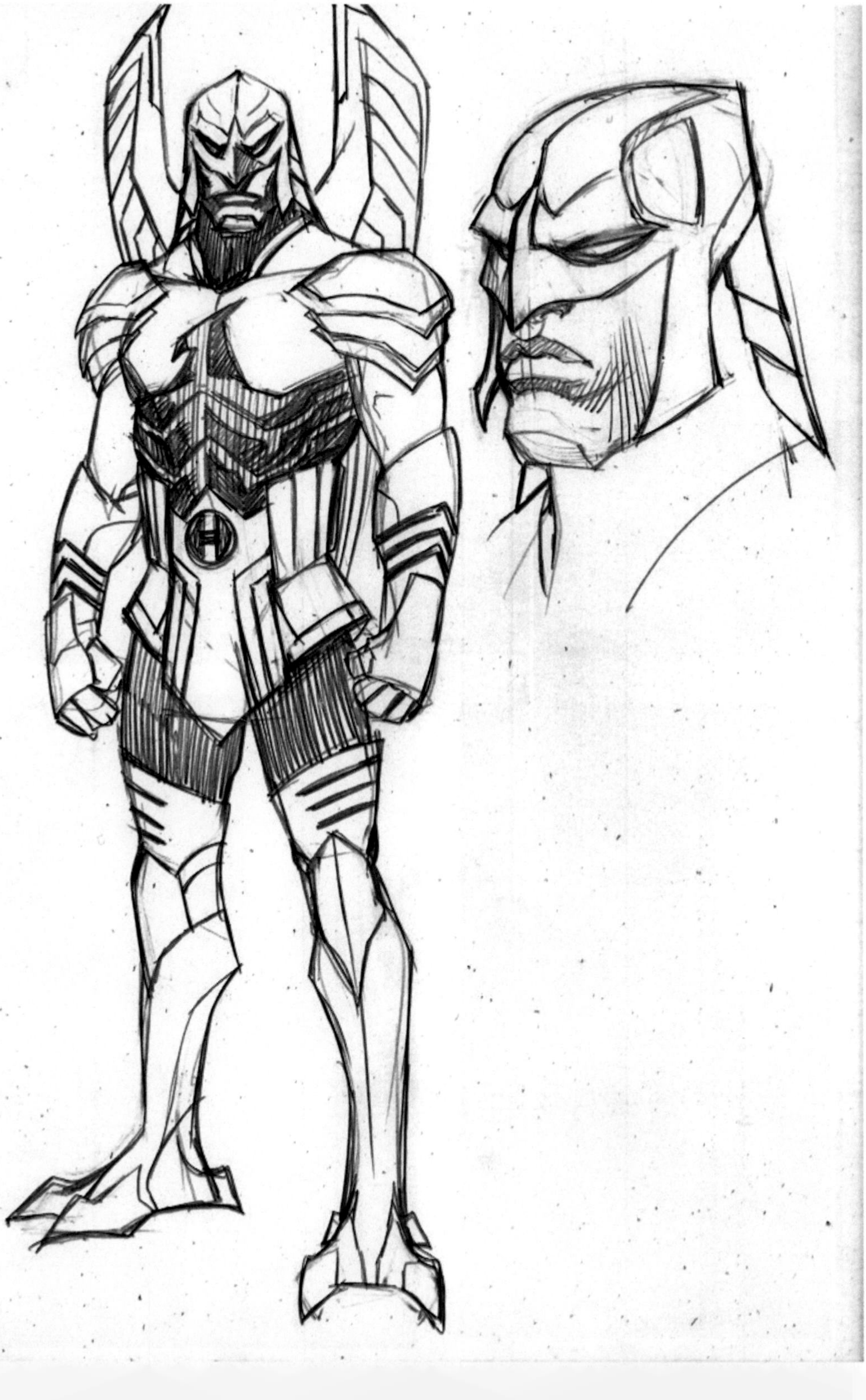

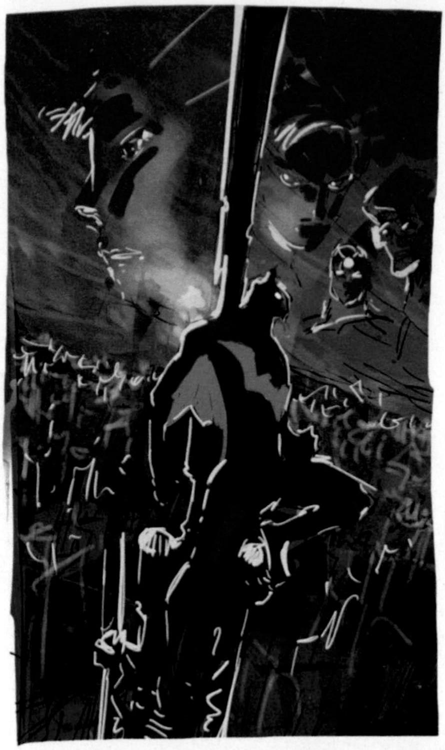
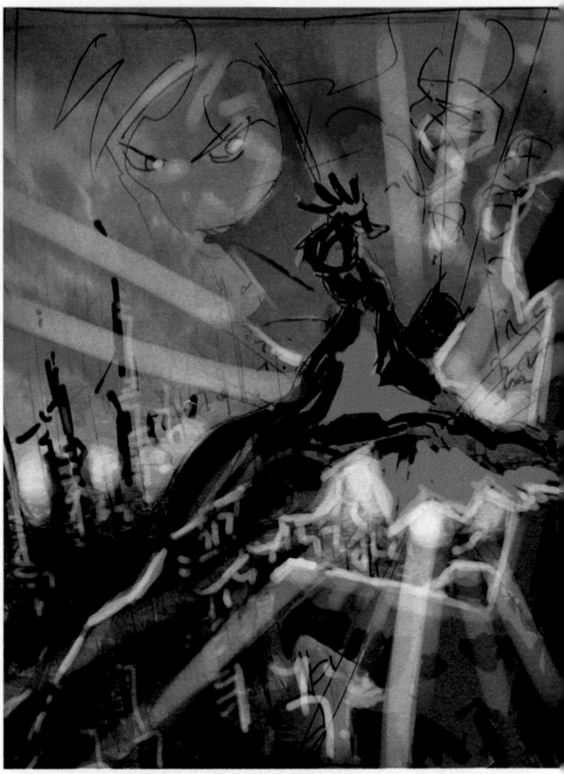
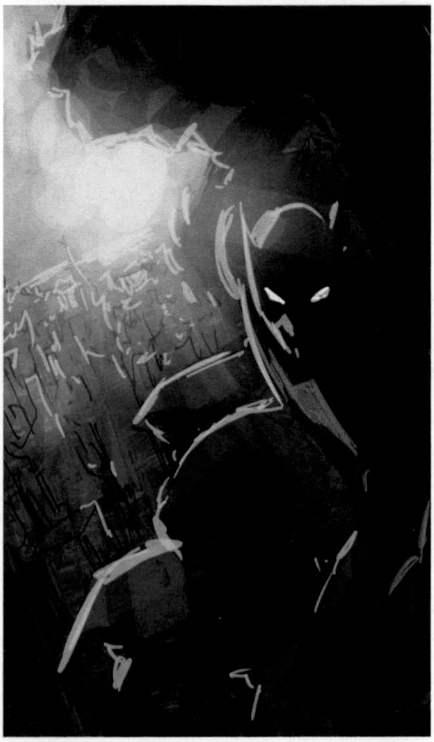
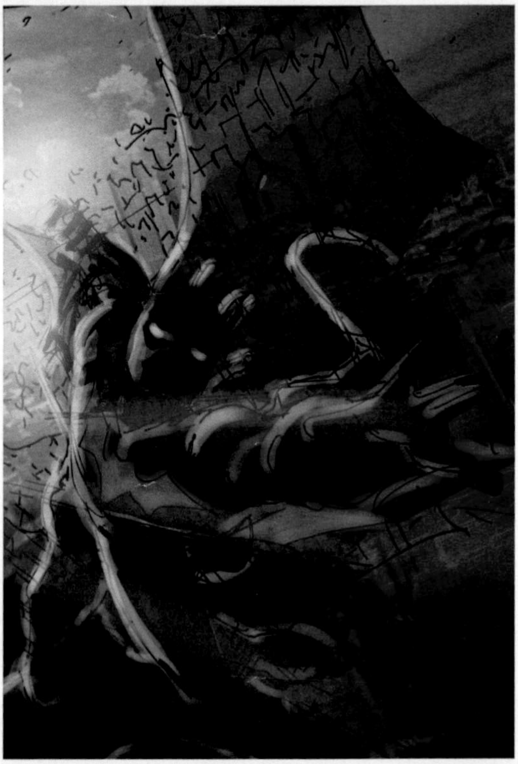

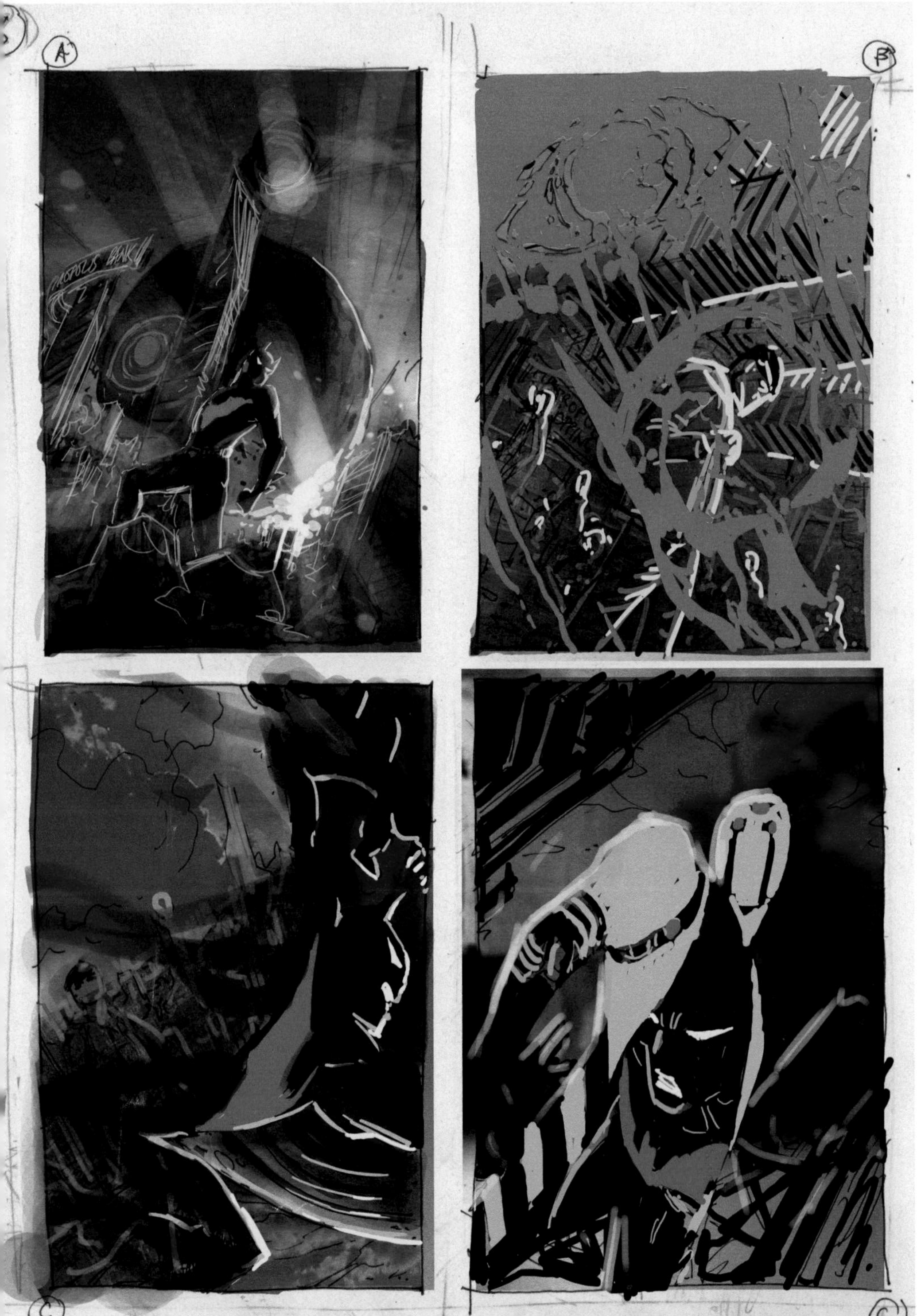
A
B
BANK
C
C

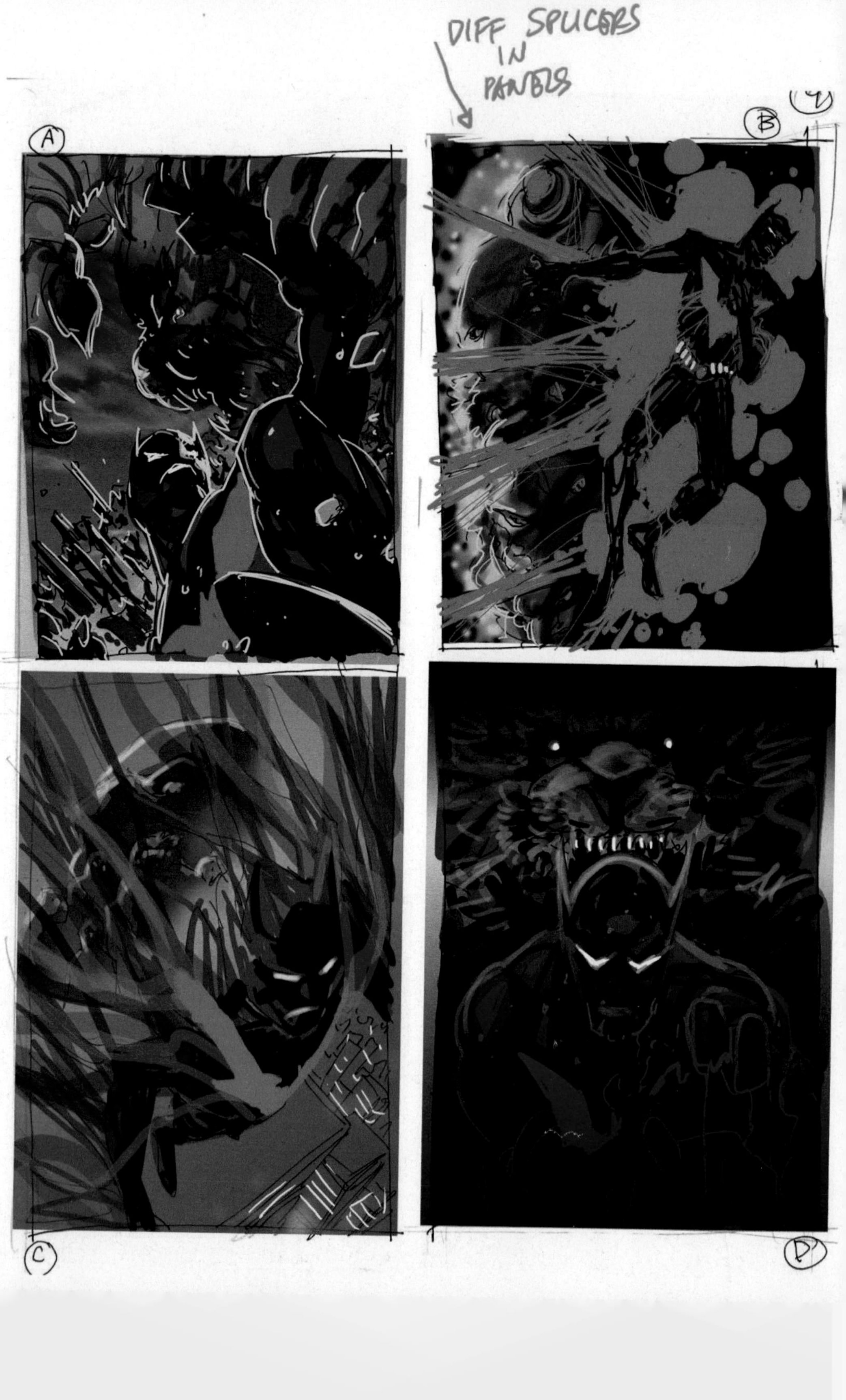
DIFF SPLICERS IN PANELS
A
B
C
D

B

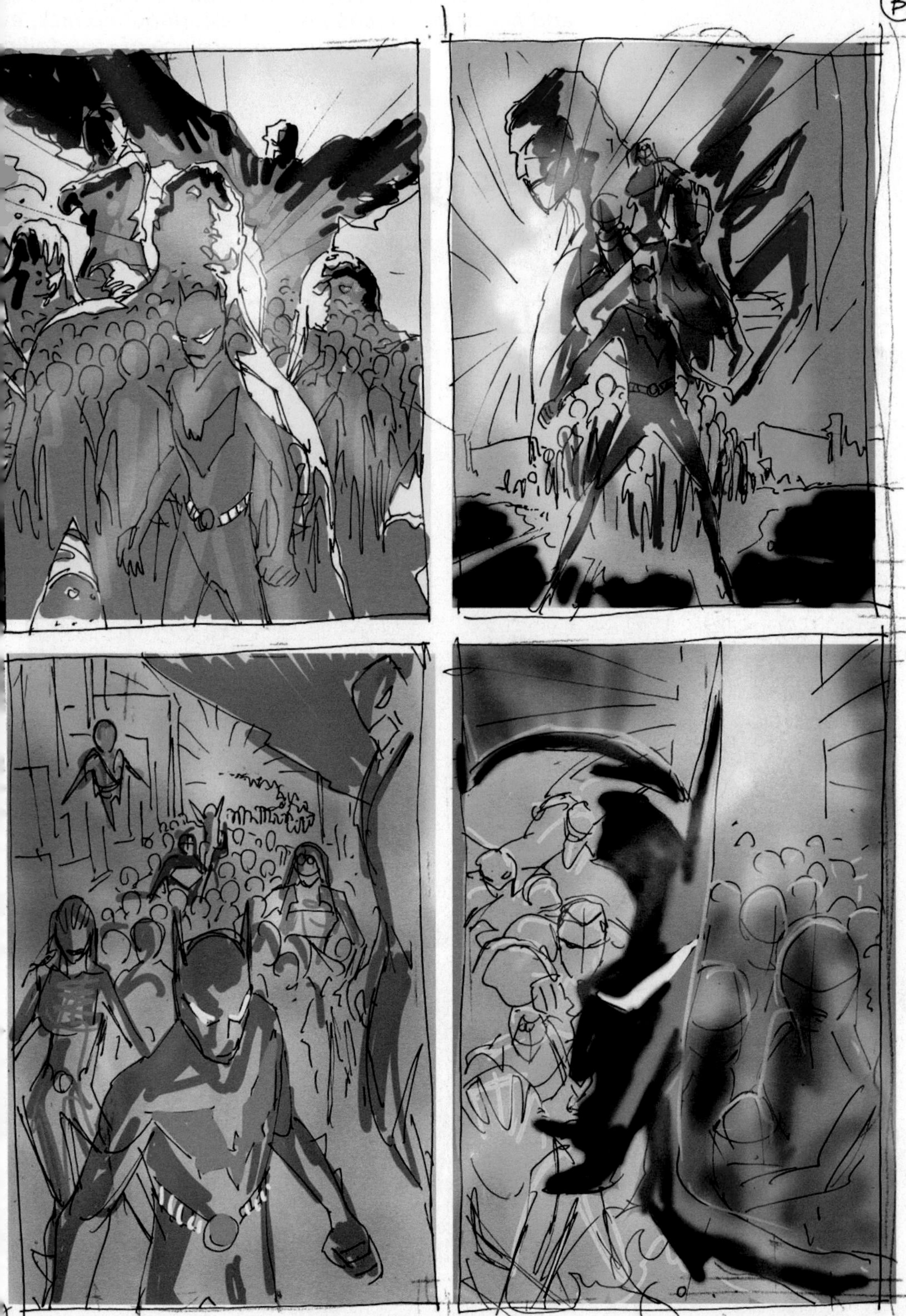

D